Roland Barthes

Roland Barthes was one of the most in[ ]
tieth century, but why should the reac[ ]
concerned with him? Martin McQuillar[ ]
on Barthes, addressing his political and institutional inheritance anu
considering his work as the origin of critical cultural studies.

This stimulating study:

- provides a biographical consideration of Barthes' writing
- offers an extended reading of his 1957 text *Mythologies* as a text for
  our own time, drawing Barthes' work into a historical relation to the
  present
- examines his connection to what we call cultural studies
- features an annotated bibliography of Barthes' published work.

Thought-provoking and insightful, *Roland Barthes* is essential reading
for anyone who is interested in the writings of this key theorist and his
continuing relevance in our post-9/11 world.

Martin McQuillan is Professor of Literary Theory and Cultural Analysis
and Dean of the Faculty of Arts and Social Sciences at Kingston
University, UK.

Transitions critically explores key figures in literary theory. Guiding the
reader through the poetics and politics of critical thinkers, **Transitions**
helps direct the student's own acts of critical analysis. As well as transforming the critical developments of the past by interpreting them
from the perspective of the present, each study enacts transitional
readings of a number of well-known literary texts.

General Editor: Julian Wolfreys

transitions

General Editor: Julian Wolfreys

Published titles

Forthcoming titles

Transitions
Series Standing Order
ISBN 0–333–73634–6
(outside North America only)

You can receive future titles in this series as they are published . To place a standing
order please contact your bookseller or, in the case of difficulty, write to us at the
address below with your name and address, the title of the series and the ISBN
quoted above.

Roland Barthes

(Or the Profession of Cultural Studies)

Martin McQuillan

First published 2011 by
PALGRAVE MACMILLAN

Palgrave Macmillan in the UK is an imprint of Macmillan Publishers Limited, registered in England, company number 785998, of Houndmills, Basingstoke, Hampshire RG21 6XS.

Palgrave Macmillan in the US is a division of St Martin's Press LLC, 175 Fifth Avenue, New York, NY 10010.

Palgrave Macmillan is the global academic imprint of the above companies and has companies and representatives throughout the world.

Palgrave® and Macmillan® are registered trademarks in the United States, the United Kingdom, Europe and other countries.

ISBN 978–0–333–91457–1   hardback
ISBN 978–0–333–91458–8   paperback

This book is printed on paper suitable for recycling and made from fully managed and sustained forest sources. Logging, pulping and manufacturing processes are expected to conform to the environmental regulations of the country of origin.

A catalogue record for this book is available from the British Library.

A catalog record for this book is available from the Library of Congress.

10 9 8 7 6 5 4 3 2 1
20 19 18 17 16 15 14 13 12 11

Printed and bound in Great Britain by
CPI Antony Rowe, Chippenham and Eastbourne

Contents

General Editor's Preface

Transitions: *transition* –, n. of action. 1. A passing or passage from one condition, action or (rarely) place, to another. 2. Passage in thought, speech, or writing, from one subject to another. 3. a. The passing from one note to another. b. The passing from one key to another, modulation. 4. The passage from an earlier to a later stage of development of formation ... change from an earlier style to a later; a style of intermediate or mixed character ... the historical passage of language from one well-defined stage to another.

The aim of *Transitions* is to explore passages, movements and the development of significant voices in critical thought, as these voices determine and are mediated by acts of literary and cultural interpretation. This series also seeks to examine the possiblities for reading, analysis and other critical engagements which the very idea of transition – such as the transition effected by the reception of a thinker's *oeuvre* and the heritage entailed – makes possible. The writers in this series unfold the movements and modulation of critical thinking over the last generation, from the first emergences of what is now recognized as literary thoery. They examine as well how the transitional nature of theoretical and critical thinking is still very much in operation, guaranteed by the hybridity and heterogeneity of the field of literary studies. The authors in the series share the common understanding that, now more than ever, critical thought is both in a state of transition and can best be defined by developing for the student reader an understanding of this protean quality. As this *tranche* of the series, dealing with particular critical voices, addresses, it is of great significance, if not urgency, that the texts of particular figures be reconsidered anew.

This series desires, then, to enable the reader to transform her/his own reading and writing transactions by comprehending past developments as well as the internal transitions worked through by particular literary and cultural critics, analysts, and philosophers. Each book in the series offers a guide to the poetics and politics of such thinkers, as well as interpretative paradigms, schools, bodies of thought, historical and cultural periods, and the genealogy of particular concepts, while transforming these, if not into tools or methodologies, then into conduits for directing and channelling thought. As well as transforming the critical past by interpreting it from the perspective of the present day, each study enacts transitional readings of critical voices and well-known literary texts, which are themselves conceivable as having been transitional and influential at the moments of their first appearance. The readings offered in these books seek, through close critical reading and theoretical engagement to demonstrate certain possibilities in critical thinking to the student reader.

It is hoped that the student will find this series liberating because rigid methodologies are not being put into place. As all the dictionary definitions of the idea of transition above suggest, what is important is the action, the passage: of thought, of analysis, of critical response, such as are to be found, for example, in the texts of critics whose work has irrevocably transformed the critical landscape. Rather than seeking to help you locate yourself in relation to any particular school or discipline, this series aims to put you into action, as readers and writers, travellers between positions, where the movement between poles comes to be seen as of more importance than the locations themselves.

Julian Wolfreys

Acknowledgements

I would like to thank everyone who contributed to the production of this book. I would like to thank the editorial staff at Palgrave Macmillan for their extraordinary patience, especially Sonya Barker and Felicity Noble. I would like to thank Julian Wolfreys for his unstinting support throughout the writing of this book. I would also like to thank Eleanor Byrne, Robert Eaglestone, Graham Allen, Simon Morgan Wortham, Nicholas Chare, Mark Currie, Derek Attridge and Stephen Barker for their various contributions known and unknown. The writing of the extended essay that forms the core of this book was made possible by a grant from the Arts and Humanities Research Council.

This book is dedicated to my friends in the north, where life is good.

The image of le Petit Diouf on p. 112 is reproduced courtesy of *Paris-Match*.

If I had to define myself it would be as a 'philosopher', which does not refer to a degree of competence, because I had no philosophical training. What I do is philosophise, reflect on my experience. This reflection is a joy and a benefit to me, and when I'm unable to pursue this activity, I become unhappy.

Roland Barthes, interview 1978, *The Grain of the Voice*
(p. 307). See pages 3 and 7 for discussion.

Introduction: Roland Barthes, About This Book

The aim of this book is to ask: why should the reader of today (or tomorrow) attend to the text of Roland Barthes? It is not in a straightforward sense an 'introduction' to Barthes as an explication of the basic theories and paradigms to be found in Barthes' work. There are two very fine books that already fill this niche: Jonathan Culler's *Barthes: A Very Short Introduction* (2002) and Graham Allen's *Roland Barthes* (2003). There have been posthumous publications by Barthes since these books first appeared but these late books 'signed' by Barthes do little to undo the lucid comprehension of his work offered by Culler and Allen. These books should be read alongside this present study by any student reader wishing to gain a foothold in Barthes' text. The opening chapter of this book is an account of the life and textual production of Roland Barthes. This introduction is necessary because this 'bio-bibliography' directly impinges upon the work that follows as an account of the complexities of the theory-writing life. Readers who feel themselves to be suitably familiar with Barthes' biography might wish to proceed straight to Chapter 2, 'Reading Roland Barthes in a Time of Terror'.

My own book responds to a different 'introductory' concern with regard to Barthes. It sets out from the premise that while the conceptual basis of what is called today, in an Anglophone context, 'cultural studies' is derived from the translation of work by Barthes in the 1970s, the figure of Barthes himself is almost entirely absent from the present theoretical scene. This suggests to me that a work of theoretical archaeology is required to understand this current situation. In particular, the substantial work to be found in this book is an extended reading of Barthes' 1957 text *Mythologies*, published in English in two volumes, *Mythologies* (1972) and *The Eiffel Tower* (1979). The gap between the

French text and its English-language reception, a veritable theoretical 'life-time', is telling. While the leap between Barthes' concerns of the 1950s and the post-human, cultural studies reader of today is substantial, the impact of Barthes in the intervening years was considerable, transforming (along with others) every channel of the Anglophone humanities. This includes the terms under which a text or a thinker might make an opening within the academic space itself. The widespread and popular appeal of Annette Lavers' 1972 translation of selected essays from Barthes' original is no longer matched by the specialist distribution of Barthes' seminar today or his recently published diary texts. The entire 'academediatic' space had shifted in this time. The connection between the complicated thought of the university and the multi-platform journalistic scene has become entirely attenuated. This mutation is formed of several related paths, on the one hand the specialisation of academic literary and cultural criticism, on the other the increasing domination of metropolitan culture by a reductive mediatic apparatus predicated on the logic of the market. In truth, as Barthes' own *Critique et Vérité* (1966) argues, this situation has always existed to a degree. However, our present situation is particularly acute as the twenty-five years between these two publications by Barthes in English have witnessed the almost complete dismantling of a critical sub-culture in Europe and North America (this includes Australia, of course) and the stratification of niche markets according to academic interests. Barthes' own career, which moved between journalism and research institute, post-Liberation small presses and the Collège de France, would no longer be possible; as much for the professional requirements of the university as for the inhospitality of the media to complexity. Barthes' life is a case study in the possibility of the impossible. The fact that he lived it and moved between the competing demands and idioms that he did is testament to the form of survival as invention characteristic of the theory-writing life.

This situation, as is always the case with the present, is considerably complex. While cultural studies has transformed the university and broken down, irreversibly perhaps, disciplinary boundaries across the humanities, it remains aporetically estranged from the mediatic space upon which it comments. On the contrary, the reductive power of journalism more frequently than not positions 'cultural studies' as an object of scorn, in some way less 'scholarly' than traditional disciplinarity such as 'philosophy', 'history' or 'English literature'. In this sense, those importantly engaged in the media have a blind spot over the media itself as a subject, which is thought not important enough for scholarly study. Equally, the academic apparatus treats the media as an arena to be both desired and feared: one should be wary of becoming ensnared in its reductive power and so no longer able to speak as a 'professor'; at the same time the professor should desire to profess across all the channels of communication. What interests me about Barthes is the way in which it is possible to read his text today in light of these transformations. The epigram that keeps guard over this book, from an interview Barthes gave in 1978 towards the end of his writing career, is suggestive of the value and difficulty presented by Barthes' work: 'If I had to define myself', he says, 'it would be as a "philosopher"'. This term is in inverted commas, for who would ever have the resources to lay claim to the purity of such a provenance? He recognises that this appellation 'does not refer to a degree of competence, because I had no philosophical training'. Rather, Barthes is a philosopher of tomorrow, one whose philosophy is more than philosophy: 'what I do is philosophise, reflect on my experience. This reflection is a joy and a benefit to me, and when I'm unable to pursue this activity, I become unhappy.' I would like to suggest in this book that cultural studies is the philosophy of the present, the philosophy that as philosophy attends to the present as its subject. The semioclast-philosopher is the one who analyses and then draws the practical and effective consequences between the philosophical heritage and the dominant political and cultural structures of the present, which are called into question and put under transformative stress by the events of the present itself. This is a form of critical intelligence, a habitual mode of critical reading and writing in the world, that I would like to suggest places Barthes in a tradition of Enlightenment thought and that I would wish to salvage from his legacy and the legacy of cultural studies today.

One might characterise a text such as *Mythologies* as the 'origin of cultural studies'. It is a text that makes its entrance(s) (1956, 1972, 1979) under singular circumstances that are revealing of the general aporias of cultural studies. The argument is made here that while the French academy today eschews 'cultural studies' as an Anglo-Saxon disciplinary disease, of course the migration of French thought is the 'origin' of a certain cultural studies. France, one might say, had its cultural studies moment long before this soubriquet entered into the vocabulary of the English-speaking university. In fact France had its cultural studies moment at a particular historical conjuncture, which we might describe as the French Empire's own 'war on terror', between the eclipse of the relative liberalism of the Mendès-France government and the military coup d'état that brought De Gaulle to power. This period in French history might be said to be its own 'war on terror' not because this phrase is a just syntagm that maps one historical moment onto another but precisely because it points to an instant when ideology and the political realm overspill the previously-thought-possible-or-acceptable. As with the years between 2001 and 2008 in the United States and United Kingdom, 1954 to 1958 in France were dominated by an assault on colonial privilege and the overwhelming, unilateral, repressive response of Empire, which justified military and judicial actions of all kinds, domestically and internationally. It is under such circumstances that Barthes produced his *Mythologies*, at once the most trivial aspect of his scholarly output and his most significant intervention in both the academic and mediatic realms. While the reading offered here presents this parallel, it is not systematically concerned with the events of our own contemporary moment (this has been done elsewhere). Rather, the concern follows a double braid. On the one hand, it seeks to reclaim Barthes as a thinker of Ideology and to recover Ideology itself as a theoretical term beyond its normative inscription. On the other hand, it attends to a wider structure of response and responsibility for theory and the scholar.

One possible answer to the question of why the student of today (tomorrow) should read Barthes revolves around the issue of historical pertinence. The answer is not directly that the time of the mythologies is also our time, or, that Barthes explains our time for us through historical similarity. Rather, the text of Barthes, before, during and after the *Mythologies*, walks the tightrope between scholarly-theoretical research, commentary on the here and now, and an intelligent intervention in the public realm. The text of Barthes did not affect the course of the Algerian War of Independence in the way that Émile Zola's polemic may have influenced the events of the Dreyfus case in 1898, nor will a belated reading of Barthes redirect the course of the world war between the Christian west and its others. The temporality of theory does not run along this course. Rather, and here is the first aporia of cultural studies, the task that cultural studies (and by extension all theoretical-political inquiry) is engaged in by reading *today*, is the longer, decades and century long struggle over the transformation of the forms of intelligibility for the present. Those who lack patience with the philosophical's seeming inability to make an impact in the present moment (to intervene in the here and now) lack historical perspective. Give it two hundred years or so and philosophy and theory change everything. Cultural studies is nothing if it is not the philosophy of the present moment. I want to suggest that Barthes is, to use his own term, a 'logothete' (a founder of language or initiator of discourse). Just as he identifies Sade, Loyola and Fourier, he is someone who has created a discourse, the means by which theory can address the present as both scholar and citizen. That is to say, Barthes, knowingly or not, invented cultural studies. However, the value of Barthes is more than this particular inauguration. Instead I would like to emphasise in this study an understanding of Barthes as a writer. That is to say, the value of Barthes today lies in the way that his work is concerned with writing as such, with the symbolisation of language itself, as the envelope of understanding. It will be a frequent gesture in this book to suggest that Barthes' own theoretical insights are either limited or have been superseded by subsequent work. However, what remains today of Barthes is his immersion in the idiom of his writing as a transformation of the means of intelligibility. This is what makes Barthes part of a great Modern tradition of theory-writers, such as Benjamin and Adorno, Arendt and the late Derrida, who dared to move their writing between genres and realms of meaning, as a writerly and philosophical intervention beyond philosophy itself. I do not wish to reclaim the term 'public intellectual'. Who could say this phrase today with a straight face? Barthes was not a public intellectual, at least not in the sense that this term is frequently used. Indeed, Barthes was considerably reluctant to take on this role, as exemplified by a contemporary such as Sartre. Rather, the value of Barthes' writing is precisely that it is inhospitable to the terms of reference of the 'public intellectual' as such. Whenever Barthes makes a public intervention it is always in the name of 'dumbing up' the public realm rather than reducing his thought for ease of transmission. Consequently, Barthes is not necessarily remembered as a 'political thinker' in the way that Sartre is, but equally, I would argue, Barthes' writing remains infinitely more 'relevant' to the reader of today than does Sartre. This is because what we find in Barthes is an attempt to open up new channels of interrogation and self-questioning as a space for thought in the face of the unexpected appearance of the present, while in Sartre one will only ever find the application to events of an already considered philosophy. Barthes risks the powerlessness of his writing in the jaws of the powerful inertia of the political realm and by the otherness of his writing effects a discernible movement in an arena that can neither master alterity nor ignore this thought. It is this version of Barthes, as the theory-writer of Modernity that I would wish to salvage from amid the intellectual furniture of post-war France. Of course, as I will go on to argue, the choice is never between Barthes and Sartre, never a case of either/or. Not if we are to move beyond the hermeneutic seal of academic readership, in order to redefine reading itself as a general practice and a way of life.

Finally, the reason why we should read Barthes today is because in doing so we will become better readers. So much of the text of Barthes lies before us waiting to be reread, reassembled and re-evaluated. The theoretical tradition must always recognise itself as a tradition, which inevitably means the constant return to the texts of the tradition in order to turn them around and to open up new directions in the present. To my mind Barthes remains a considerably under-read author today. I hope that this study will give others a reason to explore more widely and wildly the text of Barthes.

*

It is traditional for books in the Transitions series to conclude with readings of literary texts 'after the manner' of the theorist to whom the book is devoted. In the case of Roland Barthes I do not feel that such an approach would be either possible or productive. Which Roland Barthes would we choose to imitate, if imitation were called for? Will it be the Barthes of 'Structural Analysis of Narrative', which would call for a full-blown categorisation of the structural elements of a given text? What benefit would the reader derive from such an exposition of a typology that they could not receive directly, and better, unmediated from the structuralist Barthes? Will it be the Barthes of *S/Z*, which would call for a forensic examination of a text at the level of the letter, the signifier, the code and every minimal unit of sense? Entertaining as this would be, for the author, what use will it serve for the reader of today who wishes to mobilise the spirit of Barthes beyond a technical application? Will it be the Barthes of the *Mythologies*? Good reasons will be given for believing that any attempt to revive myth-hunting *per se*, in the style of Barthes, would not be unproblematic today given Barthes' profound influence on those who are now the conductors of our present mythology, from the advertisers to the spin doctors. Will it be the index-card writing Barthes of the book on Michelet, or the later autobiographical, fragmentary Barthes of his final texts? Will it be the Barthes of his seminar, or the Barthes of his texts on fashion or the *Empire of Signs*? All of these Barthes would be in some way radically heterogeneous. There is no one single Barthes for us to copy. Barthes is plural, there is more than one. Such would be the point of my thesis in this book. The interest in reading Barthes today lies not in the curiosity of an obsolete hermeneutic methodology that can be reapplied today to literary or cultural texts. Rather, what is engaging about Barthes is precisely his fluidity, adaptability and persistent heterogeneity when faced with the contingency of the present and the evolving intellectual scene. It is this spirit of a heterodox, writerly and critical Barthes that I wish to reclaim rather than the specificities of his technical operations and vocabulary. The pedagogical challenge of Barthes does not fall within the locus of such an exposition today; rather it lies in an altogether more compelling and demanding place. Given the radical disjuncture between theoretical thought and the public space today and the example that Barthes sets us of the critical-writer-theorist, the question that lies before the reader of Barthes is: what resources can we find in Barthes' own response to his particular historical situation that will assist us in determining a new criteriology for distinguishing between comprehending and criticising/justifying the world that surrounds us today?

The book therefore concludes in two ways. First, there is a text that responds to one of the persistent themes of the longer study of Barthes in this book, 'An Answer to the Question: What is Cultural Studies?' This essay responds to Barthes' own, late self-definition as a philosopher (see epigram above) and examines Barthes' relation to what we call cultural studies and the relation of cultural studies to the philosophy of Enlightenment critique. This chapter is therefore an important step in justifying the particular reclamation of Barthes that this book attempts. Other prolonged considerations of the questions raised by the essay 'Reading Roland Barthes in a Time of Terror', such as the trope of 'cultural archaeology' and the question of an alternative philosophical history of ideology, will have to wait for another occasion and another philosophical return. However, neither of these promised excursions will be possible without first properly placing Barthes and the philosophical heritage of cultural studies. The book concludes finally, as the Transition series requires, with an annotated bibliography of Barthes' published work, which will point the reader towards Barthes' expanded corpus and hopefully to a compelling re-examination of the texts of Roland Barthes.

1 R.B.: Bio-bibliography

Roland Barthes and Jean-Paul Sartre died within three weeks of each other in the spring of 1980. Barthes' funeral in the town of Urt in the Bayonne region of south-west France was attended by a handful of his close friends; Sartre's funeral in Montparnasse in Paris attracted a crowd of over fifty thousand mourners along a two-hour route. Today, the name of Sartre is instantly recognisable in the media as a touchstone for the 'committed intellectual'. In contrast the name of Roland Barthes is readily familiar to humanities academics and students of cultural studies or literary theory, perhaps to the readership of 'elite liberal' publications such as *The London Review of Books*, but has little currency with a more general audience. However, what remains untold in this scenario is the fact that from the perspective of today the majority of Sartre's cold war political interventions look disastrously misjudged, while his philosophy and literature appear, on first inspection, to be somewhat dated, while the majority of the text of Barthes seems, to the theory-hound, fresh and vital some thirty years after his death. Now, Sartre is a fascinating writer, a complex and compelling figure who deserves to be read and reread: we will never be done with Sartre. However, there is no time for that here, this is not a book about Jean-Paul Sartre. Rather, I would like to suggest that while the public response to the death of these two thinkers points towards the ways in which different idioms of writing and different modes of living the philosophical life are appreciated by a public audience, there remains a subterranean route through which thought lives on. In this respect, while Sartre's highly visible public engagements make for an epic biography, Barthes' relative academic isolation would tend to indicate what is often mistaken for 'political quietism'. On first appearances, the schematic division between the life and times of Sartre and those of Roland Barthes looks like a choice between a figure such as André Gide and a Marcel Proust. The one provides the model for the 'engaged' writer, the other the one who never leaves his study. Thankfully, the choice is never between one and the other, Sartre or Barthes. However, while the text of Sartre now looks like a bridge in the history of ideas, the significance of Barthes' writing continues to irrigate the humanities today. This then is the first question we must ask: what is the relation between the biography of Barthes and the text of Barthes? In particular, what significance does this biography have in the reading of Barthes today?

Barthes, of course, offers one possible answer to this question in his text 'The Death of the Author'. Here Barthes does not deny the link between the transformative process of writing and the biographical experience of a writer. On the contrary, this is a constant theme of much of Barthes' writing on those authors who spoke to him enough to make him feel compelled to write about them: Michelet, Sade, Flaubert and so on. Rather, Barthes' object in this essay is to initiate a new idiom of reading that provisionally untied the reader from the tyrannous culture of the Author and the critical authority that stood as the expert witness able to unlock the relation between book and biography. So, let us not too easily dismiss the life of Barthes simply because Barthes once wrote about the need to consider more than just the life of an author when reading literature. Instead, what I would like to propose here is that the life of Barthes, while hardly dramatic in the way that Sartre's might be considered, tells a singularly interesting story about the dilemmas and contradictions of the theoretical and writerly life. I do not hold by Heidegger's famous dismissal of the biography of Aristotle: he was born, he thought, he died. By this calculation, the life of Aristotle is of no interest to philosophy; it is mere anecdote in contrast to the rigour and precision of a philosophical system. On the one hand, it may be possible to read productively and to admire philosophical writing without knowledge of its author (this would be the point of Barthes' own essay). However, on the other hand, this is not a proposition that will hold with any degree of rigour itself as soon as one scratches the surface of the philosopher's biography. I am not suggesting that we will find in the life of Barthes a key to unlock the secrets of his text; rather I am suggesting that the act of writing in whatever genre is always in some significantly complex way autobiographical. This is the case even, and doubly so, when the writing in question seems at its most distant from a biographical source. There is nothing more autobiographical than the administrator's report, nothing more revealing of the life of the bureaucrat, their concerns and influences. It is through such texts that one might effect a psychoanalysis of the institution. Nor am I proposing that we can read backwards from the text of Barthes to explain the life of its author, the choices he made, the actions and consequences that followed from them. Rather, I am proposing, as a general difficulty in writing and reading about writing, the absolute uncertainty over the proper relation between the life of an author and their writing. Just as the writer cannot programme the life to 'walk the talk' that their writing has proposed, neither can the reader adequately determine the true relation between the text of a life and a body of writing, the one being inextricably contaminated by the other. All that the reader and author can do is to affirm this impossibility and to work through their reading and writing to render the difficulty ever more effective as a problem worthy of consideration. It is in this spirit that I would like to approach the biography of Roland Barthes as an allegory of the aporias of cultural studies, or something like the public-political understanding of theory and philosophy. In this chapter I present Barthes' life as a case study rather than developing this theoretical aporia. The issues raised in this chapter will run through the more properly theoretical text that follows in Chapter 2.

*

Roland Barthes was born on 12 November 1915 in Cherbourg. His father was stationed in Cherbourg as a naval lieutenant during the First World War. He was a Catholic from the south-west of France; Barthes' mother was a protestant from Alsace in the east. Louis Barthes died in action before Roland was a year old, in command of a patrol boat (the *Montaigne*) in the North Sea beyond the Cap Gris-Nez. Barthes was raised a protestant by his widowed mother and as with the children of the French military who die in conflict was 'adopted by the state', although he officially became 'a ward of the nation' only in November 1925 after a civil court decision in Bayonne. After her husband's death Henriette Barthes moved south to live with his family. Here Barthes went to primary school after the war in the Arènes district of Bayonne until June 1924. At this time Barthes was a little Basque kid with a southern accent, often belittled for its cultural associations with the rural and the pre-modern, the French equivalent of a Yorkshire or Norfolk accent, or a Southern US drawl. In 1924 Roland Barthes and his mother moved to Paris where he went to school, ironically, at the Lycée Montaigne. The Barthes lived in several flats during this time but never moved outside St-Germain-des-Près. Roland spent his school holidays in Bayonne with his grandmother and aunt. The Lycée Montaigne faired only marginally better than Louis Barthes'

patrol boat, being occupied as a German staff headquarters during the
Second World War, with the subsequent destruction of all the school
records that covered Roland's time there. In April 1927, the unmar-
ried Henriette gave birth to Barthes' half-brother Michel Salzedo. The
father was an artist and ceramist who lived near Bayonne. He never
lived with the Barthes brothers; instead Henriette brought them both
up on her war widow's pension and her modest income from book-
binding in the Rue Jacques-Callot in Paris. Thus, Barthes' childhood
was one of unconventional living and considerably reduced circumstances within the context of the Parisian bourgeoisie. From 1930 to
1934 Roland Barthes attended the Lycée Louis-le-Grand, which sat just
behind the Sorbonne, and was recognised as a school for the privileged classes and the future elite. Barthes was a prize-winning pupil
(records show him receiving prizes and certificates in 1931 from His
Excellency Dinu Cesiano, 'special envoy and Minister Plenipotentiary
of His Majesty the King of Romania'). The archive shows the teenage
Barthes to be a reader of Jean Jaurre and a self-identifying 'socialist'.
    In 1934, with Hitler in power in Berlin, and Paris the site of increas-
ingly anxious activity (including the mobilisation of the far right in
France), Barthes' academic progress was checked by pulmonary tuberculosis as he prepared for his baccalauréat exam. He was sent from Paris
to recuperate in Bayonne. Barthes was able to sit part of the examination but was unable to continue his studies in Paris; instead his family
moved to the village of Bedous in the Pyrenees for the benefit of the
mountain air. After this brief hiatus, and having missed the chance to
sit the entrance exam for the École Normale, Barthes returned to Paris
in October 1934 to enrol in a classics degree at the Sorbonne. Here the
undergraduate Barthes pursued his love of drama with the Ancient
Theatre Group, performing the classics in the main courtyard of the
Sorbonne, not far from where he would eventually be knocked down
and fatally injured on his return from lunch with François Mitterrand
in 1980.
    Barthes was exempted from military service in 1937 on health
grounds and in the years before the outbreak of the war divided his
time between study, his ancient drama group and exploring Europe in
the twilight before the all-encompassing war against fascism: including trips to Greece and Hungary. In 1939 when war was declared
between France and Germany Barthes was ruled permanently unfit
for service. He applied to teach literature in the *lycée* and found a
post in Biarritz in the south, taking his mother and brother with him.

However, after the defeat of France and the foundation of the Vichy government in July 1940, Barthes returned to Paris, *en famille*, and taught as a 'supply teacher' across two schools while continuing to study in the occupied city. By November 1942 Barthes had suffered a pulmonary relapse and applied for a place in the student's sanatorium at Saint-Hilaire-du-Touvet in the Isère in the Alps between Grenoble and Chambery. At this time tuberculosis sufferers such as Barthes were described as being 'positive' and the purpose of institutions such as Saint-Hilaire was as much to isolate the patients to control the spread of the disease as to attempt any sort of a cure. There were several sanatoria in Saint-Hilaire but the village was only accessible by a funicular railway built for the express purpose of servicing the institutions. There was a very real prospect that Barthes could spend the rest of his days in the sanatorium, with his 'positive' identification every bit as much of a possible death sentence as the diagnosis of HIV positive today. However, the student sanatorium encouraged its patients to continue their studies and placed an emphasis on the redemptive value of culture as a cure for corrupted lungs. So Barthes saw out the war in a hospital in the Alps, reading and writing, and developing his thoughts towards the book that would become his first significant work, *Writing Degree Zero*. At Saint-Hilaire he read voraciously and discovered the work of Gaston Bachelard. Diverted from his classical education at the Sorbonne, these years in the library at Saint-Hilaire were really Barthes' theoretical education, undertaken in the most unusual of circumstances on a mini-campus of unhealth with its reading groups and lecture series, and at a distance from professorial oversight.

In the summer of 1944 France was liberated far from the isolated scholars of Saint-Hilaire. In fact the Isère itself, a stronghold for the German army, was not liberated until the following summer. Notices appeared one day stating that a new regime had been established in Grenoble and the Vichy-supporting director of the sanatorium discreetly disappeared to be replaced by a Jewish doctor returning from the United States. While the rest of France was liberated Barthes remained a prisoner of his illness. However, in February 1945 Barthes was transferred to the university sanatorium at Leysin above Aigle in Switzerland as part of a charitable exchange funded by Swiss bankers. His routine changed little and in Switzerland he read the complete works of Michelet in between treatments. Here he met George Fournié, a student three years younger than Barthes, but who had fought with the POUM in the Spanish Civil War aged seventeen and later joined the Resistance in France. Fournié encouraged Barthes' reading of Marx and introduced him to writing by Trotsky, which sat alongside Barthes' reading of Michelet's *History of France*. Barthes finally left the Swiss sanatorium in February 1946 after a prolonged period of reading. Like Lenin he had learned his future Marxism in the quiet cantons of Switzerland.

Between Bedous and the various sanatoriums Barthes had spent in total some eight years in isolation; like a Proust confined to read but not yet write. In autumn 1946 his friend the diplomat Philippe Rebeyrol (who had completed his studies while Barthes convalesced) offered Barthes the opportunity to escape the austerity of post-war Paris where Barthes was yet to be reintegrated into intellectual life. He took up the post of librarian at the Institute Française in Bucharest where Rebeyrol served as a cultural attaché. At the same time Barthes was attempting without success to find a professor in Paris willing to supervise a doctoral dissertation based around his Michelet project. However, George Fournié introduced Barthes to Maurice Nadeau, a fellow militant from the International Worker's Party and now editor of the cultural section of Camus' post-war publication *Combat*. It was through Nadeau that Barthes would originally publish *Writing Degree Zero* in *Combat*. The route through which authors come to writing, or more specifically come to be recognised through publishing, are always revealing of the nature of that writing. In this case we have a High Theorist whose path into the academy does not pass through any easy institutional route. Barthes' undergraduate education had been disrupted by war and illness. He was never to find a doctoral supervisor. His early career as a critic and theorist passed not through the École Normale (the usual path for the French elite) but via librarianship and journalism. During this time Barthes was an autodidact working outside the French higher education system. This fact is suggestive of two things: first, that it ought to be possible, in principle, to engage in theoretical-critical reflection without the university; and, second, that the boundary between university research and intelligent thought in the public realm is undoubtedly complex and porous. Barthes' 'higher education' was of a less formal type than that offered in the rue d'Ulm but nevertheless his concentrated reading during his years of medical isolation constituted an equivalent experience of sorts. The point here is that while in the biography of writers there is never writing without reading (biography in this sense is always a matter of biblio-biography), thinking of a theoretical nature such as Barthes' can emerge from outside the university, or on the cusp of the university, in a way that was independent of, but related to, the 'public research project' of existentialism in the post-war publications and exchanges of Sartre and Camus, itself distinct from, but not inimical to, normative humanistic and journalistic discourse. *Writing Degree Zero* appeared in *Combat* on 1 August 1947, described by the editor as the product of 'a young, unknown writer. [Who] has never published any work, not even an article'. *Writing Degree Zero* was not translated into English until 1970.

In late 1947 Barthes took his notes on Michelet and his mother with him to Romania. Here he stayed for the next two years running the library and organising Francophone cultural events while the country slipped ever further into the grip of the Soviet sphere of influence. The Institute Française was a welcome island between the growing Stalinist influence and the alternative of Anglo-Saxon culture and the Marshall Plan. The institute and its library also provided a key resource of French language books to the universities in Bucharest, once again placing Barthes at the boundary between the university and public education. With the abdication of King Michael I in December 1947 the People's Republic of Romania was founded. The French Institute served for a while as an irritant to the new regime in a diplomatic to and fro, before the Romanian government expelled the staff of the institute at the end of July 1949. Barthes' name did not appear on the list of those expelled and he was able to stay on until September of that year when a second list was issued. As a believer in dialectical materialism Barthes seemed less concerned with the regime's expulsion of the French diplomats than the prospect that he might miss out on employment with Rebeyrol in his new posting in Egypt. He organised a final musical concert and, as reported by his biographer Louis-Jean Calvet, spoke to the audience of the long march of history:

> The critical function of French science, scholarship and thought has been carried out through the centuries by millions of French teachers and intellectuals, from Montaigne to Valery, Gerson to Marc Bloch. It constitutes a solid historical fact in comparison with which the closure of a library or the departure of a cultural attaché are laughable, in historical terms. Thus it is with absolute peace of mind that I reflect upon the future of this institute. What matters is the spirit it conveys and this has already been borne out and championed by history itself. History could never deny its own march.[1]

With that the twenty-two year old Barthes put the lights off in the institute and left the Romanians who had just emerged from the dark wood of fascism only to be eclipsed by the night of Stalinism. Before he left he arranged for the transfer of the library books to the university as a lamp of enlightenment hiding in the shadows of the shelves of other pulped trees. Europe's last representative (the one who had fallen off the list and was left behind, the librarian having not been bothersome enough to power to have been on the original roll call) departed with his mother on the last train under the Iron Curtain.

He was redeployed to Alexandria, a Franco-British trading post, in 1949, where an interest in French culture among the local educated represented a subtle slight at the English sphere of influence. Barthes worked here as a lecturer in French at the university along with the newly arrived Algirdas Julien Greimas, who later became a prominent thinker of structuralism and semiology and would teach with Barthes in Paris. Greimas introduced Barthes to Saussure's *Course in General Linguistics* and to Roman Jakobson. As a consequence of his status as a consumptive, an Egyptian government commission refused Barthes the official title of '*lecteur*' and Barthes left Egypt at the end of the academic year in 1950, leaving behind his conversations with Greimas and the Arab boys he had found easier to pursue than the more discreet Romanians or the sensitive friendships of his sanatorium years. On his return to Paris he took a job in the Cultural Affairs section of the Foreign Office where he dealt with programmes to teach French as a second language. He turned down posts as a language assistant in Cambridge and Bologna, before deciding to concentrate on his independent research in Paris. He pulled together into a book the texts he had written for *Combat*. At the same time (1953) Barthes started to write for *Les Lettres nouvelles*, a magazine founded by Maurice Nadeau after he left *Combat*. The *Lettres nouvelles* column was to form the basis of Barthes' *Mythologies*, when in 1957 he collected a selection of his 'mythologies of the month' into a single volume. In these texts Barthes puts his semiology and Marxism to good use, as he ranges over a diverse set of texts and objects to uncover the ideological obfuscations of 'petite bourgeois' culture. It is no accident that Barthes' theoretical approach to popular culture should emerge from counter-cultural publications of the post-Liberation left rather than the French universities of the 1950s. At this time Barthes was a clerk in a government office, writing in his own time and working to establish a name in journalism.

Writing Degree Zero was published as a book by *Editions du Seuil* in the last quarter of 1953 and by this time Barthes also had a contract to write a study of Michelet in the 'writers today' series, also for *Seuil* (critical summaries of Barthes' texts appear in the annotated bibliography accompanying this volume). In November 1953, with the help of Greimas, Barthes secured a grant from the CNRS (Centre Nationale de Recherche Scientifique) to pursue a new PhD project on 'the vocabulary of the social question in 1830'. He left the Foreign Office to commit himself to writing and research but found his new funded project tough going, while being compelled to teach French to foreign students at the Sorbonne to make ends meet at the age of thirty-eight.

The financial pressures on Barthes began to ease when his grandmother died in 1953, leaving him a legacy, having previously refused to assist his mother after the birth of Barthes' half-brother out of wedlock. The execution of the will was complex and drawn out but the very idea of an inheritance (including a smelting works, which he would never run but could sell) gave Barthes hope to persist with his writing. At the same time Barthes founded with others the review *Théâtre Populaire* a journal devoted to a Brechtian view of drama. Bernard Dort, a fellow editor of *Théâtre Populaire*, introduced Barthes to the *nouveau roman*, in particular the anti-novels of Alain Robbe-Grillet. Robbe-Grillet's work seemed to offer an alternative to Camus or Sartre and an example of writing at degree zero. However, all this activity, along with the draft of his Michelet book, distracted Barthes from his CNRS project.

Michelet par lui-même was published in the spring of 1954, having been the twelve-year, slow burn product of his sanatorium reading. The research for this book came to define Barthes' practice as a writer: compiling daily over a thousand index cards on Michelet with notes and thoughts, classifying and combining them in alternative combinations before settling on a publishable structure or set of themes. This strategy of filing and indexing before the advent of the word-processor or laptop served Barthes well in the years of published work that followed. However, it served him less well with the CNRS, which refused to renew his two-year contract as a trainee researcher when he failed to produce a coherent and convincing report on his research into the vocabulary of the social question. Once more the doors of the academy seemed closed to Barthes. He fell back upon *Théâtre Populaire* and the editor at Arche, Robert Voisin, who had originally commissioned the journal, took Barthes on as a literary adviser to the press, augmenting his position at *Théâtre Populaire*. After his departure from the CNRS, Barthes worked at Arche in the afternoon and wrote at home in the morning, in the maid's room above his mother's flat in the Rue

Servandoni. He called his next writing project 'the sociology of daily life', which later became *Mythologies*.

With his grandmother's legacy settled by spring 1955 (Barthes was later to lose much of it in poor investments advised by Philippe Rebeyrol's uncle Pierre Davy) Barthes pursued his criticism and theoretical innovation independent of the university. He was involved in a polemical exchange with Albert Camus (treated at greater length in the next chapter) in which he outed himself as a 'dialectical materialist' and seemed to side with Sartre in the hysterical and sterile dispute between the two men. In December 1955 Barthes met a twenty-nine year old Michel Foucault for the first time. The two obviously had much in common and a long friendship began with the two meeting regularly in Paris and Morocco before a falling-out led to estrangement in 1964, which was only resolved many years later when Foucault nominated Barthes for his position at the Collège de France. Barthes was elected to the Collège with a majority of one vote.

By April 1956 Barthes was beginning to distance himself from *Théâtre Populaire*, having secured another research assistantship at the CNRS, this time in the sociology department, and working flat out on the publication of his *Mythologies*. The book was formed of texts written mostly for *Les Lettres nouvelles*, the first of which (the famous text on wrestling) appeared in 1952. It was topped with the essay 'Myth Today', which Barthes wrote in the summer of 1956, combining semiology with a Marxist critique of bourgeois culture. Once again it is possible to discern in the editing of this book the practice of arranging indexed and archived texts into the structure of a new volume. The only difference from the Michelet text was that the 'mythologies' had been previously published elsewhere. The finished book appeared at the start of 1957, again published by *Seuil*. Like the Michelet book it did not have the same impact as *Writing Degree Zero*, partly because it was a collection of previously published material, partly because the France of early 1957 was not yet fully prepared for the era of 'theory' and its associated vocabulary. Barthes wrote his own blurb for the original edition, stating 'For the past three years, R.B. has been trying to carry out a "committed" form of criticism, including his reading of literature such as Robbe-Grillet, his work at *Théâtre Populaire* and the mythologies in *Les Lettres Nouvelle* and *France-Observateur*'. Two things are striking about this self-definition. First is the obvious link, but subtle shift, between Sartre's notion of 'commitment' and a 'committed criticism' – that is, a writing rather than a straightforward 'doing'. Second is the use of the initials 'R.B.', which most directly refer to Brecht's practice of referring to himself in the third-person as B.B. (although Bridget Bardot could also lay claim to this acronym). Philippe Sollers was later to fiction-alise Barthes as the character Arbee ('Erbé') in his novel *Les Femmes*, and most of Barthes' close friends would affectionately call him RB. However, the Brecht reference is indicative of where Barthes under-stood himself to be as a writer at this time.

In 1956 Barthes became involved with the journal *Arguments*, edited by Edgar Morin as a non-partisan space for exchange between social-ist and Marxist thinkers without the flavour of oversight from the Communist Party. His engagement with *Arguments* would serve as a stepping stone between *Théâtre Populaire* and later the theoretically orientated *Communiçations* and *Tel Quel*. Barthes was now working on his second CNRS project on the subject of fashion. In 1958 Barthes asked Claude Lévi-Strauss to supervise this doctoral research but the anthropologist turned him down on the grounds that his work was too literary. However, Lévi-Strauss did point Barthes towards reading Vladimir Propp's *Morphology of the Folktale*, which was to draw his attention to the possible relation between narrative structure and sem-iology. Once again Barthes failed to progress at the CNRS and again, as with Michelet, a doctoral project would became a book, *Système de la mode* (*The Fashion System*). By now Barthes had published three books and reams of journalism and reviews. Not only had Barthes demon-strated that he was beyond the need for training as a research student but his innovative writing surely made a poor fit with the requirements of academic protocols in a doctoral thesis. However, the academic qualification would undoubtedly unlock doors for Barthes. He pub-lished much of his work on fashion in a series of articles between 1957 and 1960 in non-academic journals.

The year 1960 marked a turn in Barthes' life. First, he was appointed *chef de travaux* in the sixth section of the École Pratique des Haute Études in the department of economics and social sciences. Second, he began to put distance between himself and the world of publishing and journalism that had been his base for so long. Notably relations with Maurice Nadeau and Bernard Dort became strained over Barthes' refusal to sign the Manifesto of the 121, or 'The declaration of the right to insubordination in the Algerian war', an open letter of support for those on trial for channelling arms and money to the FLN in Algeria (signatees include Sartre and Nadeau, as well as Maurice Blanchot, André Breton, Guy Debord, Marguerite Duras, Henri Lefebvre, Alain

Resnais, Françoise Sagan, Robbe-Grillet, Françoise Truffaut and Simone Signoret). The manifesto supported the right of political dissent against French colonialism in Algeria, and the rights of deserters and conscientious objectors in the French army, condemned the use of torture by the French military, condemned the doctrinal timidity of the French Communist Party, and without explicitly stating it offered clear support to the legitimacy of the FLN's violent struggle on the eve of the trial of the Jeanson network. Francis Jeanson was an associate of Sartre who had acted as a *porteur de valise*, ferrying papers and weapons to the FLN. To refuse to sign was as much a refusal of Sartre's interventionism as it was a suspicion of the FLN's own sectarian elimination of fellow travellers. The list of who did not sign the manifesto is as significant as those who did.

At the École Pratique Barthes became involved, along with Christian Metz and Tzvetan Todorov, with the journal *Communiçations* that came out of the 'Centre for the Study of Mass Communications'. Here Barthes published several of his most celebrated essays for the first time, including 'Introduction to the Structural Analysis of Narrative', 'The Rhetoric of the Image' and 'Elements of Semiology'. The war in Algeria ended with independence in 1962 and the years that followed led to a growing rift between the French Communist Party and its student wing. This was the time of Barthes' entry into the university proper and his growing reputation as a theorist and critic. By 1962 Barthes had become a Director of Studies at the École Pratique and in the years that followed began to increase the rate of his published output: *Sur Racine* (1963), the collection *Essais Critiques* (1964), *Critique et vérité* (1966) and *Système de la mode* (1967). His work in *Mythologies* had began to catch the eye of the advertising industry, which read it not so much as a searing critique of capitalist ideology as a blueprint for successful advertising strategies. Barthes was briefly employed as a consultant to the state-owned Renault company to analysis their marketing campaign. It is for this reason that, as Umberto Eco puts it, a Barthesian or Lacanian critical analysis of advertising or popular cultural forms has limited value today, because all the advertising and television executives have read their Barthes and Lacan better than the students and academics.

The first translation of Barthes into English came in 1970 when Annette Lavers (a Frenchwoman living in England, later Professor of French at University College London) translated *Writing Degree Zero* and 'Elements of Semiology' in the one edition for Jonathan Cape in

London (the two texts were published separately in the United States by Hill and Wang). The version of 'Elements of Semiology' appeared with a preface by Susan Sontag. An English-language edition of the mythologies followed in 1972, although it accounted for only around half of the French original. The remaining essays would be published several years later in 1979 as the book *The Eiffel Tower and Other Mythologies*. Barthes' appearance in English is then somewhat belated: 1972 was certainly not 1957, and Barthes' own writing had moved beyond *S/Z* and *L'Empire des signes* in 1970 to *Sade, Fourier, Loyola* in 1971. So Barthes became a radical structuralist for the English-speaking world at a time when he himself had long since evolved from these positions.

Two years after Barthes published his book on Racine (a collection of previously published texts from *Théâtre Populaire* and elsewhere), the Sorbonne lecturer Raymond Picard published a pamphlet entitled *New Criticism or New Freud?* Picard was a contemporary of Philippe Rebeyrol at the École Normale Supérieure and the editor of the prestigious *Pléiade* edition of Racine. The pamphlet made special mention of Barthes' text on Racine but also attacked other so-called structuralists such as Lucien Goldmann, describing the structuralist technique as using 'pseudoscientific jargon to make inept and absurd assertions in the name of biological, psychoanalytic and philosophic knowledge', with 'the mixture of impressionism and dogmatism set to a modernist rhythm of indetermination' making 'it possible to say absolutely any stupid thing'. The pamphlet is not dissimilar in its uncomprehending tone and self-contradicting argument to any of the anti-theory rants one might have found from 'traditional' 'humanist' professors in the Anglo-Saxon academy of the 1980s, best exemplified perhaps by figures such as Raymond Tallis or Allan Bloom. Barthes responded to Picard in the text *Criticism and Truth*, which in part deals with Picard's own unacknowledged theoretical position and vocabulary and in part makes a case for the theoretical investigation of literature beyond the traditional critical discourses of the university. Picard's attack on Barthes and the others carried the weight of the Sorbonne's disapproval of the late-to-academia Barthes and his theoretical discourse. The École Pratique, which also housed Jacques Derrida, is a noticeably different type of institution from the Sorbonne. Other anti-Picard polemics followed from Jean-Paul Weber (also slighted by Picard) *Néocritique et paléocritique* and Serge Doubrovsky's *Pourquoi la nouvelle critique?* The media declared it 'the war of the critics' and Picard's polemic only served to draw attention to the academic subculture of structuralism, elevating it to the status of a new movement in criticism. The whole episode resembled the simulacra of conflict suggested by Barthes' own 1952 essay on wrestling, with the public performance of pre-rehearsed positions that never truly deal a decisive blow against one another. However, as a mediatised episode it came to be understood as the most significant public polemic between 'intellectuals' since Sartre's scathing review of Camus' history of revolution in *The Rebel* in 1951. News even reached the Anglo-Saxon press, giving rise to the interest that later led to the translation of Barthes into English.

In May 1966 Barthes made a visit to Tokyo to teach a seminar on the structural analysis of narrative at the Franco-Japanese Institute. Obviously taken with Japanese culture he subsequently visited the country three more times between 1966 and 1967, producing the material that would give rise to the 1970 publication of *The Empire of Signs*. In October 1967 he visited Baltimore in the United States where he participated in the now famous 'The Languages of Criticism and the Sciences of Man', a seminal moment in the history of theory in the Anglo-Saxon academy. He delivered the paper 'To Write an Intransitive Verb' at an event where Jacques Derrida first met Paul de Man, and Jacques Lacan, Roland Barthes, Lucien Goldmann and others first landed the longboats of so-called 'structuralism' on the shores of the American humanities. By 1967 Barthes' work had begun to take a subtle shift away from the structuralism evident previously. In the academic years 1967–9 Barthes' seminar at the École Pratique was on 'The structural analysis of a narrative text: Balzac's *Sarrasine*'. This work later became *S/Z*, published in 1970, in which Barthes makes a considerable leap from the sort of structural analysis of narrative he offers elsewhere, for example in his 1966 essay on Ian Fleming's *Goldfinger*. *S/Z* is still concerned with linguistic codes and classification, but the level of analysis of the lexia and the formulation of the difference between the *scriptible* and *lisible* (writerly and readerly) text begins to take Barthes' critical reading in a new direction towards the problems of textuality rather than structure as such. Julia Kristeva had joined Barthes' seminar in 1965 and one can readily see in Kristeva's early work the semiological influence of Barthes as well as their joint displacement of any strictly structuralist model. The seminar at this time was also attended by the structural narratologist Gérard Genette, the psychoanalytic film theorist Christian Metz and Philippe Sollers, then editor of the journal *Tel Quel*, later novelist and husband of Julia Kristeva. *The Fashion System*, published in 1967, represents Barthes' last attempt at the systemisation of signification. *S/Z* concerns the difficulties of rigorously upholding any such system in the light of the polysemy of meaning and the active participation of the reader. Derrida's *Of Grammatology* and Lacan's *Écrits*, both published in 1967, were significantly to alter the direction of Barthes' thought.

By the time the events of May 1968 began to unfold in the streets beyond the École Pratique, Barthes was an established academic: of the left but neither a member of the Communist Party nor affiliated to the more radical edge of a journal such as *Socialisme ou Barbarie*. Barthes was not part of the ephemeral publications that arose at this time like *Action* and *L'Enragé* – these belonged to another generation. Barthes reportedly had little enthusiasm for the *eventéments*, seeing them as the product of narcissism and an unacknowledged assertion of the petit bourgeois. By this Barthes probably meant that the disregard for study or theorisation and the emphasis on an unreflective utopia on the part of the students demonstrated that this was a revolution without thinking. This was in marked contrast to Foucault, Goldmann and others who actively engaged with the student movement as an important articulation of the revolutionary link between the proletariat and the intellectuals. Barthes offered to teach a seminar entitled 'language and the student movement', an offer that was impolitely declined on the grounds that this was no time for seminars. However, it was, it seemed, a time for the proliferation of committees. The students who attended Barthes' and Algirdas Greimas' seminars joined forces to form an action committee on language, which discussed the ideological underpinnings of semiology and structuralism. Barthes and Greimas attended the committee on alternate days, neither allowed to intervene but only to answer questions from the student participants. On one of the days that Barthes was not present, Catherine Clément arrived in the midst of discussion. Clément later co-authored *The Newly Born Woman* with Hélène Cixous and later still became a novelist and professor of philosophy. She declared, 'I've come from the general assembly of the philosophy department. We just passed a motion which concludes "it is obvious structures do not take to the streets"' (Calvet, 1994, 166). While Barthes had not been present to receive this news from the philosophical assembly, a giant poster appeared in the corridor of the first floor of the Sorbonne the next day which read, 'Barthes says: Structures do not take to the streets. We say: Neither does Barthes'. The phrase 'Structures do not take to the streets' took on a life of its own and came to be used as a slogan of protest in the anti-establishment upheavals that took place across Europe and the USA in the summer of 1968. Of course, Barthes had not said this and in fact it demonstrates a considerable confusion as well as a considerable theoretical difficulty. On the one hand, a good deal of heterogeneous work (including that of Barthes and Foucault) had been obscurely lumped together under the singular plural 'structuralism', and there was an assumption that these epistemologically radical and academic projects had a direct connection to social and political revolution. On the other hand, the resolution suggests that such theoretical scholarship in the academic humanities cannot have a relation to political action and that in fact the events of May 1968 were as much a reaction against the theoretical as they were against more obviously sedentary hierarchies in French culture. The misattribution to Barthes is secondary order confusion. It is possible to see why Barthes had little time for the unreflective excesses of the revolutionary committees of May 1968. The relations between theory and practice, writing and revolution, thinking and doing are porous and unpredictable. 'Action' in this sense is never straightforwardly either theoretical or material and never fully not material or not fully theoretical either. It is, of course, the nature of the political crisis that there is little time for the necessary reflection that would do justice to the urgency of the crisis. If the revolution is no time for a seminar, more often than not a seminar is just what the revolution needs. As Lacan later suggested, May 1968 demonstrated on the contrary that in fact structures do clearly take to the street. No doubt the mistaken attribution came out of Sartre's dismissal of structuralism as bourgeois, reducing the human to a maker of structures rather than history. Sartre spoke in the packed main lecture theatre of the Sorbonne on 20 May 1968. Barthes spent the day at a meeting of the editorial board of *Tel Quel*.

Barthes continued his seminar on Balzac before accepting an offer to teach in Morocco the following academic year at Rabat University in September 1969. Here Barthes taught to an appreciative and theory-hungry audience, while in Paris seminars were frequently interrupted by militants seeking to destroy the class-based university system. In relative calm Barthes produced the manuscripts for *The Empire of Signs* and *S/Z*, while enjoying the privileges of the French sex tourist in the bathhouses of late sixties Morocco. Barthes writes about his sex life at this time, as well as in Paris, in the text posthumously published as *Incidents*. Barthes returned to the École to teach in September 1970. His seminar was now taught to a packed lecture theatre of several hundred, with Barthes speaking from the stage under spotlights at the hall owned by the Société Française de la Théosophie. Futile attempts were made to limit the numbers to enrolled students only, but by now Barthes was himself a 'myth' and his seminar a fashion. At the same time Barthes refused once again to put his name to prominent political interventions led by academics, the prison-reform *Groupe d'Information sur les Prisons* and the gay-rights group *Front Homosexuel d'Action Révolutionnaire*, both founded in 1971 and whose members included Foucault, Deleuze and Cixous. Instead Barthes dedicated his time to the *Tel Quel* group and their textual attempt to dialectise cultural semiology and political practice.

In early 1971 Barthes published *Sade/Fourier/Loyola*, a book concerned with its eponymous 'logothetes' who had dared to found new discourses. The book works around the construction of a Sadean grammar and the identification of biographemes in the work of each logothete. Here Barthes is close to his earlier work on Michelet. *The Pleasure of the Text* followed in 1973: with Barthes nearly sixty his writing had taken a decisive turn, or perhaps return, from the categorisation of structure to biography and pleasure. Pleasure was very much a coming topic in 1973, a year after the publication of the *Anti-Oedipus* by Deleuze and Guattari. At the same time *Tel Quel* had made a noticeable shift from communism to Maoism, with which Barthes was publically identified by association but which is nowhere present in his writing. In April 1974 a delegation from *Tel Quel* toured China at the height of the Cultural Revolution: Barthes was there along with Sollers and Kristeva and the publisher François Wahl (Lacan was due to tour but had withdrawn at the last moment). Having had little time for what he saw as ideological excess in Paris in 1968, Barthes reportedly had a wretched time in China while struggling to fulfil his duties to his friends. Notably, he failed to meet the expectations of his readership after *Mythologies* and *The Empire of Signs*, offering no commentary on the Cultural Revolution beyond the short text in *Le Monde* entitled 'Alors, la Chine'. Here he describes China as 'not coloured in ... peaceful ... prosaic'. There was no pleasure to be taken in this trip. In contrast, Kristeva produced her *Chinese Women* as a result of her engagement there. An edition of the journal Barthes kept during the trip, *Carnet du voyage en Chine*, was published in 2009.

In 1975 Barthes turned his theorisation of pleasure and biography onto himself with the publication of *Roland Barthes by Roland Barthes*, part auto-biographeme, part study of textuality and writing.

Maurice Nadeau commissioned Barthes to review his own book for *La Quinzaine littéraire*, offering a criticism of *Roland Barthes by Roland Barthes* by Roland Barthes in which he suggests that the author 'Roland Barthes' is the one person who cannot write truthfully about the life of Barthes. Just as it is not true to say that structures do not take to the street it is equally untrue to say that books such as *The Pleasure of the Text* or *Roland Barthes by Roland Barthes* are removed from the political. It very much depends what one means by 'the political', a question much of theory attempts to open up. However, it is fair to say that the later Roland Barthes has travelled a distance from the interests of the mythologies and *Critique et Vérité*. This is in part because Barthes himself has created the path by which such a distance might be measured. But it is also correct to say that one should not be surprised at the older Barthes of 1973 for failing to denounce Pinochet's seizure of power in Chile because the younger Barthes of 1957, despite our assumptions about the mythologies, fails to mention the Suez crisis or the retreat from Dien Bien Phu. There will be more to say on this point in the next chapter.

Between 1974 and 1976 Barthes lectured on 'The lover's discourse' and gave his seminar on Flaubert's *Bouvard and Pécuchet*. In 1976 Barthes was elected to the Collège de France as chair of 'literary semiology'. In his report on Barthes' candidacy Michel Foucault described Barthes as a 'fertile cultural phenomenon', suggesting of Barthes' work that 'these voices, these few voices heard today outside the universities, do they not form part of contemporary history? And should we not welcome them among us?' (Barthes had approached Foucault to support his application, not the other way around). Interestingly, Foucault characterises Barthes as a phenomenon coming from outside the university, one that has made its way inside and can no longer be resisted. This is suggestive of not only the way in which his peers appreciated Barthes but also the way in which we might think of something like 'theory' or 'cultural studies' as neither fully of the university nor strictly outside of it. Certainly, it points to a curious professionalisation of theory as an academic subject, Barthes having travelled from *Combat* to the Collège. *Fragments d'un discours amoureux* was published in 1977, three months after Barthes' inaugural lecture at the Collège de France, another mix of carefully arranged index cards on the auto-biographemes of reading and pleasure. However, *A Lover's Discourse* was an unexpected literary success and was the first of Barthes' books to sell in substantial numbers. It brought him a wider readership and television appearances. Meanwhile, the translation of his work into English lagged behind, still clearing the back catalogue of his early publications. This was evident at the June 1977 conference on Barthes at Cerisy-la-Salle, where the Parisians who attended Barthes' seminar in Paris were several decades in advance of speakers who came from the English-speaking academy.

In October 1977 Barthes' mother, Henriette, died. Barthes lived with her in the flat on the Rue Servandoni until the end. In his final book on photography, *La Chambre Claire* (*Camera Lucida* in English) Barthes writes with great pathos of the singular and 'unqualifiable' loss of his mother. Barthes had long held an interest in the visual, had his own practice as what he called 'a Sunday painter', and had written on film and art at length. There have been several exhibitions of Barthes' painting and graphic work in 1976 and 1977 and posthumously in 1980 and 1981. His book on photography and the posthumous collection *L'Obvie et l'obtus* (*The Responsibility of Forms* in English) are suggestive of the importance to Barthes of the study of the visual and of Barthes to the study of the visual. In 1978 Barthes was at the height of his fame and attempted at his own behest to write a weekly column for *Le Nouvel Observateur* in the manner of his 1950s mythologies. 'The Roland Barthes Column' ran from 18 December 1978 to 26 March 1979 before he abandoned it, the circumstances of 1979 being very different from 1956. Demystification did not seem to be quite as straightforward as it had been, while it is more difficult to critique the media from within than from without. For example, the celebrity Roland Barthes dined with the Shah of Iran's family at the same time as a popular uprising was displacing his *ancien régime*.

Barthes' lecture course at the Collège de France for the year 1977–8 has been published posthumously as *Le Neutre* (*The Neutral*). In 1979 Barthes drew together a collection of texts on Philippe Sollers and published, in response to Soller's frequent requests, *Sollers, écrivain*. Between 15 April and 3 June that same year, in a moment of respite between public engagements and media appearances, he wrote the text of *Camera Lucida*. As an act of mourning for his dead mother it is a delayed response but if that is all that the book was then it would be of limited interest. Rather, the text economically draws together the best of Barthes as a synthesiser and systematiser as well as a reader and a self-analyst, an observer of detail and a general theoriser, poet and writer. The production of the book took Barthes to the end of his life, with him cancelling a trip to Tunisia in January 1980 to deal with the proofs. On 25 February he went to lunch with the socialist presidential candidate François Mitterrand, leaving on his desk the untyped manuscript of an essay on Stendhal entitled 'One always fails to speak about the things one loves' for a conference in Milan, and in his typewriter a single sheet that read, 'A few weeks ago, I made a brief trip to Italy. When I arrived at Milan station, it was a cold, foggy, filthy evening …' On the way back to his flat after the lunch at 3.45 p.m. Barthes was knocked down by a van on the Rue des Écoles outside the Sorbonne. He was taken to the *Hôpital de la Pitié-Salpêtrière* where he died after a month of visitors and minor operations. He died of pulmonary complications after a tracheotomy designed to ease the effort to breath and speak after the accident. Finally, Barthes' respiratory difficulties had undone him.

The diary that Barthes kept in his last years was subsequently published as *Incidents* (1987), detailing his cruising and reading habits, and as *Journal de deuil* (2009), concerning his life without his mother. A collection of interviews, *La Grain de la voix* (1981, *The Grain of the Voice*) duly followed. The collections *L'Obvie et l'obtus* (1982), *La Bruissement de la langue* (1984, *The Rustle of Language*) and *L'Aventure Semiologique* (1985, *The Semiotic Challenge*) were guided into publication by Françoise Wahl at *Seuil* in the years following Barthes' death. It is difficult to complain about the posthumous collection of disparate texts since this is the index card approach that Barthes frequently took during his life. More recently the seminar on the *Neutre* was published by *Seuil* and translated into English by Denis Hollier and Rosalind Krauss, and a project is under way to publish what remains of Barthes' seminar. A surprising amount of Barthes' shorter texts remain untranslated into English and it would seem that R.B. will remain a force in academic publishing for a while yet, even if the theoretical scene has moved on from his most immediate concerns. Each new publication by Barthes should be treated like the discovery of a rare genus of orchid, even as the likelihood of discovering more diminishes and the quality of each offers diminishing returns. Barthes' art and writing was the subject of a retrospective at the *Centre de Pompidou* in 2002.

*

The life of Roland Barthes is suggestive of a number of difficulties that confront academic writing today: the aporetic relationship between the avant garde of thought and political endeavour, the circular relation between the university and the space of the media, the traditional strain between the study of popular culture and academic disciplinarity, the internal resistances between theoretical thought and its others, the specialisation and professionalisation of that thought as an academic activity undertaken by professors who profess theory, and the difference between commentary and critique (political or cultural). The remainder of this book is an attempt to work through these issues by returning to Barthes' 1957 work *Mythologies* as an opening into the wider text of Barthes and Theory, as a contribution to contemporary debates on the intersections of culture, media, literature, politics and academia. As such I hope that the book follows the spirit of Barthes and is more of a book 'on' Barthes or 'about' Barthes than a more obviously dutiful act of scholarly retrieval and depositing might otherwise be. In this sense, I hope that it will be of some use to the reader.

2 Reading Roland Barthes in a Time of Terror

I would first like to make a distinction which may seem somewhat specious to you, but it is quite valid to me: between 'the political' and 'politics'. To me, the political is a fundamental order of history, of thought, of everything that is done, and said. It's the very dimension of the real. Politics, however, is something else, it's the moment when the political changes into the same old story, the discourse of repetition. My profound interest in the attachment of the political is equalled only by my intolerance of political discourse. Which doesn't make my situation very easy. My position is somewhat divided, and often guilt-ridden. But I think that I'm not the only one, and that at present most people, at least most intellectuals, have a guilty relation to politics. One of the essential duties of today's avant-garde would be to address this problem of the intellectual's guilt in regard to politics.

Roland Barthes[1]

And so I will again take up my poor life, so tranquil and dull, where sentences are adventures.

Gustave Flaubert

Roland Barthes died in the Saltpêtrière hospital, Paris, on 26 March 1980 at 1.40 p.m. from pulmonary complications after a road-traffic accident a month earlier. Dying when he did, Barthes was to know nothing of the accelerated transformations in the material conditions of western and global culture that characterised the subsequent three decades. He knew nothing of the Internet, climate change, nanotechnology, satellite television, the end of state communism in Europe, so-called globalisation, energy wars, global Jihad, and all the *bêtes noires* of the contemporary scene. And yet Roland Barthes remains a significantly important influence on academic writing today. This has been achieved seemingly in almost the complete absence of a substantial body of readers of Barthes at this moment. On the one hand, Barthes remains the unquestioned point of reference for the intellectual jus-tification of what is known in the Anglophone humanities as cultural studies (a term Barthes himself never used). On the other hand, little attention is paid today to the actual reading of Barthes, outside of a recuperation of Barthes as a late-flowering queer theorist.[2]

In his posthumous volume, *Privileging Difference*, Antony Easthope was heard to grumble bad-temperedly, 'are people still reading Roland Barthes? I suspect not …'[3] Easthope's complaint on this occasion was not an affirmation of Barthes' irrelevance but a swipe at those fashion-conscious academics that were, in his view, blithely and blindly living in errors that Barthes' work had exposed long ago. It is perhaps one of the greatest ironies of Barthes' after-life that in fact he is now read much more profoundly in France than in the United Kingdom and the United States. In 2002 his work formed the basis of a retrospective exhi-bition at the Pompidou Centre,[4] while Julia Kristeva's *Centre de Roland Barthes* ensures that Barthes' writing is the focus of active research in France today. In Britain, despite the almost universal influence that his semiological analysis once held in the humanities, I cannot think of a single monograph written this decade (outside of introductory guides) that treats Barthes' writing as a productive theoretical force for the con-temporary moment.[5] Certainly Roland Barthes knew nothing of queer theory, eco-criticism, post-colonialism, post-humanism, disability theory or minority studies. He can also be grateful that his untimely death exempted him from the managerial (counter)revolution that has transformed the role and conditions of the transglobal university today. Such a situation might lead us to ask the question: why should the student of today read Roland Barthes beyond the appreciation of a particular moment in the history of cultural inquiry? When one reads Barthes (that is, really reads Barthes, widely and in detail, beyond the canonical prescriptions of a short seminar on structuralism) one finds that his writing is as close to the present moment as the still, distant beauty of Henri Cartier-Bresson's black and white photogra-phy. It simply cannot be claimed any more that Barthes is a writer of the contemporary scene. It is almost thirty years since he last took up a pen. His world is one of auteur cinema, French colonial influence, closeted homosexuality, handwritten letters, the death penalty in Europe, McCarthyism and Poujadism.

It was a world in which the national media concerned itself with debates over the literary interpretation of Racine. In other words,

Barthes' writing is firmly located in the specifically French culture that emerges from decolonisation, through the foundation of the fourth Republic, and the political aftermath of 1968 and the final retreat of de Gaulle to Colombey-les-deux-Églises. This history is of course, as Barthes once said of Michelet's concerns, 'as concrete as toothache'.[6] Barthes' writing is occupied by the general leftist concerns of this moment but it never came into contact with Mitterrand's age of neo-liberalism or the epoch of the *banlieue*. By locating Barthes in this way I have no wish to denigrate him. On the contrary, I would like to do justice to Barthes and that means accurately discerning what Barthes' writing does not do as much as what it might have to say, and thereby not making excessive claims for the prescience of his writing or its attachment to our own present moment. Rather, by reading Barthes in this book I would like to reclaim a certain Barthes, for there are no doubt many, from the one with which most Anglophone critics might be familiar. In so doing I will attempt to find in the text of Barthes reasons to return to him again and again in this present moment of the so-called 'war on terror' and the war on thinking it has become.[7]

Writing a book such as this would be, as Paul de Man says of Barthes, 'trying to make a monument out of a man who is about as monumental as a Cheshire cat'.[8] I must confess that having accepted the authorship of this book as an assignment, I was until recently one of Easthope's tardy readers. I admit with shame that it is many years since I picked up Barthes in a sustained fashion, outside of the requirements of teaching a survey course on literary theory. I have always had a fondness for Barthes' late 'theory-poetry', especially the book on photography and *Fragments of A Lover's Discourse*, but it is some time since as a graduate student writing a dissertation on narrative theory I spent several months cocooned on the sixth floor of the University of Glasgow library working my way systematically through Barthes' back catalogue from *Writing Degree Zero* to *Camera Lucida*. However, in my later doctoral studies and in the intervening years, Barthes has not held for me the enthralling intellectual necessity of say a Jacques Derrida, Paul de Man or Hélène Cixous, or that thinkers such as Deleuze and Guattari, Georgio Agamben, Jacques Ranciere or even Slavoj Žižek have for others of my generation. I have then returned to Roland Barthes after a period in which cultural studies has simultaneously held hegemonic sway over the humanities as a form of interdisciplinary cultural analysis (to the extent that disciplinary study itself is becoming an endangered species for scholars under the age of forty) and also fallen into decline as a singular practice dedicated to the transformation of the academy and to challenging the canonical assumptions of high culture. Today everyone does 'cultural studies' and correspondingly few remain wedded to cultural studies as a nomenclature for their own theoretical endeavours. The problem that this presents, it seems to me, is that given this situation Theory, *theory as such*, Theory as an Anglophone mobilisation of French thought and philosophy, has lost its way and runs the risk of simultaneously abandoning disciplinary practices such as philosophy and literary studies to the reactionary influence of pre-theoretical humanism, biographers and 'creative practitioners', while shrouding itself in the numbing blandness of interdisciplinary relativism.

Perhaps this is the future and Theory should not attempt to reassert the value of disciplinarity when it has done so much to decentre the very idea of value itself. However, I believe that Theory (High Theory, the sort of Theory that so profoundly transformed the humanities in the 1980s and that still gets me out of bed in the morning) has lost its way because it has lost sight of its own history. Theory, if it is anything, is a negotiation with the tradition of western thought as a commitment to a certain mode of reading as questioning and cultural inquiry. Theory, therefore, must also negotiate its own tradition. This is what riled Antony Easthope in the last weeks of his life. The study of Theory, then, ought to be at least in part an encounter with its own history as the unfolding of an opening in thought. Easthope's point would be that people ought to read Roland Barthes still and return to his texts (and the countless other texts of the theoretical tradition), the appreciation and study of which is only in its infancy, but that are routinely skated over in the acceleration towards newness in Theory. Here is a genuine aporia for theoretical production, that in order to remain committed to Theory as an avant-garde practice of questioning and inquiry it is necessary to keep apace with the rhythm of newness, while to remain committed to Theory as a sustained and rigorous negotiation with thinking itself it is necessary to pay due respect to the long sweep of that thought, including Theory's own history. In the light of this speculation, titles such as 'Forty Years of "Structure, Sign and Play"' are to be as welcomed among the current generation of theoretical users as much as designations such as 'New Directions after Post-Humanism'. Accordingly, I would like to ask in this book, to paraphrase the Derrida of *Glas*, what remains for us today of a Roland Barthes?

The structure of Roland Barthes

The first point to be made here is that it is not the case that structuralism is an irrelevance, although it is certainly unfashionable now, and as an active technique for cultural analysis is the preserve of those living in denial about its own structural insufficiencies.[9] Rather, the work of structuralism as a project has been displaced into other theoretical domains. On the one hand, textual analysis maintains its vitality and rigour through a critical relationship to continental philosophy, while on the other hand, the radical work of breaking the vessels of traditional modes of criticism must inevitably give way to reflection and diaspora within theory itself. That is to say that structuralism is structurally important in the history of theory. It should also be said that for Barthes, his structuralist episode really represents only a fraction of his sizeable output and in many ways might be thought of as an aberrant interlude in a writing career that begins in critique and ends in self-analysis but that is committed throughout to the avant-garde. As far as structuralism goes Barthes had all but abandoned it by the time he came to publish *Le Plaisir du Texte* in 1973. We might describe his structuralism as 'aberrant' in the sense that it is only one Barthes in a series of 'Bartheses' that has been given singular attention and raised above other equivalent moments in Barthes's oeuvre by the anthologisers and editors of Theory. It might be said of him that he was not so much a structuralist but a writer who wrote, for a while, about structure. He was only ever an amateur when it came to structuralism. The important thing about Barthes was not that he advanced the work of Saussure, Jakobson, Benveniste, Lévi-Strauss and Hjemslev, but that in 1953 he was aware that literary criticism ought to attend to the resources of linguistics if it wished to make good on its commitment to literary language. It is not even the case that Barthes was a significant herald for this work: much of it had been around for a long time before he emerged on the scene (*The Course in General Linguistics* dates from the time of the *First* World War). Barthes is important for structuralism because in his critical writing he manages to mobilise the terms and tropes of structuralist linguistics in a polemic and innovative way that popularises a methodology for cultural analysis. He is the *bricoleur* of his own writing, raiding from anthropology, linguistics and psychoanalysis to articulate an opening in the institution of literary criticism, which is still being felt today even if the trumpets used to bring down those walls are now muted and pointed in a different direction. This is to say that the significance of Barthes for theory is not so much his actual theorisation (at least in his structuralist phase) but the fact that he was a writer who articulated Theory in a way that enabled it to begin its transformative journey through the academy. I do not think that to say Barthes was a writer more than a theorist is to belittle him in any way. On the contrary, to my mind this is a considerable accolade, because so few theorists can write (as we are often told). It is also, I will contest in this book, the very thing that I wish to redeem about Barthes at this present moment. I find in Barthes' texts an irresolvable difficulty between his life as a writer and his political inclinations. He is what I have called elsewhere a textual activist.[10] The two epigrams that guide us here are indicative of this difficulty that is given a massive legibility in the text of Barthes. On the one hand, there is the theorist who is absorbed by the necessity of the political but alienated from the compromises and broken promises of the realm of public politics, 'My profound interest in the attachment of the political is equalled only by my intolerance of political discourse. Which doesn't make my situation very easy', says Barthes. 'My position is somewhat divided, and often guilt-ridden. But I think that I'm not the only one, and that at present most people, at least most intellectuals, have a guilty relation to politics.' The guilt arrives from the sin of omission, from non-action according to familiar signposts of what might constitute political activity. However, the relation between the material realm and the all-powerful otherness of writing follows complicated, surprising and unpredictable paths. For a theorist to remain a theorist they must commit themselves to their practice, namely theory. There is a difference between the philosopher and the professional revolutionary but the two are linked if only by invisible threads. The theorist is the one who sits at her desk in the early morning, where, as Flaubert says, 'sentences are adventures', writing in the name and memory of a politics from which their person, if not their writing, are necessarily removed with all the inevitable, good and bad, consequences that follow from this. My study of Barthes is really an attempt to explore this difficulty and to respond to Barthes' 1975 suggestion that it is the business of theory to know itself by addressing 'this problem of the intellectual's guilt in regard to politics', with Barthes himself providing us with a singular case study. This is a familiar aporia perhaps but to my mind it is the generative melancholic matrix out of which his entire textual career emerges, and it is the very difficulty that makes him such a modern and vital figure for us today. We shall have to be careful with the use of this term 'matrix' for it is a gendered metaphor, one that returns all ideology to the Mother (there will be more to say on this later).

As Jacques Derrida noted as early as 1966, 'If it recedes one day, leaving behind its works and signs on the shores of our civilization, the structuralist invasion might become a question for the historian of ideas, or perhaps even an object. But the historian would be deceived if he came to this pass: by the very act of considering the structuralist invasion as an object he would forget its meaning and would forget that what is at stake, first of all, is an adventure of vision, a conversion of the way of putting questions to any object posed before us. And, unexpectedly among these, the literary object.'[11] Let us begin by saying about structure that as a concept it is as old as philosophy itself and fundamental to the way in which we categorise and describe the universe. As such the traditional notion of structure upon which the philosophical tradition relies is one that gives a centre or fixed origin to a moment of presence. This idea of structure provides the rubric for stability, balance and organisation, as well as limit and the restriction of play within any given system or operation. As a structuring principle, structure is thought of as organising coherence and only allows for a play of elements within a total form defined by the structure itself. In this sense, philosophy's traditional idea of structure presupposes a notion of play restricted by a fundamental and reassuring ground. Here 'play' is intended as much to mean pliability and 'give' in a dense material as it is in its ludic sense. This ground can take the form of a centre, origin or end, and while play such as substitution, transformation, condensation, permutation and so on can take place, they do so in a set of relations defined by the ground and traced back to the ground as a fixed and stable point. This point is itself beyond play and could be said to be outside the structure itself even as it gives rise to the structure as the fixed locus of this point as an origin. It is this appreciation of the structuring principle that is shared by all theologies (with God or the transcendental at their centre), all humanisms (with Man or consciousness at their centre) and all metaphysics (with essence or presence at its centre).

The history of Modern thought is the history of a series of interruptions to this onto-theological understanding of structure: Nietzsche's critique of truth, Freud's displacement of the conscious sovereign subject, Heidegger's 'destruction' of Being as presence. However, Nietzsche, Freud and Heidegger are all caught up in a circular relation to the version of structure they oppose: Nietzsche must make truth claims about the unreliability of truth, Freud can only describe the unconscious using conscious discourse, Heidegger must rely on the language and inheritance of metaphysics to destroy the certainty of metaphysics. Hence, each displacement draws into itself the whole history of that which is being opposed and so becomes the latest point of that history, structured by the very structure under question. This situation is systematic and one can give oneself up to it in ways that are more or less knowing, or more or less in keeping with expectation. Marx is a good example of this insofar as he attempts to disarticulate the structure of social production through revolutionary practice only to stay tied to a structuring principle for the social (and a hierarchical one at that) on the other side of revolution. Or again, when in *The German Ideology* he and Engels identify philosophy as the very essence of ideology but are compelled to use philosophy to prove this. There will be more to say regarding Marx later. The so-called 'War on Terror' is another example of this problematic. How can one continue to use this term? Surely it must be abandoned straightaway as soon as one places the joint substantives 'war' and 'terror' in doubt. However, how can we abandon it without giving up any hope of criticising and challenging the discourse that gives rise to it? Equally, if we continue to retain it in some careful way, how can we avoid falling into its logic and assumptions? Having made this point, it will be our premise in this book, as it is for Derrida in 'Structure, Sign and Play' that 'we can pronounce not a single destructive proposition which has not already had to slip into the form, the logic, and the implicit postulations of precisely what it seeks to contest'.[12]

Now, what we call structuralism (of which Barthes' early work is considered a part, if only as a mobilisation and application of the work of others) is a particular case in point within this history. Structuralism considers itself to shake the metaphysics of presence through its attention to the concept of the sign. Barthes' own diagrammatic representation of the sign is taken from the essay 'Myth Today'.

Barthes's famous, and expensively copyrighted, diagram of the operation of Myth can be found on page 115 of the Annette Lavers translation. It suggests an inversion in signification that occurs during Mythology in which the sign itself (the conjunction of a signifier and signified in language) is appropriated entirely as the signifier of the myth that retains a hidden signified as part of its ideological action.

Later I will say a considerable amount about the way Barthes describes the operation of the sign in the essay 'Myth Today' (one ought to attend to Barthes' own words rather than offer a reduction of a formulation). However, insofar as his basic model of the sign is derived from Saussure it involves the idea of a 'signifier' referring to a 'signified' and different from its 'signified'. On the one hand, this division is an attempt to explain the archaic philosophical difficulty of the diremption between the sensible and the intelligible, the empirical and the conceptual, between seeming reality and language. However, if one accepts the motivation for such a division, namely that there is no fixed or stable (privileged or transcendental) signified and that the field of signification is thus without limit or ground, then the very idea of the 'signifier' itself must be quickly abandoned. The notion of the signifier is defined by the opposition between the sensible and the intelligible and so cannot overcome this distinction. To speak of the 'signifier' in a semiological way is to insist on the difference between this signifier and its signified. The wholly figural nature of language means that the 'concept' of the signified as a concept can in no way be separated, even methodologically, from the signifier. Accordingly, language is referential to nothing but itself and this signification has no fixed anchor in any real or pre-linguistically true signified. Hence, signification is without limit. Saussure's idea of the sign depends on a division it cannot explain and that, if it recognised it, would radically displace its own determination. However, one cannot easily do without the idea of the sign because to give up the metaphysical complicity involved in the idea of the sign would be to abandon the possibility of any critique directed against that criticism. This is the very problem of structure itself. To derive a radical notion of the signification independent of the sign would be to reduce the opposition between the sensible and intelligible and so have no leverage on this aspect of the problem by denouncing the system that produces the distinction. The alternative is not to dismiss the sign and its assumed division but to work with this division to question the ways in which the history of the sign (which includes structuralism) founds these concepts. In this way, one is not stepping outside of semiology but accepting as Barthes does that language contains within itself the necessity of its own critique. To think that one can escape the problem of language by abandoning the history of the language of language would be to fall straight back into the very division between the sensible and intelligible that has been the basis of our criticism of the sign.

Therefore, reading Roland Barthes today (or at least that part of Barthes that falls within the ambit of 'structuralism') is not a matter of denouncing structuralism as a misunderstanding of signification but of working with structuralism as part of this history of structure as a concept. To question systematically the ways in which structuralism grounds and uses concepts would be to find within structuralism resources for language's own internal critique, without risking the fall into errors that Barthes and structuralism have already identified. This strategy is a particularly important necessity given that so much of my reading of Barthes will involve itself with the division between the writing of social criticism and the effects of that criticism in a 'real' world one supposes to be beyond that writing, when in fact the opposition is another systematic production of an ancient structuring division between the sensible and the intelligible. The purpose of reading this part of Barthes will be to affirm a certain aspect of Barthes' so-called structuralism. While Barthes remains wedded to a fundamentally metaphysical idea of the sign and indeed in the early part of his career all of Barthes' concepts are metaphysical through and through, there remains an impulse in his work that would like to imagine interpretation otherwise. Barthes, under the influence of Marxism, seems to yearn for access to an unalienable reality but is prepared to live in the necessity of semiological exile. However, he simultaneously affirms the play of writing and the internal logic of the symbolic. This is the writerly Barthes I would wish to recover, who regularly abandons ground and turns away from origins to attempt to pass beyond humanism and onto-theology. This can be shown in various precise ways in relation to 'classic' texts by Barthes, such as 'The Death of the Author' or 'From Work to Text', the first of which posits the demise of a theological model of reading as revelation in favour of an active countersignature of a text in the play of critical reading, the second of which, in attempting to define the structure of a text without anchoring origin or *telos*, does so without appeal to any other reassuring limitation on the domain of play. I think the reason to read Barthes today is bound up with this issue: no doubt Barthes the methodological structuralist is frequently in conflict with the *scriptible* Barthes, but what a careful reading of Barthes might show is the ways in which the text of Barthes deals with the problem of metaphysical complexity. Barthes' work as a social critic is at its least effective when he imagines himself beyond the ideology he critiques, but the more cunning and subtle Barthes is a game of hide and seek as an internal resistance to the structuring circle of structure. Such critical self-awareness and commitment to the interminable task of writing to defy the gravitational pull of ideology is surely a history worthy of study at a time when lessons on critical consciousness need to be learned.

Although Barthes says of himself that he was never more than an amateur in linguistics (Barthes 1985, 213), in many ways he is quite the critical technocrat, he will happily borrow from any source that will yield effective critical results for him – *whatever works* would seem to be his theoretical model. It is not necessarily the case that the many areas and texts from which he borrows are in any way mutually compatible. I think that Barthes finds in structuralism not so much a life's cause as an opening onto a degree of critical rigour he had been seeking since his research on Michelet: the sort of 'control over technical problems of language' that Paul de Man speaks of in the interview with Stefano Rosso.[13] Elsewhere, Barthes might have called this a critical '*passion du sens*'.[14] De Man himself might have recognised it as the desire for mastery and closure that characterises all critical texts and at the same time condemns criticism always to misread (i.e. foreclose a reading too soon).[15] It is also what makes Barthes a modernist writer, one whose ambit revolves around a self-reflection on what it means to write itself. I would like to suggest that in this sense Barthes is one of the important figures of a modernist avant-garde whose work is still in progress. It can be said to be Modern because of its almost ascetic seriousness that desacralises the author, its intention beginning and ending in language itself. As Barthes describes the innovations of modernist writing, 'We can find what we call text, writing and therefore avant-gardism, in writers of the past such as Proust, Michelet, Brecht; it's not a question of 'form' (still less of formalism') but of impulse: whenever it's the body which writes, and not ideology, there's a chance the text will join us in our modernity.'[16] However, one can readily see the fairly rapid departure Barthes makes from full-scale structuralism under the influence of Lacan and Derrida. The contrast would be between the Barthes of *Elements of Semiology* (1964) or 'The Structural Analysis of Narrative' (1966) and, say, *S/Z* (1970) or the essay on Poe's 'Valdemar' (1973). At the risk of accepting Barthes' own self-report at face value, he outlines this trajectory in diagrammatic form in *Roland Barthes by Roland Barthes.*

As Barthes states of his own relation to theoretical formation since structuralism, 'On that subject, I've changed position completely. I did indeed think at first that it would be possible to determine one or more models from the study of texts, to work toward these models by induction in order then to go back to the works themselves by deduction. Greimas and Todorov, for example, continue to pursue research directed toward a scientific model. But Nietzsche's writings and what he says about the indifference of science have been very important to me. Both Lacan and Derrida have confirmed my belief in this necessary paradox: each text is unique in its difference, however saturated it may be with cultural and symbolic codes, repetitions, and stereotypes.'[17]

The insistence on the diagram of course points to a not entirely renounced love of the structural. The point I think for Barthes as a literary critic is that while a study of structure remains necessary, the work of Derrida and Lacan (and even Barthes' close friend and student Julia Kristeva) show it to be itself structurally insufficient. In other words, Barthes' writing drifts out of a commitment to semiology on the apprehension that structuralism is not structural enough. It fails to account adequately for the complexity and self-immolating deficiencies of structuration. On its own the structural analysis of narrative is only of forensic interest; knowing how *Goldfinger* is put together is not the same thing as knowing what *Goldfinger* means.[18] As Barthes puts it in the essay on the Eiffel Tower as early as 1956, 'every visitor to the tower makes structuralism without knowing it' (Barthes, 1997, 9). This is because unlike other texts the structure of the tower is presented immediately and unvarnished. However, this immediate apprehension is not sufficient to understand the significance of the tower or why 'Maupassant often lunched in the restaurant at the top of the Eiffel Tower though he did not care for the food' (Barthes, 1997, 3) because it was the only point in Paris from which one did not have to look at the thing. It might also be said here that Barthes' subsequent writing does not make a significant contribution to deconstruction or psychoanalysis either. Again, it would be Barthes' *forte* to mobilise these terms into a critical practice rather than to augment their theoretical endeavour.

But 'Which structuralism are we talking about?'[19] Barthes' debt to Derrida is only occasionally to be found in explicit textual references to the younger man. In 1972 Barthes was asked to contribute to an edition of the journal *Les Lettres Françaises* dedicated to the work of Derrida. Whether out of genuine lack of time or out of diplomacy Barthes wrote to the editors that he was too fatigued to contribute but went on to say enough in his brief response to encourage Jean Ristat to publish the letter in full. In it he points out that he belongs to older generation than Derrida and his readers but accordingly this has meant that Derrida has had an affect on Barthes' mature work. The semiological project was already advanced in Barthes' writing 'but it risked remaining enclosed [*enfermé*], enchanted by the phantasm of scientificity but Derrida was one of those thinkers who helped Barthes understand the philosophical and ideological stakes in his won work, 'he disturbed structure, he opened the sign: he is for us the one who unhooked the end of the chains'. He praises Derrida's readings of literature (Artaud, Mallarmé, and Bataille) as 'decisive' and 'irreversible'. He describes Derrida's texts as 'a sort of incessant deterioration of our intellectual comfort (that state where we comfort ourselves by what we already think)'. While regretting that he is unable to contribute Barthes notes that he would have liked to worked on the idiom of Derrida's writing which he describes has having 'something of the intimate about it, which is fascinating: its solitude comes from what it will have to say'.[20]

*

I mention Barthes' relation to Derrida here not because I want to suggest that Derrida is the *übermensch* who puts structuralism to flight, or that all of Derrida 'disproves' in some way all of Barthes. That would be a sterile debate and would anyway require a considerable analysis of both oeuvres to demonstrate the absurdity of any such claim. Rather, I have taken this route via Derrida to indicate how pointless an activity it would be for me to produce a fully elaborated distillation and demonstration of Barthes' structuralism only to advise my readers to move on from it as Barthes did himself. Barthes' writing is in its own way quite deconstructive enough to be going on with.

Theoretical evangelism

Let me pause here and say that I find in Barthes' defence of structuralism something compelling and to be greatly admired. It is part of the historical significance of Barthes that through his polemic against Raymond Picard and the orthodoxy of the Sorbonne elite whom he metonymically represented, Barthes was present at a moment of step-change in critical thought. To say he was 'present' is to do him a disservice. He was the John the Baptist of Theory. He cried in the wilderness for a theoretical approach to the humanities. He was the herald of cultural studies. It is not that one could recreate or repeat the conditions of this moment to lay claim to Barthes' importance for us today: theory is not the barbarian at the gate that it once was, the spectre haunt-ing the academy of old Europe. Rather, it is by a historical relation between then and now that Barthes' defence of theory has significance for us in the present. Theory today does not stand in the same relation to the university as it did during Barthes' early career as a polemicist. A sea-change has occurred within the humanities, whereby theory or interdisciplinary 'cultural studies' has not only emerged as a powerful motor for scholarly endeavour but in fact has, as the dominant species in the academy, come to endanger the health of the disciplines, such as literary studies or art historical studies, from whence it emerged. Cultural studies, in its pre-eminent form, as the easy interdisciplinarity that moves between high and low culture and across a range of media via a set of 'theoretical' methodological manoeuvres, has proven so popular and seductive for a generation of scholars and their students that entire areas of periodic scholarship now resemble the last enclaves of an endangered species. When sojourning as a head of an art school in the United Kingdom I tried repeatedly to hire a junior lecturer who could teach Early Modern art history (as far as the requirements of the national benchmarking document on art history are concerned Barthes is correct when he says of the *Guide Bleu* that in bourgeois culture 'it is almost impossible to conceive a History of Art which is not Christian and Roman Catholic' [Barthes, 1972, 75]). This proved impossible, either because newly graduated doctors of Renaissance art history did not want to come to my art school (which is entirely pos-sible) or because there were no newly graduated Renaissance scholars to be had. There were, however, any number of highly qualified and distinguished 'cultural analysts' who if appointed to the post would be prepared to cover the Early Modern period if required. This is not to complain about the loss of traditional crafts. Rather, I would suggest that when 'Theory' becomes the mainstream in this way it is no longer doing the work of avant-garde thinking that is the remit of the theoreti-cal (and cultural studies) as such, and as a career choice can no longer be worthy of the name 'Theory'. I am worried that these graduates could not teach European art of the Renaissance but could teach cul-tural studies because it means that Renaissance art is no longer on the agenda of 'cultural studies' as a theoretical problem. In this way both the study of the Renaissance and the pursuit of theoretical endeavour are impoverished. When universities in the United Kingdom can no longer produce scholars of Early Modern art history or eighteenth-century literature, say, then it is hard to reach any conclusion other than that the humanities, under the influence of theory and cultural studies, are in an interesting moment in the transition of authority and its cultural transmission. I say this not out of a conservative impulse or for any reactionary reason. On the contrary, the questions of literature and art are far too important to be left to diminished connoisseurial, 'historically' (of course such discourse understands little of what history is) or biographically dependent disciplines.

The point is that if theory, in its interdisciplinary guise as cultural studies, has lost sight of literature and art as an object then it has lost its guiding principle. There are several important and contradictory corollaries to add to this.[21] First, just as theory and interdisciplinarity have become commonplace across the arts and humanities, their visibility as a practice has receded within freshly irrigated and transformed disciplines integrating such gestures into their own vocabulary and protocols without recognition or appreciation of their origin or tradition. In this way, the insights of theory are assimilated while the avant-garde impulse of theory is simultaneously excluded from these disciplines, which hold onto their occult power as disciplines unaware of their internal mutation and self-harm. To identify something like augmented disciplinarity in this way may seem like a contradiction of my original point concerning the interdisciplinary humanities. Not so, the two difficulties inform one another to create our present situation. One might characterise the problem as follows. In presenting itself as an intervention called Theory, theory must necessarily lay down roots in a presence that its own work must constantly seek to undermine. Theory is always in retreat from this presentation, leaving behind a trace of a form that we call Theory in the academy. In this sense Theory is always in anticipation of its own disappearance, which is also its own entrance into institutional life. The death of Theory is itself a theoretical concept and just as any monotheism implies the necessary retreat and death of God as an active participant in the world, so too the death of Theory must result in something like an institutional Mono-theory-theism as the legacy of its disappearance. So, on the one hand the passage of Theory through disciplines results in both its retreat and the leaving of its hardly visible tide-mark on those disciplines. On the other hand, the wash through of Theory must also leave behind an institutional Mono-Theory-Theism that stands as a totem to the disappearance of the theoretical impulse itself. In a complex interplay between resurgent anti-theoreticism in disciplines wishing to be left to their own devices and the Theory-soup of interdisciplinarity taking centre stage, Theory itself, if there is any, is doubly squeezed and erased. In this sense, I take 'Theory itself' to mean the commitment to a mode of questioning that ties itself to, and is in no way independent of, idioms of cultural inquiry, such as literary study, philosophy or art histories.[22]

Hélène Cixous once told me, 'We have taken the Bastille but not the Sorbonne'. Part of the kettle logic that attacks Theory is to label it both, and simultaneously, popular and elitist, both fashionable and esoteric. The first half of Barthes' *Criticism and Truth* challenges this argument with vigour and wit. If today, in 2010, one wanted to construct an argument as to why, in the face of the banalisation of the university by management and government and the reduction of thought in public life by mediatic culture, something like 'post-structuralism' or deconstruction or an avant-garde of critical thought was more important and relevant than ever, one might begin with this text by Barthes. Paul de Man described it as Barthes' 'greatest mythology'.[23] He begins by pointing out that the 'new criticism' that Picard opposes in his 1965 attack (*Nouvelle critique ou nouvelle imposture*) on Barthes' *Sur Racine* of 1963 has a history. Barthes suggests that this 'new criticism', what we might elsewhere call 'Theory' but that had not been unfortunate enough to be ontologised as such in 1965, begins with the inevitable experience of reappraisal of culture after the Liberation. Others argue for an alternative origin for 'Theory'. Robert J. C. Young points to the post-colonial origins of the deconstruction of western logocentrism and the significance of Algeria as a place and cause for a generation of thinkers in France.[24] Robert Eaglestone suggests that the decentring impulse of theoretical 'postmodernism' (his word) can be attributed to a fascination with the indescribable destabilisation of the holocaust.[25] The problem with attributing any such onto-genetic origin to something like deconstruction, as both Young and Eaglestone do, is that as a point of origin such origins must themselves always already be in deconstruction and can never be originary enough to escape being the effect of the cause they themselves are said to produce.[26] It would take us on too long a detour to do justice to Young's and Eaglestone's arguments here so I will limit myself to saying that both scholars are fully aware that there is no single, autonomous origin of something like deconstruction or 'postmodernism'. However, in Barthes' 1965 text he is keen to draw an explicit line between the 'new criticism' of the fifties and sixties in France at the modernist tendency of the avant-garde. The citation of the Liberation as an appropriate starting point for an identifiable opening in critical discourse is suggestive, because it explicitly ties this sort of writerly practice to a counter-cultural turn. In particular it relates the history of this 'new criticism' to a productive cultural and publishing apparatus, which flourished during the years of the Resistance in France and out of which a certain post-war literary idiom emerged. One might think here of the journals *Combat* and *Les Temps Modernes* or the publishing houses such *Editions du Seuil*, which all emerged from the underground publishing scene of the Resistance into national media outlets after the Liberation. Barthes, as a young man in his twenties, spent the war in a sanatorium recovering from a bout of tuberculosis. The point is not to 'heroicise' the new criticism as being the product of the Resistance in France; there will be something to be said later about Barthes' difficult relationship to Sartre and Camus, for example. Rather, the suggestion would be that this modernist tendency passes through a culture of resistance that is explicitly a counter-culture of opposition and critique.[27]

It is the business of an oppositional discourse to oppose, and the effect is systemic rather than given. However, it is also true that an oppositional discourse must have something to oppose and that this thing must be a worthy opponent. The editors and publishers of the Resistance had the occupier and the collaborator in their sights, the new criticism has an analogous (if not similar) deathly and inertial cultural target in mind. Barthes will make his object what he calls 'bourgeois culture' and as a critic of it he will always remain caught within its orbit, circulating it and drawn towards it in the eternally compromised high-wire act of the 'semioclast'. However, there remains throughout Barthes' writing, from *Sur Racine* onwards, a commitment to a certain avant-garde of thought and to the counter-cultural possibility. It is difficult to reconstruct today the exact historical specificity of Barthes' counter-cultural capital at the moment of publishing *Criticism and Truth* (or indeed the cachet associated with the post-Liberation left of Sartre and Camus: they are not the same thing and in important respects are opposed; in this respect Barthes is thus oppositional to opposition itself). In particular, when so much of contemporary academic and intellectual life is now led by the homogenising influence of corporately owned publishing houses and media outlets, it is difficult to reimagine the very idea of a counter-cultural possibility. The Internet has a certain value in this respect but as a tool that relies on the inventiveness of the techno-science of privatised research its frequent gestures of resistance are all too easily trammelled up and appropriated by the power its users seek to subvert. For example, the newspaper *Liberation*, founded by Sartre and others in

1968, is now owned by a nominally right-wing 'press baron' who, while wishing to maintain its distinctive (but now modified) editorial voice (because otherwise a certain corner of the market would go unserviced), has brought the newspaper within the culture of mediatic capitalism with a 'restructured' workforce and as part of the Rothschilds media group. Counter-culture and opposition is no longer the patrimony of youth. Rather, we now all live an ironic relation to the channels of communication which produce the meaning that envelopes us. I am preparing to speak of what the text of Barthes may have to say to us today about this situation. However, let us return presently to the issue of the counter-culture of complexity.

In his response to Picard, Barthes considers it 'normal' that 'a country should periodically review… the things which come down from its past and describe them anew in order to find out *what it can make of them*'.[28] For us today this includes the text of Roland Barthes, but here Barthes is referring to the inherited canon of classic French literature, which in his opinion is due for reappraisal. This reassessment of the values of French culture would be an appropriate activity after the Liberation (although Barthes' own owl of Minerva arrives belatedly on the scene to identify this enterprise with such a cause). This would be a case of what Derrida terms, in relation to Marx after the collapse of the Soviet Union, assessing 'the state of the debt';[29] that is, the act of inheritance that must affirm the inheritance by distinguishing and choosing that which one wishes to inherit. It is also the avant-garde impulse that Harold Bloom terms 'the anxiety of influence' in which each generation confronts and must creatively 'misprision' the authority of their predecessors – as we will attempt to do with Barthes himself in this book. Barthes sees Picard's polemic as a conservative reflex of one generation against this 'normal' impulse. The arguments that are used against the new criticism are, according to Barthes, those used against 'all avant-garde movements … people have discovered that these works are intellectually empty, verbally sophisticated, morally dangerous and they owe their success to snobbery alone'.[30] This, says Barthes, is the assault of a certain obscurantism that attacks Theory as precisely obscurantist while disguising its own obfuscation and lack of detailed analysis with the ideological cloak of the normative. This is an important reaction because it betrays a suspicion of a discourse without comprehending it. The reaction thus betrays itself, projecting its own faults (of a lack of understanding or discursive clarity) onto the object whose difference it suspects. Thus, the constitutive lack at the heart of normative discourse, which Theory has already taken as its theme, is turned back onto Theory and Theory is criticised for an objection it first formulated with regard to the normative. Such a situation might be understood as systemic of such encounters or, as Barthes describes it in his text, a kind of scapegoating, 'a primitive rite of expulsion of a dangerous individual from an archaic community'.[31] Normative criticism approaches its assault on the new as if it were, says Barthes, 'a job belonging to public health, which was bravely undertaken and whose successful completion affords relief'.[32]

I do not wish to rehearse here the opening salvos of what in Britain were called the 'theory wars', in America the 'culture wars' and in France the '*la guerre de professeurs*'.[33] Why, incidentally, this unreasonable and disproportionate metaphor of mortal combat? Here is a mythology that would take some unpicking. Allowing it to pass for the moment, however, it should be noted that on the one hand it is not unusual today to find the disciplinary professor resistant of the theorist even though the disciplinarian has, as a disciplinarian, taken on board all the insights of the theorist without recognition and continues to feel able to eschew the theorist. Disciplines would like nothing better than to be left alone to sediment. It also should be said that the place where theory now most frequently and intensely runs up against this charge of obscurantism is in the media, which has taken on the mantel of 'normative' biographical and contextual criticism as it has migrated from the academy, pushed out by the complexity, even 'specialism', of theoretical approaches. It is in the reductionism of the media that the worst sorts of calumnies are replayed about the 'intellectually empty, verbally sophisticated' and 'morally dangerous' obscurantism of Theory. Media representations of Theory and the representation of Theory in the literary and artistic culture at large is a huge topic.[34] It is caught on the horns of the aporia identified above, namely the double bind Theory finds itself in between on the one hand an institutional resistance to theory within disciplinarity and on the other the disconnect between normative 'public' discourse and the academic specialism of theoretical language. The example of deconstruction and the refusal to read the work of Jacques Derrida, and especially Paul de Man, would make a suitable topic for a whole book-length study. However, it is by no means a straightforward question of inside and outside the university: the contemporary art gallery, for example, proves a hospitable place for the conceptual. I do not think that this point needs to be prolonged too long, however. A basic familiarity with the mediatic presentation

of culture today in newspapers and on television should leave us in
no doubt that, as Barthes suggested some time ago, we continue to
live in the epoch of the cult of the author and of attendant bourgeois
criticism.[35]

The point is not, I think, to expect the mediatic space to become
friendly to the complexity of Theory. Rather, the transformation of critical thinking that the theoretical opening initiates and which begins
in universities should be thought of as a mutation in the experience
of thought which may take decades and centuries to play out. The
seduction of a possible response to Picard's argument (and it is everywhere) would be either to imagine that the theoretical impulse could
be diluted to suit television, for example, and so transform it as a channel of communication (the dilution indicating that the transformation
has not been of television) or to imagine that critical thinking should
retreat to specialist publications and media outlets as an intellectual
sub-genre (here the so-called normative retains its dominance, having bought off the challenge of theory, as Baron de Rothschild caters
for the readers of *Liberation*). Rather, in this situation the task for criti-
cal-theoretical thought would be: by what strategy and style could
a new writing interlace the motifs of complexity and critique in an
avant-garde practice that ranged across disciplines and media, that
spoke several languages and produced multiple texts at once as a possibility of the counter-cultural, parasitic upon and augmenting of the
more archaic structures of culture in general? This is a process that
can neither be accomplished within a modest time-frame nor result
in a domination of critical culture by the theoretical, which is by its
nature avant-garde and so must remain, at least in part, oppositional.
The significance of such an entirely conceptual, biblio-political, textual activism would be that today it retains the possibility of a culture
of resistance to homogeneity and reduction in thought as well as the
material order it addresses. Theory offers the possibility of a counter-
culture of thought, which takes as its object and goal the invisibility of
complexity in contemporary, western and globalised discourse. Such,
it seems to me, are the stakes suggested by Barthes' extraordinarily
insightful *Criticism and Truth*.[36]

Now, Barthes is concerned with the place of literary criticism in
the academy. As one who could not find a supervisor for doctoral
research (Lévi-Strauss turned him down) and who twice did not have
his contract renewed as a researcher at the CNRS, only returning
to the academy after the success of his published articles in critical

journals and magazines, Barthes was more than acutely aware of the inertial power of the normative within the institution. Despite his late and distinguished election to the Collège de France in 1976, it should be remembered that he was only elected by a majority of one following the sponsorship of his candidacy by Michel Foucault. Barthes learnt his theoretical 'radicalism' not in the university but in the sanatorium at Saint-Hiliare-du-Touvet where he spent the war discussing Marx and Trotsky with Georges Fournié, who had fought in the Spanish Civil War and who introduced Barthes to the emerging post-Resistance presses after the Liberation. The first version of 'Writing Degree Zero' appeared in *Combat* in August 1947. This experience of mountain top isolation in a sanatorium during the war renders an entirely different meaning to the idea of 'committed criticism'. Barthes' continual reluctance to join the fray and his melancholic detachment from the stupidity of political discourse has more in keeping with the observations of Proust than with the actions of Sartre. When reading through Barthes systematically, one becomes overtaken by an overwhelming sense that Barthes as a writer and semioclast was constitutionally unable to become involved in a political world that extended beyond epistolary exchange. An involvement of the sort that characterised much of Sartre's activity would have ruined the very sense of what Barthes calls in *Mythologies* sarcasm as 'the condition of truth'. In this respect Barthes would seem to be the textual activist *manqué*, so close to his own portrait of his beloved Voltaire as the saddest of writers. The melancholic, hermetic Barthes was never able to actualise the aporia in a productive way that imagined writing as a ranging practice that overspilled the critical page to circumvent and outflank the stupidities of public discourse. The closest he ever came to achieving this was in his *Mythologies* of the 1950s, which have themselves given rise to so much bad faith and to what we now call cultural studies.[37] However, this is to misunderstand the relationship of theoretical practice to material politics: there is no bridge to be crossed from one to the other. The one resides within the other as the scholar resides in the world, because coordinates cannot be measured without position.[38] It is a particularly Anglo-Saxon illusion to imagine that a theoretical discourse is necessarily and esoterically divorced from the prevailing 'normality' or 'pragmatism' of something like liberal parliamentarianism, just as it has been a striking, but now defunct, academic illusion to imagine the easy dismissal of theory by normative criticism.

The counter-cultural possibilities of Barthes' writing should not, however, be over-stated. In *Criticism and Truth* he is well aware that western society does not consume 'critical commentaries in the way that it consumes films, novels or songs'.[39] Rather, we might understand the debate between the 'Old' and 'New' critics in France in the 1960s as an example of a wider phenomenon that Barthes' writing highlights, namely the ways in which an inherited tradition (novelistic, critical or political) takes on through the act of inheritance a verisimilitude that needs to be challenged as not natural but contingent. Just as the verisimilitude of the realist novel must be addressed by modernism and the critical verisimilitude of 'authorial biography' must be demystified by the new criticism, so the appearance of a political verisimilitude in western democracies, the news agencies that report them and the academic policy advisers who feed them must be challenged by an avant-garde of critical thought that imagined an alternative to the deadening discourse of the same. What is called esoteric, obscure or elitist in such a theoretical discourse is the requirement that thought and writing be imagined in a different way. Barthes' riposte to Picard is that the normalising effects of bourgeois criticism cannot tolerate 'that language should talk about language'.[40] That is to say, that it cannot bear that its own symbolic nature be exposed, cutting it adrift from the referential illusion of its own verisimilitude, that it is not a textual practice but has an essential relation to biography and truth. The same goes for the political realm in which normative political discourse cannot bear to have its own operations as a symbolic practice laid bare but must cling to its own referential illusion by expunging theoretical inquiry as *mere* textual activism. As the frequent stupidity of western political discourse demonstrates, we pay a high price for this particular obfuscation. As Barthes says, 'Our task, as intellectuals, is not politicization but a critique of meanings, a critique of meaning itself' (Barthes 1985, 156).

Barthes
―――――
Sartre

Nor is the task of the semioclast necessarily the duty of 'Sartre' either. Not Barthes or Sartre, never either/or. Rather, the role of a Barthes is to imagine thought itself otherwise. This is where the modernist avant-garde meets the possibility of an alternative politics. Sartre's politics may be progressive but they are not an alternative, they are a replay of the same, one side of a wider and more archaic structure. Barthes says of Picard, 'we know that old criticism cannot write in any other way unless it begins to think in some other way. For to write is *already* to organise the world, it is *already* to think (to learn a language is to learn how one thinks in that language). It is thus useless (though critical verisimilitude persists in expecting it) to ask the Other to re-write himself if he has not decided to re-think himself.'[41] That is to say, the semioclast changes the world by imagining a way of thinking about the world that is otherwise in a performative interpretation that transforms what it interprets. This is the injunction of Marx's Eleventh Thesis on Feuerbach, which is understood so badly by the literal minded.[42] The point of Theory is not that it offers a fashionable jargon for the pseudo-intellectual, it is that it opens up an alternative means of intelligibility that moves criticism and philosophy into something other than itself, that negotiates between the realm of thinking about the world and living that thought. For the semioclast criticism is always more than mere criticism, it is a way of being in the world that thinks productively about the constructed nature of that world. It is an alert critical consciousness that transforms the means by which the world is understood and thus the actions that one takes within it. What some see as 'jargon', as Barthes explains, is really only the foreignness of an alternative vocabulary that has been allotted according to a long forgotten disciplinary 'gold rush', 'in which each discipline (a concept which in fact derives from the way universities organise their work) is conceded a small language territory, a sort of terminological miner's claim whose confines one cannot leave'.[43] This division of jargon is entirely arbitrary but results in current usage being 'promoted to the dignity of a universal language', says Barthes.[44] It is the task of the alert reader to actualise meaning in a textual overspill between what Hélène Cixous calls 'auto-bibliography' and the meanings in operation in the world, to challenge given models of understanding, writing and thinking because this is the necessary challenge of questioning inherited modes of being in the world. This is an irreducibly conceptual process, it cannot be otherwise as an event of thought, it is textual through and through.

Barthes has his own particular project in this regard, which explains a great deal about his relation to political culture. As a writer of a particular modernist inclination Barthes imagines his task is 'not to enter into an easy relationship with an average of all possible readers, it is to enter into a difficult relationship with our own language: a writer has greater obligations towards a way of speaking which is the truth for him than towards the critic of the *Nation française* or *Le Monde*'.[45] What his critics characterise as 'jargon' is for Barthes the mobilisation of a certain vocabulary that allows for the description of a way of thinking about thought itself, speaking about language, and writing about writing which is necessary if we are to move beyond the model of verisimilitude and what Edward Said calls, in the text that replaced de Man's unpublished review[46] of the *Mythologies* in *The New York Review of Books*, the self-evident 'thereness of things'[47] that prevent us from understanding thought and the world as anything other than inherited nature. Several things follow from this for Barthes. First, the task of the writer such as himself (he never makes a claim for his own identity beyond this appellation, except as a teacher) is that of the semiotic adventurer, voyaging at the frontier of intelligibility to expand our consciousness of the world. Second, such an enterprise cannot be reduced to fit the demands of those forms of communication that rely upon simplification and banality for their operation. This is not a revo-lution that will be televised because it is precisely an attempt to move beyond the terms of understanding allocated to us by such media. The semioclast cannot be accountable to the media because the media is the exact cause of their critical impulse to imagine thought other-wise. Third, and here is the difficulty for Barthes that his present read-ers may or may not wish to avow as part of his patrimony, it is not clear that Barthes himself ever felt his own writing had effectively made the negotiation between the symbolic adventure and the material world.

He was himself an admirer of what he called 'logothetes' (founders of language or initiators of discourse), by which 'the book transmi-grates into our life'.[48] Sade, Fourier, Loyola and Derrida are among the examples Barthes cites as such innovators, inventors of new ways of reading the world. Modesty and decorum, as well as his own habitual and splenetic melancholy, prevents him from citing himself as a 'log-othete' but five decades after the publication of the *Mythologies* and the transformation of the academy by cultural studies (and everything that falls out from it, such as identity politics and so on) I think it is safe to say that Barthes was just such an initiator. Perhaps, the task today for the reader of Barthes is to move beyond the operational intelligibil-ity provided by Barthes, to remove Barthes from Barthes, and to pursue a new opening in the spirit of Barthes that would mean leaving behind the semiological and 'popular-cultural-interdisciplinary-studies' as the very inheritance that Barthes today would challenge as a sedimen-tation of thought. Perhaps. But such a task of course begins by reading the text of Barthes as a point of departure. There is, of course, nothing older or more hackneyed than calls for the new. The innovative discourses of a Loyola or a Barthes do not spring authochthonously from ivory towers. Barthes' writing is on the one hand part of the modernist and symboliste tradition of writing in French that he admires so much and on the other it is a 'bricolage' of other signs and 'sorties' in circulation on the French intellectual scene at the time of its writing. For these reasons Barthes considered Flaubert as 'the first modern writer: because he accedes to madness. A madness that is not representation, imitation, realism, but a madness of writing, a madness of language'.[49] He borrows heavily from anthropology, sociology and historiography as well as philosophy and literary criticism. Barthes' writing is a proprietary, hybrid blend of all these borrowed things out of which something genuinely new emerges.

His dispute with Picard is that since language is always multiple (without this there is no literature) then the text of criticism is also always multiple. As soon as you understand this criticism can never be the same again. It is no longer a universal meta-language used to understand the eternal greatness of the classics, but an adventure in writing that moves the symbolic object beyond itself into a productive negotiation with meaning in the world. Accordingly, as an expanded practice, criticism becomes difficult to disentangle from literature itself, philosophy and critique. The binary division between critic and literature becomes porous and writing overspills between the two. Literature then becomes a question not of reference through fiction but of the fiction of reference. Classical distinctions between the literary and the material are no longer rigorously tenable as a 'new criticism', itself an innovation in writing, takes up the semiotic challenge of exploring the frontiers of intelligibility and meaning. In order to get to this point, Barthes' own texts pass through a structuralist and post-structuralist bricolage in the human sciences. They adopt and in part invent and reinvent a series of terms in order to allow Barthes conceptual leverage on the process of critical writing in order that he can outflank traditional oppositions and decentre sedimented forms of intelligibility, so that he can catch his thought on the cusp of a self-reflection where sight sees sight and hearing hears itself listening. This new conceptual order that Barthes constructs as a provisional and precarious platform out into the frontiers of writing is what his critics call 'jargon'. It is a frequent accusation thrown at other initiators of radical theoretical discourses such as Derrida, Lacan or Deleuze and

Guattari. For Barthes it is an opening in the possibilities of meaning and thus of existence within a world of meaning. It is a question of how one experiences thought and the sign. He asks Picard (if Picard is indeed the addressee of *Criticism and Truth*), who attacks him according to the protocols and vocabulary of traditional criticism and who subsequently is speaking a different language from Barthes, 'Would you blame a Chinese (since new criticism seems to you to be a strange language) for the mistakes he is making in French *when he is talking Chinese*?'[50] For Barthes, the suggestion would be that the distinction between modes of being between critical verisimilitude and semioclasm is as distinct as that between understanding the world in French and understanding the world in Chinese. However, this is to beg the question of translation. I would suggest that the difficulty for Theory is not finding a third, neutral or 'meta' language into which both the normative and the theoretical can be translated because the normative by default already occupies this position. Rather, after its own institutional success in the form of cultural-studies-after-Barthes Theory can no longer be satisfied with a self-description as a foreign language. After so-called globalisation (which simultaneously makes a world and withholds its privileges) such a distinction between Theory and its normative other is no longer tenable. After the globalisation of Theory and cultural studies (the presentation and retreat of Theory) surely the theorist can no longer console themselves with Barthes' description: the symbolic adventure has moved elsewhere in a world whose *caps* are melting at both ends.

Barthes today

I have confessed that it has been a few years since I last turned to Barthes for my daily theoretical bread. In part my return to Barthes today is in response to a commission. Barthes would have appreciated that: he claimed only to write for commissions and never for a pre-elaborated project of his own. Disingenuous as the claims of writers might be, especially the claims of writers who have famously pointed out the disingenuousness of writers' claims, there remains perhaps the question: why respond to this commission and not any other? Why would Barthes be of interest today? I think the answer to that lies as much in the term 'today' as it does in 'Barthes'. Our historical moment is considerably complex and crowded. I will not reiterate the problems of the present moment here, they are all around us and pal-pable. I trust they are at the front of the mind of any reader who has persisted with this book so far. If I may lay specific examples to one side for a moment, examples that would require patient and individual responses, I would like to speculate on the wider field of cultural pro-duction in which such examples operate, derive their meaning and in turn augment through their own immanence within the field.[51] I would like to speculate as to what the text of Barthes might have to say to this cultural field. Perhaps, at this moment, right from the very beginning, we have already entered into an irresolvable difficulty with Barthes. The suggestion I am making is that when reading Barthes today, it would be most productive to turn his texts towards the cultural field rather than, say, 'politics' (let me suspend this term in quotation marks for the moment), which might seem more germane to our current condition. At first glance the text of Roland Barthes is one that primarily concerns itself with culture, high and low: wrestling, fashion, soap powder, Greta Garbo, the Marx Brothers, James Bond, Flaubert, Poe, Balzac, Proust. It is through commentary on this textual scene that Barthes alludes to and accedes to the political but there is, seemingly, little in Barthes that attends to the normative political discourse of parties and policies *per se*. The position of Barthes is that of the textual activist who sits aside the fray, sharpening his pencils, painting his water colours in the sun room in the house in Provence, quietly despairing of the stupidity of the political culture that fills the pages of *Le Monde*. I find in Barthes an exemplary figure for our time, Barthes today, the melancholy of a critical thinking that cannot cross over into the public space because that space is so hostile to its complexity and because that thought would fail to be critical enough should it reduce and banalise itself in order to become accepted by that space.[52]

In truth this is a familiar, even classical, condition for the writer, separated by writing from the world they write about, caught in a supplementary logic where their writing is part of the world their position as writer throws them into anterior relief against. Political culture remains separated from the world of critical thought because politics likes it like that and requires that 'action' have a relation of anteriority and utility to thought. The textual activist seeks critical lev-erage on the world by attempting to undo this division in a practice of writing-politics that decentres the conceptual order upon which such a division and its categories rest. This writing-politics, a new crit-ical writing of the present, calls for an engagement and commitment of the writer as a writer in an interminable and ever vigilant rewriting of the political. In this way, the boundaries of 'political culture' as a sub-culture become indistinct and the critical writer accedes to its textual structure as a discursive and ideological formation. Such a degeneration of the boundaries of the political is a prolonged process, fraught with difficulties, false exits and falls into closure. The mutation of political culture, initiated by the textual activist, may take centuries but although painstakingly slow it is irreversible. Barthes' text stands at the opening of the transformation, like the planting of a flag that cracks the surface of a glacier; a crack that slowly spreads with time to open a fissure, that becomes a opening, that becomes a gorge running the length of the mountain, opening it up, inch by inch, until it becomes not a crack in the surface of a mountain but the very space that defines a new arrangement between cliffs and valley, ground and air. If Barthes is morose when faced with the brute materiality of political idiocy, perhaps it is because as the planter of the flag he could not begin to appreciate the ways in which his own demystifications of culture could begin to open up spaces in the glaciers of the academy and politics. Such would be the self-pitying delusion of the critic, the confusion between the response of their own proximity and the significance of their action. Barthes was able to see this historic and untimely significance in the text of Michelet, what he calls 'the vegetal character of historic growth',[53] but not in his own writing. Barthes here seems to suffer from both the mourning and melancholia that affects those of the left nostalgic for a certain idea of now disappointed revolution, and simultaneously caught in a structural impasse of something like the non-messianic, what Rei Terada has termed 'politics after expectation'.

To speak then of 'Barthes Today' is to say a great deal about the temporal disruption that connects a body of writing to the present and to the very idea of a 'today': the 'today' of a here and now, of an urgency, as well as the 'today' that implies Barthes' yesterday. To ask what remains of Barthes today is already to suggest that Barthes is a thing of yesterday: that his today is already our yesterday. The reader who wishes to ask what Barthes means for us today is caught in the act of dragging a yesterday into the present. This cannot be done by a temporal dislocation that flips a text of the past onto the present and treats it as a text of the present. Rather it only makes sense to ask this question as a consideration of the historical relation (as a play of differences) between Barthes' text as a text of the present (his present, about the present as such) and our present. Accordingly, theory today, or even cultural studies, literary studies and the humanities in general, would then be occasioned to identify the text of Barthes as part of its own history. It would be necessary to recognise that in some curious way Barthes made us, and that in a significant way we all remain, in part, 'Barthesians' today. Such would be the after-effect of the vegetal growth, the historic entanglement, of Barthes' writing. It is difficult and contradictory then for cultural studies, say, to ask what does Barthes means today because the very idea of today that this question depends upon owes a debt to Barthes who first inaugurated a discourse of 'the today' in cultural studies. Cultural studies would be caught holding Barthes to account via a notion of 'today' that it has derived from the text of Barthes itself. The relevance of Barthes today is that Barthes is a thinker not of today (our here and now) but of today as such (an insistent and persistent critic of the here and now).[54] This much cultural studies owes to Barthes; Barthes owes it to the tradition of Enlightenment critique to which he belongs, running through Benjamin and Adorno back to Kant, to cite only a few minimal and inadequate indices.[55]

To ask this question concerning 'Barthes today' is to prepare to read Barthes' own text 'Myth Today', the methodological supplement that retrospectively imposes unity and clarity on the run of short texts written between 1954 and 1956 and collected in the book *Mythologies* (1957) (and subsequently translated into English across two separate books, *Mythologies* (1972) and *The Eiffel Tower* (1979)). The idea of the 'today' in 'Myth Today' is then considerably complex. The chronological 'today' referred to here is already dated before it migrates into English. The decade that Barthes comments on is that of McCarthy and De Gaulle, of Greta Garbo and Tony Curtis, of the Abbé Pierre and Pierre Poujade. This is a 'today' of French culture that has already passed through the transformations and radicalisation of the sixties before it reaches the English-speaking academy. Barthes' 'today' is always already too late for the scene that it enters, already too late for that transition between revolution and recuperation that marks the waning of the sixties into the seventies in the west (if we are prepared for the sake of argument to work momentarily with these unyielding epochal units). By 1972 Barthes himself had moved beyond Sade (1971) to 'the pleasure of the text' (1973). The Anglo-American scene in which Barthes' text belatedly appears is that of Nixon and Kissinger, Vietnam and Watergate, the Angela Davis trial and the Munich Olympics. John Berger's admiring review of Barthes' book in *New Society* is concerned with Berger's own application of 'Myth Today' to an analysis of *The*

Observer's front page (6 February 1972) reporting a civil rights march in Glasgow one month after Bloody Sunday, when the British army opened fire on a civil rights march held by Catholics in Derry, killing thirteen and energising the cause of the IRA. Here Berger is occupied with the importance of bringing the today of 'Myth Today' into his own present, making Barthes' today his own. In this sense, the question of Barthes-in-English has always been the question of 'Barthes today'.

Ever since the published translation of *Mythologies* in 1972, the primary question for Barthes has been: what relevance does this collection of texts on the cultural scene of the mid-1950s have for us today? The answer to this is, I think, that Barthes is significant not because he is a critic of Poujade and De Gaulle but because he is like Arendt, Benjamin, Adorno, Marx, Voltaire and Montaigne before him, a thinker of the idea of 'today', today *as such*. January 1972 is a curious 'today' for me, because it was the month in which I was born in Glasgow, not so very far from where the civil rights march reported on by *The Observer* took place. I am, then, the same age as Barthes, at least the same age as the English Roland Barthes. Thinking the present, the question of 'today', is always a thinking of autobiography, of one's own mortality, ends and limits. This is a significant issue for critique and the writer-textual-activist that in their critical thinking philosophy becomes the counter-signature of their own autobiography. Any piece of critical writing on the present is always an act of autobiography. The question posed as the question of 'today' is also a question concerning tomorrow. To ask what is the relevance of Barthes today is to ask what will be the meaning of Barthes tomorrow: what will the reader of tomorrow do with Roland Barthes? It is thus a question of one's own future as well. The question of the future of cultural studies, literary studies, the future of the humanities in general. What is the future of my own autos, perhaps of the autos in general, how will it write and think tomorrow as a result of reading Roland Barthes? In considering the today of Roland Barthes, dear reader, you are also considering your own future, how you will think and read after encountering this book and by extension the wider text of Roland Barthes.

The question is both 'what is to be done with Barthes today?' but also 'what is to be done with the "what is to be done with Barthes today?"'? The whole apparatus of cultural studies and the urgency of reading the 'today' as a primordial schema is at stake in this question. How might one begin to think about thinking about today in such a way that was not merely thinking about today such as it has been thought about yesterday by others like John Berger but also Roland Barthes himself? The traditional manner, if like the architecture of certain cities on the western seaboard of America one considers 'tradition' to be adequately attributed to the last fifty years, in which the question of today has been asked, following Barthes, is in the form of the synchronic. The urgency of today calls for a synchronic intervention in the manner of a classical structuralist analysis. It is to address the here and now by concentrating on its singularity in a methodological vacuum from either the historical, philological past or the impossible arrival of a tomorrow. This synchronic analysis of today is of course necessary from the point of view of immediacy but it is also and purely metaphysical. Its method relies upon a strictly metaphysical apprehension of temporality and history as temporality. There is of course only ever this vulgar temporality, the *distentio* and the *extentio*, the yesterday, today and tomorrow. There is no other concept of time and yet it is by this reckoning that the question of today takes on the value of an immediate presence even though we might know from reading Augustine, Heidegger and Derrida that this present moment never arrives and is never fully actualisable as a present. The idea of 'today' as it is used in a formulation such as 'Myth Today' or 'Roland Barthes Today' then covers a more complex historical conjunction and temporality. By 'today' here we really mean a today (the war on terror, climate change and so on) that is already our immediate past and that, having passed away, we are called upon to rationalise and categorize. It also refers to the consequences of this past, that which will arrive from the future as a result of this irrecoverable and unrepeatable past. 'Today', in this sense, never happens. There is no myth today, there are only ever myths of tomorrow and myths of yesterday that require to be read in order to prepare oneself for tomorrow. Such a scenario might begin to complicate the synchronic assumption, which predicates the very idea of 'Myth Today'.[56]

What then is the meaning of 'Today' today? Would it be possible to disturb the schema of political and philosophical thought that gave primacy to the present question as the question of presence, while continuing to take responsibility for the pressing urgency of the 'today' today? This is a question that cannot be answered directly, I think. It must be returned to the act of reading from which it emerges as that reading opens up the text of Barthes, yesterday's text, to its possible future. Today the question of Roland Barthes is the one he poses himself in 'Myth Today': how shall we read today? So it goes, when it comes to Barthes. For Barthes' essay it is always a matter of 'today'. It has been an unbearable, eternal day for myth since 1957. This day will not end, as long as Roland Barthes has a future, that is to say as long as Roland Barthes has readers. Therefore, let me submit 'Myth Today' to an inquiry that considered both its past (which is to say its own future, 1957 to the present) and its future (which is to say, the possibility of its own past as an estimation of what 'history' will make of this text). 'Myth Today', yesterday, today and tomorrow; the myth of 'today' and the myth of 'Myth Today'. 'Le Mythe, aujourd'hui', 'Myth Today' but also 'Myth nowadays', 'Myth at present'. These second and third options for translation place a slightly different emphasis on the idea of 'today', an emphasis that is not quite as clean cut as the Anglicised or journalistic 'Myth Today'. The French even has a comma that separates 'le Mythe' from 'aujourd'hui', 'Myth, nowadays', 'Myth, at present', because this is a synchronic analysis of 'Myth', how it works today, at present, captured and dissected. The pause between 'Myth' and 'Today' in the French indicates Barthes' own distance from the absolute urgency of the 'today': the unstable stepping stone between the writer and the world, ivory tower and down and dirty, theory and practice.

Barthes/Marx I

'Myth Today' is a creative misprision of *The German Ideology*. There can be no other reason to read Barthes' essay unless one is contemplating the radicalisation of reading. If we ask the question, what remains of a Barthes today (why read Roland Barthes in a time of terror?), an answer must surely begin with this essay and its significance for an appreciation of ideology. This is a term that has its own considerable obfuscations and history of appropriation through a certain Marxian genealogy. In returning to the text of Barthes I also want to open up the question of ideology to the contemporary moment and to an alternative history running from the text of Marx and Engels to so-called post-structuralism, of which Barthes-Today would be part. When universities succumb to managerialism without comment, unprecedented breaches of privacy and civil liberties are signed off in the middle of the night in the name of the 'Patriot Act' and the French legislature can, with a straight face, demand that teachers and textbooks 'emphasise the positive role of France overseas, especially in the Maghreb region, in North Africa', then it is time to reassess the work of the concept of ideology. On the one hand, it is a term that has fallen out of the present critical lexicon as a result of its association with a now largely unread, unloved and unmissed Marxist inheritance. It is not a sexy term for the present generation of cultural analysts and literary theorists. Political philosophy has moved its interests elsewhere to the deconstruction of terms from the European tradition such as sovereignty, universalism and cosmopolitanism. On the other hand, where it is used, it acts as one critical tool among many, deployed momentarily and in moderation as one might a scalpel or a seasoning bay leaf, its provenance as a concept lost in the critical melange and its place within a more general political-theoretical schema ignored or minimised. Now, let me state explicitly and pre-emptively that I am not concerned here with dismissing the use of 'ideology' in Marxist theory and criticism. Rather and momentarily I would like to return to the text of Marx to test it in relation to the space that Barthes opens up for thinking about ideology under the name of 'Myth'. On the contrary, by reading Marx and Barthes together I would like to encourage a certain generation of theorists to re-engage with an idea of ideology that is currently unexplored because of its perceived relation to an unadmired institutional Marxism. I do so out of a belief that the enterprise of critique (without which deconstruction or cultural studies are themselves structurally insufficient) is nothing without a functional and critical notion of ideology.[57] When Barthes puts ideology to work under the name of 'myth' he is engaged in an exemplary act of revendication, to use a term he borrows elsewhere from Brecht,[58] in which this concept from the tradition is turned around and put to use in a new and productive way. Sufficient time has passed since 'Myth Today' for us to be required to revisit this gesture and to once again explore the meaning of myth and ideology today. First, some remarks on Barthes and Marxism.

Barthes learned his Marxism in the sanatorium at Saint Hilaire-du-Touvet during the war (having been excused military service in 1937 due to his consumption). At this time he 'breathed the same informed air', to borrow a phrase from Muriel Spark,[59] as the writers and theorists of the resistance, and in particular found himself drawn to the gravitational pull of Sartrean thought. On leaving the sanatorium, as an unpublished and largely self-taught thirty-two-year-old, Barthes considered himself to be both a Marxist and a Sartrean. As his biographer Louis-Jean Calvet describes it 'he decided that his project was to combine these two philosophies in his approach to literature: to develop a "committed" literature, and to justify Sartre in Marxist terms'.

This was Barthes' intellectual position during his post-war sojourn in Romania where he worked as a librarian and cultural coordinator at the Instituit Français des Hautes Études in Bucharest. While an early text such as *Writing Degree Zero* clearly demonstrates a strong and original theoretical voice that is not yet caught up in the scientific ambitions of structuralism, it is equally suggestive of a creative thinking through of the questions of history, class and politics derived from his reading of Marx. This reading of Marx was neither especially wide nor prolonged but is undoubtedly a seminal influence on Barthes' later elaboration of his critical position, as equally significant to an estimation of Barthes as, say, Barthes' reading of the *nouveau roman*. The astute reader will wish to stop me at this point to suggest that such a determination of the meaning of the text of Barthes through biographical 'proof' would not be particularly Barthesian in spirit. Perhaps, but there is more than one spirit of Barthes. I shall return to the place of Marx in the text of Barthes momentarily; however, to say that the horizon of meaning is not saturated by the intention and biography of an author is not the same thing as saying that that horizon has no relation to the intention and biography of the author as a point of reference, as Barthes himself did frequently in his readings of literature. To paraphrase Barthes' understanding of Chateaubriand, mine is a Roland Barthes of paper. My point here is that up until the writing of the *Mythologies* Barthes was an active reader of Marx (this is of course quite different from being an active Marxist in the period before 1956). Barthes' relation to Marxism at this time is complex and is exemplified by his commentaries on texts by Sartre and Camus.

In 1955 Barthes was editing the journal *Théâtre populaire*. He and his co-editor Bernard Dort took a distinctly Brechtian line following their admiration for a successful staging of *The Caucasian Chalk Circle* at the Sarah-Bernhardt theatre in Paris. Barthes remained close to Brecht as an exemplar of avant-garde modernism throughout his career as a critic. In 1955 Sartre's play *Nekrassov* was an open attack on perceived right-wing anti-communist propaganda. The action takes place in the editorial office of a right-wing Parisian daily newspaper, *Soir à Paris*, in which the character Jules Palotin is a satirical representation of Pierre Lazareff, the then editor of *France-Soir*. In the face of declining circulation the editors are seeking sensational stories. A man arrives in the office claiming to be the Soviet minister of the interior seeking political asylum. He is in fact an international criminal who has been on the run for years. The newspaper begins to print the minister-criminal's invented memoirs containing all manner of outrageous fictions such as the Soviet Union's plans to invade France and the list of tens of thousands of Frenchmen, including MPs and right-wing newspaper editors, who will be shot when the Red Army seizes power. In the manner of a Molière burlesque the intended comedy is derived from the ways in which the criminal deceives the right-wing editors by telling them what they want to hear. Sartre does not entertain the possibility of what would happen a year later when the Red Army entered Budapest and views as propaganda the tales of similar suppression in the liberated countries of Eastern Europe after the war. Not surprisingly the right-wing French dailies panned the play and it closed after only sixty performances. Barthes defended the play in his journal,[60] finding in it a freewheeling Brechtian satire on one of his favourite tropes, 'the bourgeoisie': 'Every evening, for as long as possible, Nekrassov will liberate those French people who like me, are in danger of being suffocated by the prevalence of the bourgeois sickness. Michelet once said France hurts me, and this is why I found Nekrassov such a breath of fresh air.' Universal critical opinion, of which one should be justly wary, identifies Nekrassov as an over-long, dogmatic indulgence that makes bad theatre. On the one hand, for those on the left at this time (as the right-wing reviewer of the play and friend of Pierre Lazareff, Françoise Giroud, wrote to Louis-Jean Calvet) 'Sartre was sacred, and only pearls of wisdom could drop from his pen. If one disagreed, one was immediately classed as a right-wing bastard who had sold out to imperialism.'[61] On the other hand, at a time when Barthes was writing his critique of bourgeois culture in the mythologies, he no doubt thought Sartre's play a genuine demystification of French McCarthyism, worth defending in the face of the right-wing press. However, with this review Barthes placed himself publicly on the side of Sartre and his avowal of communism.

At the end of 1954 Barthes had reviewed, critically, Camus' *L'Étranger* and took up a similar commission to review *La Peste*. Camus read Barthes' second review before it was published and replied to Barthes in the same edition of *Bulletin du Club du meilleur livre* (the magazine of a mail order book club). Barthes' review and criticism of Camus is clearly influenced by his attraction to Sartre and as such is a decidedly un-Barthes-like text, and indeed seems to contradict much of what Barthes has to say about literature in *Writing Degree Zero* (first published in Camus' journal *Combat*, and clearly written – as Graham Allen suggests – within the ambit of Sartre's *What Is Literature?*).

The exchange with Camus is intriguing because it seems to me that both in temperament and in terms of political positions the mature Roland Barthes has much more in common with Camus than he does with Sartre. However, the Barthes of 1955 (that is, the Barthes of the *Mythologies*) aligns himself with the party of Sartre, who criticised Camus' novel as an allegory of the Occupation because it seems to suggest that fascism is a naturally occurring phenomenon and not the consequence of human behaviour or product of history (i.e. class war). Barthes' account of the novel by extension seems to criticise any attempt to write about the social in a metaphorical way and makes a call for a literal and realist fiction. How Barthes squares this with his ongoing and profound criticism of nineteenth-century Realism as the effect of bourgeois ideology is not at all clear. The confusion, it seems to me, is suggestive and symptomatic of Barthes' political instability at this time.

Camus responded to Barthes' review in a letter dated 11 January 1955. Allow me to read it to you it in a piecemeal fashion: firstly Camus tells Barthes that he cannot share his point of view concerning *La Peste* even though 'all commentary is legitimate, when criticism is done in good faith' but in the case of Barthes in would be a stretch to venture that this is what he is doing. Camus has been most put out by Barthes' review and he is really just warming up. He continues by asserting that all works of literature contain 'obvious things' that the author has the right to reclaim for himself in order to indicate the limits to which critical commentary can be used. Not for Camus the death of the author, rather something remains of his writing that must force itself upon us in light of Barthes' criticism. He goes on to respond to Barthes' review in detail in what amounts to a firm rebuttal of Barthes, and by synecdoche all the Sartre-inspired commentary on his novel. He writes to Barthes telling him that his claim that *La Peste* founds 'an anti-historical morality and a politics of solitude' is 'to devote oneself to contradiction' and to ignore several obvious examples, '*quelques evidence*' which he goes on to list. Thus Camus identifies Barthes with the Sartrean line, which he does not respond to elsewhere. He makes a special case of responding to Barthes, partly perhaps because Barthes should have known better, partly because he might be better placed than most to appreciate that responding itself is the very responsibility of the writer. Camus goes on to cite his evidence against Barthes, telling him that Camus wishes *La Peste* 'to be read in a number of different ways' even though it 'obviously concerns the struggle of the European resistance against Nazism', the evidence for this he suggests is that although this enemy is not named it has been recognised by readers in all the countries of Europe. A substantial part of the novel was published under the occupation '*dans un recueil de combat*' and, says Camus, it was only these circumstances that justified the transposition performed in the novel. He notes that *La Peste* is 'in one sense more than a chronicle of resistance. But assuredly it is not less'. The point for Camus then is that the novel as a novel is irreducibly multiple at the same time as insisting on its singularity. He goes on to propose that compared to his previous novel *L'Etranger*, *La Peste* is marked by a passage from an attitude of solitary revolt to a recognition of a community whose struggles one must share and that the evolution of his writing between the two novels can be identified through 'the meaning [*sens*] of solidarity and participation'. He goes on to say that the novel ends with the announcement and acceptance of struggles to come. *La Peste* is, Camus tells Barthes, a testimony to what will have to be accomplished in future struggles and which 'without doubt (Men, despite their own personal failings) must once again achieve against terror and its untiring weaponary [*arme*].' Having categorically rejected Barthes' characterisation of the novel as representing an anti-historical morality and politics of solitude, Camus takes Barthes' critical methodology to task, which for Camus would be to speak in the name of 'a more complete morality'. Camus tells Barthes that many of his observations revolve around the simple claim 'that I do not believe in realism in art'. This issue will be the locus of confusion and contradiction in Barthes' text. Camus rejects Barthes' claim that he 'refuses solidarity with our historic present' and suggests that the question posed by Barthes' review – namely, what would the protagonists of the novel do before the 'too human face of catastrophe'[the word used here is '*fléau*' meaning blight or scourge] as opposed to the faceless virus in the novel – is unjust. He suggests that the protagonists, 'whose experience I have translated a little', did what they did precisely against Men and at a cost that is well known. He goes on to say that faced with any Terror, they would no doubt do it again, 'no matter what its face because terror has many faces'. It is the multiplicity of terror that Camus suggests justifies why he did not name any single terror, 'precisely, in order to attack all its forms'. Here the exchange takes an interesting turn for us, connecting Barthes' confusion over metaphor with the difficulty of translation and the question of understanding and confronting 'Terror' of one kind or another. Camus' response to Barthes presents a linguistic predicament

of considerable complexity in which the elasticity of Camus' metaphorical extension snaps back into a misreading by Barthes of an imposed
metonymic insistence. Equally, in justifying his position (namely that
he is addressing all terror and not the single terror of Nazism) Camus
precisely opens himself up to Barthes' original claim (namely that by
the universalisation of faceless terror he has dehistoricised his object).
The slip between the necessity of the literal and the unavoidability
of the metaphorical leads to the mistranslation, one by the other, of
the texts of Barthes and Camus. Camus goes on to say that this is no
doubt what he is reproached for by his critics: the novel can be used to
represent all resistances against tyrannies. But says Camus this is not
something to reproach a writer for and he flatly denies that he can be
accused 'of refusing history to legitimate a tyranny'. At this point Camus
has moved beyond the text of Barthes for he immediately adds, 'this is
not your point, I know that'. He is then addressing through Barthes all
his other 'reproachers' and by extension Sartre.

  What I find interesting about this exchange is that Barthes' inchoate
position arises out of a confusion concerning metaphor. First, Barthes
reads Camus' remarkable text in an extraordinarily literal fashion. Like
other 'friends of Sartre' he assumes without question that the narrative
refers to the German occupation of France; all criticism of Camus follows from this. However, there is no point in the novel where it would
be possible to draw this inference with any degree of certainty. The
novel is set not in France as such but its southerly *departement* Algeria:
the action takes place in a quarantined Oran. The first occupation in
the novel then is of North Africa by the French, a colonial situation
that is almost entirely elided by the narrator as the milieu of the novel
is a community of middle-class white 'settlers'. There is no organised
resistance against the plague (one cannot combat bacteria in this
way) although there is a good deal of discussion about the necessity
of action in the face of spreading death. The reality of this novel is that
it is a piece of science fiction in the manner of Mary Shelley's *The Last
Man* and, as with all science fiction, without exception, its issue is the
issue of the alien and of colonialism. As much as his readers would wish
the ex-Resistance fighter Camus to fictionalise the Occupation this is
not what he does in this book: there is no attempt to denotate here,
suggestion and ambiguity is everything. As we shall see with Barthes'
understanding of signification as de Man (who knew something of the
doubleness of the Occupation) describes it, Barthes is led into a contradictory position by his failure to take a coherent line with respect to

the possibilities of polysemy. One might assume from his critique of Camus that Barthes found ambiguity in politics unconscionable. This was not the case elsewhere.

Barthes replied to Camus that his observations did not dissuade him from his point of view but they at least did permit him to better situate the debate between them. He characterises this debate as one concerning metaphor and history, reference and referent: does the novelist have the right 'to alienate [*d'aliéner*] the facts of history' and can a plague be equivalent, not to an occupation but to the Occupation? Barthes suggests that the entire book, from the epigram onwards, is based on this possibility. For Camus, says Barthes, this difficulty can be reduced to the rejection of realism in art, which Camus acknowledges that he does not believe in. However, Barthes continued by making his profession of faith for realism, or by qualification 'because realism has a weighty inheritance', what Barthes calls 'a literal art' which calls a plague a plague and in which resistance is only *the* Resistance. Such a position of course draws Barthes into the double bind of this linguistic contraction, whereby he insists that the novel be in no way metaphorical but at the same time is not metaphorical enough (i.e. more explicitly referencing the Nazi occupation of France through the trope of pestilence). Barthes is now playing on a considerably sticky wicket of his own making, calling for a literal art without metaphor, which would be no art at all. Barthes says that he sees in this literal art 'the only possible recourse against a formal morality' which would be capable of diverting the 'stubborness of facts' and the only possible respect for History 'whose ills are only remediable if one looks at them in their absolute singularity, not as symbols or paradigms [*germes*] of possible equivalences'. It is at this point that Barthes pulls a card out of his sleeve. In response to Camus request to say in what name he finds the morality of the *La Peste* insufficient, he claims that he has made no secret of it: it is 'in the name of historic materialism'. Barthes goes on to say that by his estimation 'a morality of explication' is more complete than a 'morality of expression'. He concludes that he would have said this sooner but had feared that it was 'pretentious'. Here Barthes' profession of faith is said to speak in the name of historical materialism. What tangled webs are woven by professors in the attempt to justify theory in the face of undeniable facts. Forced by Camus into a public articulation of his own political beliefs, Barthes chooses the nomination of a certain Marxism and as good as says to Camus, I side with Sartre.

*

Camus wrote to the journal editors, perhaps graciously, perhaps content for Barthes to have said all that needed to be said: 'I only wish that you retain the essential thing: it is absolutely necessary to publish the new letter from Barthes the instant it is written. I am counting on you in this matter ...' Barthes is worried that it might be considered pretentious to declare himself for a complicated Marxism; however, the clamour for self-definition was shortly to become irresistible. Shortly after this iterative exchange interest in the exact nature of Barthes' Marxism grew, and this time Barthes is forced to respond to a cutting review of his own in *Lettres Nouvelles* (July–August 1955). Starting with the epigram, citing his review '... But after all, perhaps, Mr Roland Barthes is he simply a Marxist that does not say so?' Barthes entitles his response 'Am I Marxist?'. Barthes suggests that the solicitation to answer the question conclusively whether he is a Marxist or not is ordinarily only of interest to MacCarthyists. Others 'prefer to make their judgements on evidence, if only Mr Guérin would do as they do'. To help him in his judgement Barthes suggests that Guèrin reads some Marx. He says that by so doing Guèrin would discover that one does not become a Marxist by immersion, initiation or declaration, like a Baptist, Trobriand Islander, or Muslim, 'that Marxism is not a religion but a method of explication and action, that this method demands much from those who claim to practice it and that as a consequence it requires more complexity than simplicity to call oneself a Marxist'.

*

Barthes goes on to say that while it would be more reassuring for critics if writers could allocate themselves to a group by a 'simple declaration of faith', the freedom of writing does not work in this way. The same must surely hold for Camus, especially when Barthes concludes in his response that in 'matters of literature, reading is a more objective method than investigation'. The desire for the declaration of an identifiable Marxism on the part of Guérin is surely the converse of Barthes' own attempt to nail down Camus as not Marxist enough. Either way, the need for an uncomplicated categorisation of the author and the division of literature according to political purities, in the face of the irreducible complexity of writing, leads each reviewer onto a ground where having attempted to pin down their text, the text gets up and walks away with the pin.[62]

Barthes no doubt travelled some distance from this self-description as a historical materialist in his later life and work, although I do not think that he ever went very far from the spirit of the *Mythologies* and the project of critical demystification in which he was engaged at this time. If the text of Barthes can be said to be 'Marxist' after a fashion, it is a curious and individual Marxism, one that animates a spirit of Marx seldom found in the Marxist tradition. However, one might say that rather than bending the project of modern critique towards an ortho-dox and scientific Marxism (what the vulgar call 'vulgar Marxism'), Barthes' writing reinscribes the critical potential of Marx back into a tradition of critique contemporaneous with Modernity from which it has otherwise been separated by a certain appropriative 'Marxist' discourse that condemns such philosophy as the product of bour-geois reification. Barthes is not a Marxist of vocabulary and scientific ambition, his revolutionary activity is reserved for the nineteenth-century novel, his textual activism becomes increasingly reserved and reluctant, but it is difficult to argue against Barthes as a Marx brother in spirit. Marxisms like roses have infinite variety and Barthes was a Marxist by any other name. As a textual activist Barthes was very much like Proust's aunt Léonie, who always believed that she was about to get up and go for a walk but who never left her room.[63]

Towards the end of his life two epicurean moments define the com-plexity of his personal history and of the French intellectual scene over an extended period. On Thursday 9 December 1976 Barthes along with his long-term friend and fellow *Tel-Quel* contributor Philippe Sollers attended a lunch party for President of the Republic Valéry Giscard d'Estaing at the Hôtel de Lassay in Paris. Michel Foucault had also been invited to the lunch but had declined in order to protest against Giscard d'Estaing's failure to commute the death sentence of the alleged child killer Christian Ranucci, one of the last people to be executed in France and whose clemency appeal had been hast-ily processed by the President in just ten days (considerable doubt now surrounds the solidity of this conviction). Barthes made a point of discussing his Marxism over the coffee course with the Gaullist President, asking him if he was in favour of the withering away of the state. Giscard d'Estaing is reported as replying, 'Why not?'[64] Later Barthes told Bernard-Henri Lévy in an interview, 'I went out of curi-osity, a taste for hearing things, a bit like a myth-hunter on the prowl. And a myth-hunter, as you know, must hunt everywhere.' When Lévy then reminds Barthes that his fellow-travellers on the left took rather a dim view of the lunch at the time, Barthes responds, 'There are, even on the left, people who substitute facile indignation for difficult analysis: it was shocking, incorrect, it's just not done to chat with the enemy, to eat with him. One must remain pure. It's all part of the left's *good manners*.'[65] In a displacement of Fourier, it would seem that for some you are who you eat with. Barthes' point is no doubt that critical thought is better served by engaging with a political problem than retreating to the rehearsed responses of one's own comfort zone as a socially recognised set of coordinates that identify you through the repetition of convention. At any rate it would seem that lunch with Barthes and Sollers made little impression on the policies and action of the Gaullist government. By this time Barthes and Sollers where more celebrities to be seen to be lunching with than intellectuals with whom one might engage.

Jacques Lang and François Mitterrand thought exactly the same thing when they invited Barthes to lunch on 25 February 1980, the lunch after which he was knocked down and taken to the Salpêtrière hospital: like Camus he met his death in a road accident. From his lunch with the right to his last meal with the left, Barthes' political engagements tend to take bizarrely bourgeois forms, as if he were his beloved Bouvard, politely discussing the latest ideological fashion over cheese. This is the comedy of the intellectual life, the revolutionary vanguard are by dint of education and social position irremediably of the bourgeois culture they critique from the top table. One might identify it as the auto-immunitary suicide of the bourgeoisie if it were not for the hilarious bad faith that accompanies Oxbridge Marxists' attempts to prove their working-class provenance. The Barthes brothers may have been raised by a single mother but they had no claim on the proletariat and when in May 1968 the possibility arose of a grand revolutionary alliance between the workers and the intellectuals, not only did the unions turn their back on it but so did Barthes. Barthes' sole achievement in the month of May 1968 seems to have been to organise and hold a successful masters viva defence for his student Julia Kristeva. He refused to join the barricades, citing the narcissism of the students and the petty-bourgeois roots of the events and having had his offer to teach a seminar on 'language and the student movement' turned down he spent the month of May 1968 in his mother's flat near the Parthenon reading, before escaping the hysteria of Paris by taking a long break in Tunisia where he spent his nights cruising for boys in the baths and saunas.

Barthes' de Man

In a text written for the *New York Review of Books* but rejected for publication by the editor on the grounds of its complexity, Paul de Man
offers his considered criticism of the early English-language translation
of Roland Barthes: 'despite the considerable emphasis on structure,
code, sign, text, reading, intratextual relationships, etc., and despite
the proliferation of a technical vocabulary primarily derived from
structural linguistics, the actual innovations introduced by Roland
Barthes in the analytical study of literary texts are relatively slight'.[66]
Now, it is standard practice for de Man to hold the position that all
'rival' criticism is in error compared to his own 'linguistics of literariness', but he seems to hold a special place of criticism for Barthes. This
essay is not de Man's first public commentary on Barthes. It would be
necessary to take the temperature of the question and answer session that followed Barthes' address, 'To Write an Intransitive Verb', at
the 1967 conference on structuralism at Johns Hopkins University in
Baltimore. Here de Man's questioning of Barthes' paper is cutting to
say the least and thin on the niceties of academic protocol. However,
in the text for *The New York Review of Books* de Man's take on Barthes
is more fully elaborated in a nuanced way. De Man's aim in this text
is to warn his readers against the expectation of receiving Barthes
into English as a potential innovator in criticism: 'the contribution to
practical criticism is not as extensive as the methodological apparatus
would lead one to expect'. On the one hand, de Man is quite correct.
The theoretical scaffold of structuralism that is to be found in the two
texts de Man is ostensibly reviewing, the *Mythologies* and the collection entitled *Critical Essays*, is perhaps the one part of Barthes that has
least mileage. On the other hand, de Man is rather short-sighted in
his diagnosis, failing to see (and why should he?) the ways in which
Barthes' work would give rise to an institutional practice (cultural
studies) that would come to dominate the scene of the humanities in
a way some claim the Yale School's own deconstructive comparativ-
ism did in the late 1970s and early 1980s. I would contest that this was
never truly the case but let us move on.

One of the often-neglected (outside of the circle of professional de
Man readers) aspects of de Man's own writing is his interest in ideology. De Man came from a European sensibility and had an ear for the
texts of the continental tradition. He, like Barthes, was a keen reader
of Marx and Engel's *The German Ideology*,[67] and one way of reading

de Man's own elaboration of figurative discourse is as the development of an understanding of ideology as a rhetorical illusion. Hence, it is significant when de Man names Barthes as 'primarily a critic of literary ideology'. In this respect, de Man is recognising his own concerns in Barthes. The trouble de Man has with Barthes is that Barthes lacks the necessary technical apparatus to achieve the sorts of insights he avows: 'his work is more essayistic and reflective than it is technical, perhaps most of all when the claim to methodological precision is most emphatically stated'. It is interesting to note that de Man suggests in 1972, while working in both Cornell and Zurich, that this essayistic style rather than his technical skill allows Barthes' writing to reach beyond the academic in a way that is not possible in the United States: 'the close integration of methodology with ideology is an attractive characteristic of European intellectual life ever since structuralism became a public issue in the sixties – and, for better or worse, French writers on literature are still much closer to being public figures, committed to articulate positions, than their American equivalents'. From this admission one might begin to identify an early but growing fissure between the technical discourse of the Anglophone humanities and mainstream public discourse. De Man characterises Barthes' polemic exchange with Raymond Picard as to be 'read and understood as an intellectual adventure rather than as the scientifically motivated development of a method', an adventure that is 'idiosyncratically French' and not to be transposed to the American scene. Perhaps this is true, but equally Theory in America has had its own public and institutional battles to fight. It is interesting to note that for Barthes' part his voice was much more resonate in public exchanges than that of American Theory, which tended to be the victim of character assassination: 'American criticism is notoriously rich in technical instruments but frustrated in its attempts to relate particular findings to larger historical, semantic, and epistemological issues that have made these findings possible'.[68]

De Man sees in *Mythologies* a form of 'semiocritical sociology' of which 'Walter Benjamin and Theodor Adorno are among the undisputed masters of the genre'. It is not that Barthes demonstrates any familiarity with Benjamin and Adorno in 1957 but that their 'common ancestry is nevertheless apparent from the reference ... to Marx's *German Ideology*, the model text for all ideological demystifications'. As with Marx and Engels, for the Barthes of the *Mythologies* ideology is always a question of language and it is Barthes' interest in this problematic that makes his identification of the 'fiction' or 'simulacra' (de Man's words) of Myth interesting to de Man:

> It follows that fictions are the most marketable commodity manufactured by man, an adman's dream of perfect coincidence between description and promotion. Disinterested in themselves, they are the defenceless prey of any interest that wishes to use them. When they are thus being enlisted in the service of collective patterns of interest, including interests of the highest moral or metaphysical order, fictions become ideologies. One can see why any ideology would always have a vested interest in theories of language advocating correspondence between sign and meaning, since they depend on the illusion of this correspondence for their effectiveness. On the other hand, theories of language that put into question the subservience, resemblance, or potential identity between sign and meaning are always subversive, even if they remain strictly confined to linguistic phenomena.[69]

One might note here that in contrast to Barthes in 'Myth Today', de Man characterises fiction or simulacra itself as 'disinterested', that is to say 'neutral'. It is through the agency of 'collective patterns of interest' that the ideological operation of fiction occurs. Barthes in contrast suggests that Myth is essentially of the right because its work maps onto bourgeois ideology. It is not that there are no such things as 'left-wing' myths for Barthes but that myths of the left are 'inessential' because 'revolutionary language proper cannot be mythical'. I suppose what motivates Barthes' claim is not as much a touching naivety concerning left-wing politics ('Of course [there are left-wing myths] as the Left is not revolution') as an absolute commitment to the thinking of revolution as progressive beyond any attempt to freeze or direct its possibilities. Myth is not progressive, it appropriates and conserves in an interested way.[70] Barthes between 1954 and 1957 is, then, content to hold on to a reserved idea of 'revolution', while de Man takes a much more jaundiced view in 1972. However, the value of Barthes for de Man is that his analysis of language in myth draws attention to the ways in which ideology works and might be exposed by attentive readers. The difficulty with Barthes, from de Man's point of view, is that while Barthes' social criticism seems to be effective, Barthes engenders his 'own mystification at the level of method rather than of substance'. De Man, misleadingly I think, suggests that Barthes is making a play for the 'scientific' nature of his work. In *Critique et Vérité*, which de Man cites, Barthes is quite clear in response to Picard's own similar accusation that there can be 'no science of literature'. De Man goes on to discuss the impossibility of such a science even though, he suggests, it is absolutely necessary for all literary study to go through a 'semioc-ritical process'. This is also Barthes' point in 1966, so de Man seems to be pushing his straw man through an open door via the rather selec-tive and unglossed quotation he picks up from *Critique et Vérité*. In a sense we might understand de Man's characterisation here of Barthes as an attempt to make sense of heterogeneous and conflicting mate-rial through a seamless narrative of development. Thus, de Man the great critic of the onto-genetic model of literary history falls back on just such a model in his account of Barthes, where the *Mythologies* of the 1950s, the polemic with Picard and *S/Z* are all of a piece as the con-tinual elaboration of a scientific position. Much as I admire de Man, I think this is an unjust estimation and typical of the sort of position-ing of others (or 'misprisions' one might say after Bloom) that de Man's own polemics frequently employ in order for him to then roll out his own 'correct' theoretical position.

He does this eloquently enough but has to lean on Barthes as the promulgator of a 'pseudoscience'. He describes Barthes as one drawn to the problem of ideology and the overspill of meaning, 'like a moth around a live flame, fascinated but backing away in self-defence'. This is an appropriate image for Barthes' entire relationship to social criti-cism or perhaps even politics as such, constantly and unavoidably drawn to the heat and light of its flame by the very methodology he instigates, only for his writing to find a path of retreat in order to ensure the survival of that writing. For de Man it is a question of the correct understanding of reference as an inevitable and unmovable difficulty:

> All theoretical findings about literature confirm that it can be reduced to a specific meaning or set of meanings, yet it is always reductively interpreted as if it were a statement or message. Barthes grants the existence of this pattern of error but denies that literary science has to account for it; this is said to be the task of historians, thus implying that the reasons for the recurrent aberration are not linguistic but ideological. The further implication is that the negative labour of ideological demys-tification will eventually be able to prevent the distortion that superim-poses upon literature a positive, assertive meaning foreign to its actual possibilities.[71]

I think here de Man is quite correct. While Barthes and de Man are actually quite close on this point in that they both recognise the pres-entation of 'aberrant' meaning as statement or message, for de Man

this situation is not a consequence of an additional process of linguistic diversion through the operation of Myth but is the way that all
language necessarily works all of the time. The problem for de Man
is not ideological but linguistic, insofar as language itself is always
already necessarily ideological. That is to say, there is always confusion between reference and phenomena at work in language. De Man's
slight on Barthes here is the idea that a negative piece of work like the
constant demystification of ideological inscription can ever lead to
anything beyond itself, i.e. to a pure or enlightened practice of non-
ideological signification (as in the case of the revolutionary articulation). De Man is correct about this: the negative labour, as he calls it, of
demystification cannot engender a counter 'positive' practice of writing non-ideological texts. However, again this is something of a delib-
erate mis-characterisation of Barthes, who to the best of my knowledge
never makes such a statement, and I can find no evidence in Barthes
of such a belief. As we shall see, Barthes does come perilously close
to suggesting that it is possible to uncover the true meaning of texts
shrouded in ideological myth. But equally and in necessary contradiction he is quite clear in the section 'Necessity and Limits of Mythology'
that the semioclast is forever condemned to wander in ideology. This is
an aporia of textual production that de Man would appreciate, namely
that in order to demonstrate the impossibility of an escape from ideology one must first attempt precisely such an escape by reading
ideological texts and for one's own reading to insist on such a demystification in the face of the inexorable closure of ideology around that
reading. For Barthes, if demystification is a negative labour then it is
an endless one and in its interminability calls for constant alertness. It
can no doubt lead to exhaustion and this might explain Barthes' own
methodological and social retreat, but it is the nature of the critical
that it has no final destination. In contrast, one might say of de Man
that what is remarkable about him is his confidence in the positive
affirmation of his own technical inquiry into language and that it will
lead to an understanding, even 'mastery' to use a phrase of his own, of
the complex 'over-meaning' of language.

De Man goes on to say of Barthes that given the fact that semiology cannot account for aberrant meaning as a linguistic rather than
ideological effect, it is unable to 'face the problem of the truth value
of its own interpretations'. Consequently, the semiologist, trapped in
a mistaken understanding of language, has his own meanings produced by an operation of language that he does not recognise and

so 'a science unable to read itself can no longer be called a science'. Well fine, that's the end of semiology then, if it were not for the persistent fact that Barthes never claims for it the status of a science. De Man quotes Barthes in the section of *Critique et Vérité* where he speculates that 'a *certain kind* of literary science' might be possible 'one day' (although de Man cuts Barthes' text to miss out the tentative and hypothetical nature of this 'certain kind' of science). Barthes' point is that there 'cannot be a science of the content of works', for this is the undecideable realm of criticism, which he states unequivocally 'is not a science'. Rather, Barthes speculates about a science of writing that sought not to explain meanings but the conditions by which polyvalence is possible. In this sense, Barthes is talking about linguistics, which in its present form Barthes sees as hampered by its lack of understanding of how language actually works: a position with which de Man would have some sympathy. This then is only a 'certain kind' of science because it views the scientific model of linguistics as not being scientific enough. He concludes this section, 'It will thus be necessary to bid farewell to the idea that the science of literature can teach us the meaning to be attributed infallibly to a work: it will neither *give* nor even *rediscover* any meaning', and goes on to say that 'no doubt a long road remains to be travelled before we shall have at our disposal a linguistics of discourse, that is to say a true science of literature in conformity with the verbal nature of its object'. This is because linguistics as such will always remain inadequate to this task: 'it alone cannot resolve the problems presented by those new objects which are the parts of speech and double meanings'. Barthes proposes that the assistance of supplementary disciplines of history and anthropology (i.e. cultural studies) will be required 'to describe the general logic of signifiers'. This is to say that there is no science of literature, and any version of linguistics that might arrive one day, adequate to the task of describing polyvalence, will need to be propped up by other disciplines that are themselves in no way scientific. This after all is only 'a certain kind of science'. Barthes closes *Critique et Vérité* with an appeal not to science but to the displacement of the myth of the 'critic' by the role of the unscientific reader. Now, I am not denying Barthes' attempt to elaborate a general semiology in 'Myth Today' and later in *Elements of Semiology* (*The Semiological Adventure* is a posthumous and heterogeneous collection put together by François Wahl in order to derive maximum return from the Barthes brand). Rather, I am suggesting that Barthes' understanding of the 'scientific' nature of semiology is much more open and less naive than de Man gives him credit for.

> I don't think Derrida would ever acknowledge having wished to found a science, or even ever having thought about it; besides, neither have I. In fact, as far as I'm concerned, the reference to literary science, or arthrology, or semiology, has always been quite ambiguous, very devious, and I would almost say that it is often faked. Moreover, in *Critique et Vérité*, I did speak of a science of literature, but it was in general overlooked – to my dismay, because I formulated my sentence so that this would be seen by those who pay attention to ambiguities and ellipses – that in speaking of a science of literature I had put in parentheses: 'if it exists one day'; which meant that I did not in fact believe that discourse on literature could ever become 'scientific'.[72]

Barthes does go on to say, almost straightaway, in this interview that 'the only acceptable scientific model' is that of Althusser's Marxist science, which 'disengages science from ideology', thus demonstrating that he may after all have entirely missed the point entirely regarding science as such.

Barthes does not merit a mention in de Man's essay 'Rhetoric and Semiology', which opens his unparalleled account of the figural nature of language, *Allegories of Reading*, but he is no doubt in the back of de Man's mind at this point (Barthes appears in later footnotes in *Allegories*).[73] Perhaps what is most suggestive about this encounter is what it tells us about what de Man's response might have been to the rhetoric of cultural studies had he lived long enough to witness that particular barbarian-invasion-by-invite. What also interests me here are the ways in which both Barthes and de Man are nodal points in an alternative history of ideology that runs outside the parameters of so-called orthodox Marxism's appropriation of this term. De Man cites Benjamin and Adorno as being part of a genre of social criticism, but they are also, as he points out, readers of *The German Ideology*. In turn, Marx and Engels are readers of Hegel, who is a reader of Kant. One should add Sarah Kofman, Nietzsche and Schiller to this list as readers of the problem of ideology as a linguistic problem and as thinkers who take seriously the indisociablity of ideology and language as a technical problem.

This present study does not afford me the space to elaborate this genealogy further or to point out the ways in which this understanding of language is directly related to an appreciation of language in terms of technics and tele-technology, whereby every language involves an

experience of the ideological as technics at a distance.[74] As a preliminary foray in advance of such a theorisation, we might ask whether
the term 'ideology' itself might be something worth salvaging at this
present moment. On the face of it, the classical distinction between
false consciousness and the world as it really is, stripped bare of
ideology, looks like a hardly respectable example of binary thinking in
which little thought is spared for the seemingly innocent consciousness of a world free of ideology. This will become a tricky moment for
Barthes towards the end of 'Myth Today', when the semioclast must
remain at an ironic distance from his ideology-bound object while
mired in an ideology of his own. In this sense, given that there might
be no escape from the ideological, 'ideology' as a term comes to name
a constant condition rather than a critical tool. Accordingly, one might
think of ideology as analogous to (or perhaps even the same thing
as) metaphysics, which at once would be impossible in principle to
escape and the object of an interminable critical or deconstructive
resistance. Ideology, like the poor, will be with us always. However,
despite the fact that there would seem to be no grounds exterior to
discourse from which a critique of ideology might proceed, nevertheless such a situation renders such a critique ever more pertinent.
A critique then might work according to the principle that Derrida,
for example, sets up around the term 'justice' in his reading of Marx,
whereby the undoubtedly metaphysical concept works not as a regu-
lative ideal in a critique but as the name given to a position always in
advance of an articulation from which a critique might proceed. So, it
is in the name of justice that one might begin a critique of ideology,
which is to say it is in the name of doing justice to the other excluded
by the ideological that one might begin to read against ideology. In this
sense, ideology and its critique becomes a problem of inscription and
deconstruction, with the necessary metaphysical compensations that
fall out from this as the problem of ideology is, as Tom Cohen says,
'refracted through the trace'.[75] Ideology as a category is thus a question no longer of 'false consciousness' but of 'constitutive distortion'
and the means by which the very idea of materiality itself is founded
by means of the figural. Language then, in the terms of *The German
Ideology*, is nothing other than 'practical consciousness' and ideology
would involve a transformative metaphysical process whereby both
exteriorisation and deterritorialisation of the idea occur simultaneously. It is a short step from here to the logic of the supplement and
towards the question of language and/as technics. Accordingly, one

might see that the stakes of an understanding of ideology are not straightforwardly a matter of liberation from false consciousness but are tied up with the very process of conceptualisation itself and the foundation of all and every materiality. It is this that needs to be held in mind whenever the term 'ideology' is invoked in this present study. One might say that 'ideology' itself needs to be moved on from the ideological effects of its own arrest and exteriorisation in the text of cultural studies and canonical Marxism. We will at some later date be required first to consider the ways in which ideology places the subject in a necessarily fictional relation to the real event and second to understand the ways in which ideology as a category emerges from a specifically nineteenth-century representational regime of optics and metaphysics.[76]

The ideology of Roland Barthes

One might say that Barthes has a marginal relationship to *The German Ideology*: we can find it everywhere in the footnotes and margins of 'Myth Today'. While it is true to say that one should be suspicious of the claims to 'radicalism' made on behalf of Barthes' semio-critical collection given that, as we shall see, it seems to eschew every opportunity to discuss the genuine substance of the political history of France during the period 1954–7, it should also be said that it is no insignificant matter to attempt at this precise moment, as Barthes does, a reinvention of one of the primary tropes of the Marxist tradition, namely 'ideology'. Louis Althusser's essay 'Ideology and Ideological State Apparatus' followed some twelve years after 'Myth Today' and is notable for its failure to credit Barthes' prior attempt to rethink the function of ideology as a linguistic problem. In fact one of the most remarkable things about Althusser's otherwise exceptional essay is his distinct reticence to engage with the text of *The German Ideology*. He goes so far as to say of the version of 'ideology' proposed here by Marx and Engels that 'it is not Marxist'.[77] That is to say that *The German Ideology* proposes a 'positivist and historicist thesis' of ideology, which is at odds with Althusser's own formulation in which, rather than suggesting as Marx and Engel do that 'ideology has no history' (implying that the history of ideology lies outside of itself), one should say that while ideology in general has no history (i.e. it is structurally omni-historic) ideologies do have histories and are the product of class struggle. Now, I have some sympathy with Althusser's position here although I would offer a good deal more sympathy if he actually attended to the text of Marx and Engels to discuss what they actually said. However, it is also entirely typical of a certain appropriative Marxist tradition and the purity of its avant-garde[78] that it finds one of the ur-texts of Marxism by Marx himself to be not properly Marxist.

As Sarah Kofman uncannily noted in another context, 'The camera obscura is never set right by a camera lucida.'[79] Barthes acknowledges his debt to Marx through a series of citations. He describes bourgeois Myth as transforming 'the reality of the world into an image of the world, History into Nature. And this image has a remarkable feature: it is upside down' (Barthes, 1973, 141). The footnote that follows takes us to one of Marx and Engels most famous formulations in *The German Ideology*: 'If men and their conditions appear throughout ideology inverted as in a camera obscura, this phenomenon follows from their historical vital process. …' (Marx, *The German Ideology*)'. We might note the way in which Barthes erases, as so many do, the co-authorship of the Mancunian Engels.[80] One can see that Barthes has not strayed particularly far from Marx and Engels in his consideration of Myth as ideology and appeals to the authority of Marx on a fairly straightforward level. What separates Barthes from Marx and Engels here is that Myth is a form of ideology particular to the petit-bourgeois. That is to say, Myth is the operation of ideology pertinent to the strain of 'popular' culture that he has chosen to make his object. The inversion he alludes to is the one whereby the petit-bourgeois experience comes to stand metonymically for that of culture as a whole; the rise of a French petit-bourgeois being, for Barthes, 'the key to the century'. This is also why he is so concerned by the ascendance of Pierre Poujade as a petit-bourgeois populist and the predominance of the petit-bourgeoisie among the *pieds noirs* in Algeria.

One of the reasons to be suspicious of an uncritical valorisation of popular culture in 2010 is the fact that much of what stands for 'popular culture' today is not the product of marginalised cultural sub-groups once the preserve of myth-hunters like Richard Hoggart or Dick Hebdige[81] but the product of late capitalism as a homogeneous global culture[82] ripe for consumption (one might think here of a continuum of banality that included MTV, *Big Brother*, *The X-Factor*, *Friends*, the Premier League, Paris Hilton, celebrity magazines and so on). As Barthes would frequently say, 'In my opinion, one should read anything at all' (Barthes 1985, 112). For Barthes in 1957, I think

Paris-Match occupies a different place to, say, *Hello* or *Heat* magazine does today (or even *Paris-Match* does today), and that difference is really a matter of scale. In a sense, the situation of today represents the global triumph of Myth as petit-bourgeois ideology. We live in a culture saturated by this material in a way that is different from the aspirational role it fulfilled in the 1950s, as the coming of global homogeneity as transformations in the sovereignty of states, the law and structures of trade, the efficiency of technology, the retreat of standing empires and the worldwide infrastructure of global governance (such as the United Nations, IMF and World Bank) took shape in the decade following the end of the Second World War. This emergence is obscured in 1957 by the double thread of the Cold War and decolonisation but it has endured as the historical path that links the popular culture examined by Barthes to that which cultural studies is presented with today. Thus, the inversion of the camera obscura is also a matter of intensification and transmission, whereby western petit-bourgeois culture is projected onto the planet as a universal condition. This is not to claim victory for the petit-bourgeoisie in any form of class struggle merely to remark upon the suitability and adaptability of this culture and its mythologies for the channels of communication and tele-technologies that are the 'ideological apparatus' of globalisation. To a degree we are all petit-bourgeois now because the image of our desires is petit-bourgeois through and through.

The citation of *The German Ideology* continues with two further important considerations of ideology. One of Barthes' key points concerning the universalisation of petit-bourgeois ideology is that it works by rendering a complex historical and political event as a 'natural' not-to-be-questioned given. He turns to Marx in this commentary when he asks, 'However, is myth always depoliticized speech? In other words, is reality always political? Is it enough to speak about a thing naturally for it to become mythical? One could answer with Marx that the most natural object contains a political trace, however faint and diluted, the more or less memorable presence of the human act which has produced, fitted up, used, subjected or rejected it' (Barthes, 1972, 143–4). Here he offers the simple yet authorative footnote 'cf. Marx and the example of the cherry-tree, *The German Ideology*'. The reference is to the section of *The German Ideology* on Feuerbach when Marx and Engels write, 'Even the objects of the simplest "sensuous certainty" are only given him through social development, industry and commercial intercourse. The cherry-tree, like almost all fruit-trees, was, as is well known, only a few centuries ago transplanted by commerce into our zone, and therefore only by this action of a definite society in a definite age it has become "sensuous certainty" for Feuerbach.'[83] Barthes' gloss on this passage is self-evident: the cherry tree is not natural to Europe but the product of history of importation, colonialism and often bloody narco-trade-wars. Although Barthes does not cite him, this suggestion is close to Benjamin when he contests that there is 'no document of civilisation that is not at one and the same time a document of barbarianism'.[84] As Stuart Hall suggests, what could be more British than a cup of tea with a spoonful of sugar: the tea having come from the colonisation of India and the sugar from the colonisation of the Caribbean.[85] What activity in 2010 could be more 'petit-bourgeois' than driving to the mall to buy a bargain T-shirt: the petrol in the car having been secured by global hydrocarbon production and the cheapness of the T-shirt ensured by the exploitation of cotton workers. This situation is close to the problem of structure discussed above, in which the concentration of the singular draws within it all the history of its concept in a circle of virtuous-vicious complicity. As Barthes puts it of Myth's use of synecdoche, 'the whole of Molière is seen in a doctor's ruff'.

Now, while it is Barthes himself who suggests in a subsequent footnote that 'Today it is the colonized peoples who assume to the full the ethical and political condition described by Marx as being that of the proletariat', I would like to suggest that one of the difficulties I have with Barthes here is the way in which he seems unable to articulate the complexity of his own relationship to this culture. I would suggest today that in order for the work of the semioclast to be effective in the long run it will be necessary to acknowledge our own complicity in the socio-political structures of western-led globalisation. As Barthes notes, 'Any individual, no matter how revolutionary he claims to be, who does not consider the position from which he himself speaks, is a counterfeit revolutionary.'[86] The manuscript of my book will be sent by my UK publisher to the Indian subcontinent for typesetting, where English is spoken well but labour is cheap. We cannot always have a scapegoat and it needs to be recognised that western academics are part of the apparatus of late capitalism. This is also the case for Barthes and no doubt this is the unarticulated intuition that caused the Maoist student movement in 1968 to decline Barthes' invitation to teach them a seminar. However, it is a case not of submitting ourselves to the necessity of our fate as subjects of capital but of active engagement in the ways in which one gives oneself up more or less openly to this complicity in order to render the structures of capital ever more untenable. I am not sure that we might characterise this situation on the part of western academics as 'setting out to do good' or 'telling the truth to power' as Edward Said puts it. Rather, one must simply 'set forth' regardless without fixed point or destination, even if that setting forth takes the form of an endless 'negative labour' of demystification.

Barthes offers one further footnote on *The German Ideology* in the 'Myth on the Right' section of 'Myth Today' when he outlines a taxonomy of the operation of individual myths. The second of these is entitled 'The privation of History' and opens with the short sentence, 'Myth deprives the object of which it speaks of all History.' We shall see later that the question of History is not simple in relation to Barthes' formulation of Myth. Indeed, when is the question of History ever simple? The footnote that follows reads, '… we must pay attention to this history, since ideology boils down to either an erroneous conception of this history, *or to a complete abstraction from it*' (*The German Ideology*).[87] In this sense Althusser is quite right to be critical of Marx and Engel's positivist concept of ideology because as he suggests ideologies themselves are necessarily historical through and through. Accordingly, while on another occasion it will be necessary to revisit the extraordinarily complex, contradictory and sprawling text of *The German Ideology*, one might ask apropos of Althusser, can Barthes' evident reliance on Marx for this understanding of history and ideology allow him to account for his own ideological and 'mythic' position? 'Myth Today' closes with a section entitled the 'Necessity and Limits of Mythology' in which one would expect Barthes to be quite clear about his own complications. Rather, for Barthes the mythologist is one who is 'justified' but 'excluded'. The unveiling of myth is said to be a political act based upon a 'responsible idea of language'. When Barthes uses Brecht's term '*Einverstandis*, at once an understanding of reality and a complicity with it', he is referring to the operation of Myth, not the myth-hunter who must remain distanced from the world of myth by his vocation. He speaks in a 'metalanguage' and while others may enjoy 'good French wine' or the Tour de France, saturated by petit-bourgeois ideology, the mythologist 'is condemned to live in a theoretical sociality; for him, to be in society is, at best, to be truthful: his utmost sociality dwells in his utmost morality. His connection with the world is of the order of sarcasm'. On the one hand, we might point to this notable sentence as the origin of a certain popular notion of postmodernism as an ironic relationship to the world in which we live: I know that the musical *Mama Mia* is 'cheesy' (the supposed sublime of post-modern kitsch) and technically atrocious in every way but nevertheless I am enjoying my viewing experience based on its sublime awfulness. On the other hand, we might give Barthes slightly more credit and suggest that if this sarcasm dwells at the level of the 'utmost morality' as relation to truth then this is a permanent parabasis in the same way as de Man understands irony in his *Aesthetic Ideology*, that is to say, as an irremediable interruption between meaning and an idea of reality from which we are permanently excluded.

For de Man, as with Kant, there can be no possibility of bridging this gap and one only ever resides in the middle of a world of figurality unable to reach either pole of a non-linguistic real or absolute knowledge beyond parabasis. The Barthes of this passage seems to suggest that it is the task of the mythologist to defend the truth of a reality that can be accessed through a non-ideological use of language. This is what de Man means when he says of semiology that it is a science that cannot know itself. It cannot pull itself up by its own bootstraps to see its own complicity within figural language. However, on this criterion of meaning as wholly other because it is wholly figural, it should be said that no science can ever know itself adequately to qualify as a science in de Man's terms. Just as the criticism of *The German Ideology* would be that it uses a philosophy of ideology to denounce philosophy as ideology, so 'Myth Today' uses language to identify ideology as a problem of language without recognising the ideology at work in its own language. Now, as de Man suggests in his own unpublished review of *Mythologies*, Barthes rowed back some distance from this position in later works, partly as a realisation of the methodological inadequacy of his understanding of signification in 'Myth Today', partly as a mature understanding of the limits of social criticism. However, this later reticence might be understood not so much as a 'new turn' in Barthes but as a widening of a permanent parabasis first identified in this truthful sarcasm. If disappointment could ever be expressed with Barthes it might be that if, under the influence of Derrida, Lacan and Nietzsche, he came to appreciate the difficulties of semiology, he never attempted in a sustained way to revisit the social criticism implied by the *Mythologies* in the light of his new appreciation of meaning. There was a failed attempt in 1978 to write on commission a new set of *Mythologies* for *Le Nouvel Observateur*. However, Barthes' interests and energies had moved elsewhere by then and his anger had dissipated into anxiety about his own celebrity on the Parisian intellectual scene.

By this time Barthes himself had become a Myth worthy of the work of analysis, just as he had once commented on the Abbé Pierre and Albert Einstein.

However, Barthes goes on to say in conclusion to 'Myth Today' of the task of the semioclast that 'It is forbidden for him to imagine what the world will concretely be like, when the immediate object of criticism has disappeared. Utopia is an impossible luxury for him: he greatly doubts that tomorrow's truths will be the exact reverse of today's lies' (Barthes, 1972, 157). On the one hand, one really has to admire the young Barthes' faith that the object of his criticism will disappear. On the other hand, one might note that Barthes refuses any messianic role for the social critics, 'he cannot see the Promised Land' as Barthes puts it. There is correspondingly no faith here that the situation of tomorrow will be the ideology-free utopia that de Man assigns to Barthes; rather the social critic is only afforded the role of the clerk in Kafka, in a heroic struggle of a negative labour to defend truth by dispelling lies. In fact, Barthes suggests that the mythologist 'constantly runs the risk of causing the reality which he purports to protect, to disappear'. Here towards the close of his essay he seems to be aware of the complicity between the critic of ideology and the ideology he or she swims in. The mythologist is unavoidably condemned to 'metalanguage' that both excludes him or her from ideological immanence and is itself an ideological form. After Zhdanov and Lukács, Barthes calls this situation 'ideologism'. But as he puts it, 'ideologism resolves the contradiction of alienated reality by amputation, not a synthesis': wine is objectively good but at the same time the goodness of wine is a myth. Barthes describes this as an 'aporia' and suggests that 'the mythologist gets out the best he can'. That is to say, in an economy of complicity he gives himself up to the myth of wine with the least collusion possible in order to render the myth of wine untenable. A difficulty remains here for me, however, concerning this ascetic vocation as an exclusion from social. Given all that Barthes says elsewhere concerning the death of the author as also meaning the death of the critic at the expense of the birth of the reader, is the role assigned to the social critic not just the reintroduction of the position of the suitably qualified judge at the expense of immanence and the reader's counter-signature? Barthes' mythologist is no doubt an enlightened reader and on a continuum of complicity he or she stands at a remove from the subject of petit-bourgeois ideology (but then again the petit-bourgeois subject is non-commensurate with the subject of petit-bourgeois ideology). However, working on a sliding scale of complicity is not the same as exclusion. In this sense the mythologist must be committed to a truth they can never access. Hence their work must be interminable and their demands unconditional.

In his closing pitch of the essay Barthes seems to foresee the objection that de Man renders of him. He describes this situation as 'a difficulty pertaining to our time'. Quite what he means by this is not clear: one wonders whether he is referring to Modernity as such, an emerging sense of the postmodern assemblage or the today of France's own 1950s 'war on terror'. However, the difficulty presents a choice between what he refers to as two methods:

> Either to posit a reality which is entirely permeable to history, and ide-ologize; or, conversely, to posit a reality which is *ultimately* impenetra-ble, irreducible, and, in this case, poetize. In a word, I do not yet see a synthesis between ideology and poetry (by poetry I understand, in a very general way, the search for the inalienable meaning of things). (Barthes, 1973, 158)

From this one might suppose that history itself is Ideology but Barthes seems to continue to insist in this essay on the possibility of a search for inalienable meaning that is free of ideology, even as his own argu-ment concerning 'ideologism' demonstrates the impossibility of this situation. This impossibility Barthes calls 'poetry', a catachrestic and displaced idea of poetry to be sure. I am not convinced that Barthes wishes us to walk away with the notion that the writer or poet can have access to inalienable meaning; instead, he sees that the task of the social critic, in the resistance to ideology, is also the task of the poet. To see the world as the mythologist sees it is to be a writer of human expe-rience. The task is always forlorn, as Keats would say, as the semioclast is dragged back into the maelstrom of the world they describe:

> It would seem that we are condemned for some time yet always to speak *excessively* about reality. This is probably because ideologism and its opposite are types of behaviour which are still magical, terrorized, blinded and fascinated by the split in the social world. And yet, this is what we must seek: a reconciliation between reality and men, between description and explanation, between object and knowledge. (Barthes, 1972, 159)

Reality is a philosophical concept and as such the real is an irre-ducibly textual problem. One is condemned to speak of nothing else because the very inauguration of the idea excludes us from the thing it describes just as it affects us constantly. All idioms of discourse that approach this issue ('ideologism and its opposite') can do nothing but fall into the linguistic split that fissures the social world because these discourses are precisely linguistic themselves. Whether giving up on the dream of reconciliation and adapting to the permanent condition (neither exile nor arrival) of the wholly figural and to a world of enduring ideological complicity either takes us further than Barthes' negative labour or offers an escape from the belief that one is seeking after an unguided truth, I cannot say. After all, to assert that the true condition is permanent parabasis is itself to seek to assert an unadorned truth even as we stand at the frontier of empiricism as a discursive event. As de Man puts it towards the end of the Vietnam War, just as bombs are said to over-kill, texts over-mean.[88] An awareness of the over-meaning of texts does not stop the bombs from over-killing. Perhaps it might be more appropriate to say that the chiasmus between ideologising and poeticising is not straightforward and that indeed one might well be a version of the other.

Barthes/Marx II

One might say that Barthes has a comic relationship to Marx; this is not the same thing as having an 'ironic' relationship to Marx. Barthes is a loving and admiring reader of Marx, Groucho Marx. Barthes sees in the Marx Brothers film *A Night at the Opera* an exemplary text on the problems of the sign. It is significant I think that while the structural semiology outlined in 'Myth Today' is, according to de Man, unable to account for its own figurality and continues to presuppose a reality accessible through the negative labour of demystification, the readings that Barthes gives of texts in operation tend to suggest something else. In this sense, while Barthes seems to take a positivist understanding of the real from Karl Marx (although I have suggested elsewhere that this is not how Marx and Engels' own text understands ideology and language[89]), he takes a different understanding of the real from Groucho Marx. There are three occasions on which Barthes cites this filmic text as an allegory of reference. It is first of all significant, I think, that he describes the work of the film as being 'allegorical'; that is, as a structure of meaning that says one thing while meaning another and whose sense is finally not dominated by either. The first mention of the film comes in the essay 'Writers, Intellectuals, Teachers' in the context of a discussion of the academic convention of presenting research findings in the form of a public talk:

> In the exposé, more aptly named than we tend to think, it is not knowledge which is exposed, it is the subject (who exposes himself to all sorts of painful adventures). The mirror is empty, reflecting back to me no more than the falling away of my language as it gradually unrolls. Like the Marx Brothers disguised as Russian airmen (in *A Night at the Opera* – a work which I regard as allegorical of many a textual problem), I am, at the beginning of my exposé, rigged out with a large false beard which, drenched little by little with the flood of my own words (a substitute for the jug of water from which the *mute*, Harpo, guzzles away on the Mayor of New York's rostrum), I then feel coming unstuck piecemeal in front of everybody.[90]

If we treat Barthes' aside with due seriousness not so much as a reflection of personal anxiety about public speaking but as 'allegorical' of a textual problem then it might have something to say about the issue of ideology and language. The scene is well known: Harpo, Chico and Zeppo have stolen the uniforms of three Russian aviators who are due to appear at New York City Hall to have their flying achievements celebrated by a civic reception. The three also cut off the Russian's beards to effect their disguise. At City Hall, chaperoned by Groucho, the brothers in disguise are asked to speak as part of a live radio broadcast. Rather than do so, the dumb Harpo plays for time by elaborately drinking a jug of water only for his glued on beard to dissolve, exposing the three as stowaways. The whole time the airmen have been tied up in a cabin on board a transatlantic steamer. The brothers maintain their disguise by speaking backwards with Groucho translating, offering the semblance of an East European idiom, before storming off stage pursued by the police.

I am sure that Barthes' public insecurities were as acute as any other professional academic's. In more lucid moments I often think that the 'excitement' that surrounded the posthumous exposé of Paul de Man as a 'wartime collaborator' is the consequence of a structural anxiety within the academy of having one's supposed expertise exposed as fraud by public scrutiny. In this sense, the hyperbolic discourse that constituted the so-called 'de Man affair' was (and continues to be in the iterative fictional representations of it[91]) a simulacrum of this insecurity concerning professional (and profess-orial) qualification that runs to the heart of a structural diremption between public subjects and their unconscious. However, the Marx Brothers episode, as a textual allegory, is more suggestive than this. Harpo's silence is meaningful and meaningfully comic in that it is mediated by others. Groucho offers a running commentary on his failure to speak: the Mayor urges him to say something to fill the 'dead air' of the radio broadcast, the pregnant silence in which is a reflection of audience anxiety, while the real aviators are bound and gagged in their cabin. It is through a play of competing and conflicting mediations that the silence (or non-reference, '*unsinn*', or non-sense as the German of Groucho's mother would have it) at the centre of this scene derives its meaning. The signifying effect of Harpo's non-speech is not a consequence of his own intrinsic relation to a might-have-been-said that is waiting to be revealed but rather the run and overspill of the signification produced round about him and in the construction of the comic context. Harpo's disguise as a pure signifier unable to signify in his own right comes unglued the longer he is subject to scrutiny, undone by his attempts to prolong the ruse through the consumption of the water, which in theory is designed to help him speak but is in fact a displacement that drowns his voice. Thus, one might say that if this episode is allegorical of a textual problem it is that the ideological mask (I am talking about the stolen and glued on facial hair, in case I am being altogether too allegorical myself), although constitutive of the scene, undoes itself through the very thing from which it derives its nourishment (in this case the water, the public articulation or scene of exposure). Now, this is not Barthes' explicit reading of this scene, it is obviously my own extension of Barthes' aside. Barthes does not go on to elaborate this scene further; however, he does return to the film in two other passages in his later oeuvre.

The final reference appears as one of the fragments in the text *Roland Barthes par Roland Barthes*:

> *L'emblème, le gag* – Emblem, gag
> What a textual treasury, *A Night at the Opera*! If some critical demonstration requires an allegory in which the wild mechanics of the text-on-a-spree explodes, the film will provide it for me: the steamer cabin, the torn contract, the final chaos of opera decors – each of these episodes (among others) is the emblem of the logical subversions performed by the Text; and if these emblems are perfect, it is ultimately because they are comic, laughter being what, by a last reversal, releases demonstration from its demonstrative attribute. What liberates metaphor, symbol, emblem

from poetic mania, what manifests its power of subversion, is the pre-
posterous, that 'bewilderment' which Fourier was so good at getting into
his examples, to the scorn of any rhetorical respectability (Sade, Fourier,
Loyola). The logical future of metaphor would therefore be the gag.[92]

By this we might take Barthes to mean, more explicitly than he offers
in 'Writers, Intellectuals, Teachers', that the 'logical future of metaphor'
is a permanent comic parabasis. The 'gag' is a stronger formulation
than either sarcasm or irony, the interruption is more pronounced, the
laughter as referential non-referentiality is louder and longer. The 'gag',
rather than the muffled mouths of the Russian aviators or the choking
and vomiting suggested by the English word, is said by Barthes to be
equivalent to the 'emblem'; that is, to the allegorical and metaphorical, figural nature of reference. Such figurality is, says Barthes, a 'wild
mechanics', generative and without determining author, but equally
beyond control once in dissemination, a 'text-on-a-spree'. Again and
again this film provides exemplars of textual self-subversion: the over-
crowded steamer cabin in which Groucho invites stewards and various ship services to join him (the text crammed and overspilling with
meaning), the torn contract episode when Chico and Groucho work
through an agreement to represent the young opera singer the brothers are aiding (the performative promise that fails to connote). Barthes
returns to the 'final chaos of opera decors' in another text. The understanding of the work of the signifier that Barthes develops from *S/Z*
onwards is at a considerable remove from the one outlined in detail in
'Myth Today' as semiology. I would suggest that the understanding of
textuality that Barthes arrives at as a permanent comic performance,
which 'by a last reversal, releases demonstration from its demonstra-
tive attribute' (i.e. it continues to attempt to denote despite its failure as
denotation) is within the same ambit as the appreciation of the wholly
figural by which de Man criticises Barthes in his 1972 text. Laughter
replaces sarcasm as an appropriate response to the absurdity of ideology's continued insistence on the purity of denotation. For Barthes
reading Karl Marx is as much a matter of the discursive as is the ludic
play of Groucho Marx, as he noted in a 1975 text:

> Each time I read or reread [Marx], I experience, not the wonderment one
> might feel before the founder of an important vulgate in today's political
> game, but the astonishment one feels before someone has effected a
> break in discourse, in discursiveness. On each page of Marx, there is a
> detour into the unexpected and the penetrating, even outside his system,
> and I'm very alert to that sort of thing.[93]

A commentary on the final scene of this Marxist text comes in an interview with Guy Scarpetta in 1971. Apropos of a question concerning the relation between Saussure and Derrida in his writing Barthes comments on the need 'to wean ourselves from all the philosophies (or theologies) of the signified', and goes on to suggest that:

> The Marx Brother's *A Night at the Opera* shows us this same situation (in a burlesque manner, of course: an additional token of truthfulness). In the dazzling finale, the old witch of *Il Trovatore*, a parody in herself, sings merrily away, her back turned to a complete merry-go-round of backdrops: each flat comes down only to be promptly hoisted away and replaced by another; the unwitting old woman is successively framed by different 'contexts' (all strange and irrelevant: decors from every opera in the repertoire pop out of storage and pass fleetingly in review), unaware of the permutation behind her: each line of her aria becomes a misinterpretation. This charivari is bursting with symbols: the absence of background replaced by the changing plural of decors, the coding of contexts (from the operatic repertoire) and their mockery, delirious polysemy, and finally the illusion of the subject, singing its image-repertoire for as long as the other (the spectator) is watching, believing itself to be speaking before the background of a unique world (décor) – a complete *mise en scène* of the plural which derides and dissociates the subject.[94]

What interests me about this third visit to this text is that again the significance of the film is its multiple and undecidable levels of signification in which a burlesque parody of a parody unfolds in rapid succession with an articulating subject convinced of their correctness while undercut by the 'delirious polysemy' of an unstable context (both signifier and signified, emblematic and metaphorical). The scene provides a concentrated example of the plurality of meaning that 'derides and dissociates the subject', which is as much to say, demonstrates the permanent parabasis of signification. This parabasis is not a division between false consciousness and the real but in fact constitutive of the scene and comic meaning of the articulation itself. Of course the same is true for the social critic who may stand on stage singing their plaintive aria, unaware of their comic appearance and the shifting background that undermines their articulation the moment it is uttered. The mythologist then must also attend to their own glued on beard, their Marx dressing-up costume, as well as interference from the very context they address that renders each of their pronouncements always already a misinterpretation. Let me conclude this reading of the Marxist text with Roland Barthes' favourite joke:

> A crippled man arrives in Lourdes in his little wheelchair, goes to the edge of the swimming pool and, before jumping in the water, says, 'Dear God, when I get out again, please let things be better. Dear God, when I get out again, please let things be better.' He jumps in; then he and his wheel chair are pulled out again and, lo and behold, a miracle! God has answered his prayer: there are now new tyres on his wheelchair.[95]

This is what Rei Terada will call 'politics after expectation'.

The mythology of the *Mythologies*

What is to be done with 'Myth Today' today? The contemporary reader may find several aspects of Barthes' essay intriguing and I will attempt to articulate these areas of the text before following with a more general and closer consideration of the essay. First, what strikes me about the essay 'Myth Today' is the inchoate way in which it both wishes to be a text on ideology and at the same time tangles itself up around this term, simultaneously positing semiology and myth at a distance from ideology and reducing them to it. In this way the term 'myth' is turned inside out and pulled round and about, within the ambit of ideology, undoing and redefining its own elasticity. This intuition will form the basis of the reading that is to follow. Second, what strikes me about *Mythologies* as a whole is not the number and range of topics it covers (from Tony Curtis and margarine to the Abbé Pierre and Gide) but what it seems to miss out as a synchronic cultural analysis of France between 1954 and 1956, the concluding essay having been written in early 1957. If the *Mythologies* then are a record of a monthly response to the cultural situation of France during this time, one might begin to wonder: where is the 'mythology' on Dien Bien Phu and the French retreat from Indochina, the semiological commentary on the Algerian War, the insights on the end of colonial rule in Morocco and Tunisia, the Rosenberg trial, the demystification of Suez, the exposé of Budapest and the rise of Papa Doc Duvallier? Considered in this way, what is remarkable about the *Mythologies* is not their penetrating political analysis but their almost systematic avoidance of the seminal political moments presented before them. The period 1954 to 1956 is not just any moment in world affairs and not just any moment in the history of France either, if we can forgive Barthes his curious inward looking gaze. The years 1954 to 1956 are a period marked both by an intensification in the so-called Cold War and its corollary, the decolonisation of Africa and South East Asia. This moment has its own cultural articulations, notably that of McCarthyism in the USA and the European, notably Anglo-French, responses to the colonial liberation.

Perhaps the lesson here is that 'immediate' responses to the contemporary events, such as Barthes' texts in the *Mythologies*, are those least likely to appreciate fully the significance of those events. Rushed into commentary on those events, such responses fail to do justice to those events by not taking the time to consider them adequately. However, this is a period of writing that spans two years, and while the rhythm of the monthly mythologies might be said to have a relation to the journalistic, one might be justified in expecting a growing awareness on Barthes' part of the developments that surround him and their significance for French cultural life. There are exceptions: Barthes comments that Billy Graham's crusade for the conversion of Paris can be explained as a McCarthyist episode ('France's atheism interests America only because atheism is seen as the incipient phase of Communism. "To awaken" France from atheism is to awaken her from the Communist fascination' [Barthes, 1997, 66]). There is also the Flaubertesque dictionary of diplomatic terms for use in relation to Africa and the mythology entitled '*Le bifteck et les frites*', which details the semiological importance of General de Castries' choice of chips as his first meal after the armistice in Indochina ('not a vulgar materialistic reflex, but an episode in the ritual of appropriating the regained French community' [Barthes, 1972, 64]). Other instances of Barthes' Cold War include his account of UFO spotting as a by-product of the space race (Barthes, 1997, 27) and the mythology entitled '*La croisière du "Batory"*' concerning tourist visits by the French bourgeoisie to the Soviet Union. The text '*Tricots à domicile*' that appears in the English-language collection *The Eiffel Tower* as 'Cottage Industry' first appeared in *Les Lettres Nouvelles* but not the French edition of *Mythologies*. This is a short text from 1958 in the spirit of the mythologies that treats the magazine representation of the home-life of the wife of General Massu (who commanded the Tenth Parachute Regiment during the battle of Algiers). On these occasions Barthes can be withering and uncompromisingly 'political' as he deals with significant injustice. However, it should be noted that these texts are hardly those prominent in the reception of the *Mythologies* in the English-speaking world. Rather, if one were to consult any anthologisation or citation of the mythologies in English, of which the Susan Sontag reader would be a good example but only an example, it is the texts on Greta Garbo, wrestling, the Citroën DS or the Tour de France that seem to hold most interest for the Anglo-Saxon editor. What is happening in such a selection? We might draw several conclusions. First, the translation and transplantation of Barthes into English takes place as cultural studies, as a certain idea of cultural studies as the study of popular culture. While this translation seems to be a radicalisation of Barthes (as cultural studies) it is in fact a depoliticisation of Barthes whereby the mythologies are wrenched from their historical and topographical context in the name of a more general anthropology. This is to say, second, that if one begins to read the mythologies in their entirety it becomes clear that this is very much a book 'about' the Cold War and decolonisation, issues that Barthes and his analysis are never far away from. Why should it be that in crossing the Channel and then the Atlantic so much of Barthes' political impetus has been blunted in the production of cultural studies that ironically claims such a radical guise for itself? Rather than by these historically specific yet pointed texts the reception of the *Mythologies* is dominated, it seems to me, by an attempt to understand the structuralist apparatus of 'Myth Today'. However, in all honesty (and this might just be the way things appear today to a professor of cultural theory) the semiotic scaffold of 'Myth Today' is slight to say the least and certainly one of the less interesting aspects of that essay. Hence, it might be worth revisiting some of those shorter texts as a prelude to reading 'Myth Today'.

While Barthes himself relegated the Mythologies to his 'youth' and later adopted in his writing a more melancholic, individualist and conflicted relation to the political, these early texts show an angry and indignant Barthes who manages to combine critical intelligence with political purpose. This in itself does not overcome the aporias of textual activism or necessarily mean that these texts can affect material change; rather my concern here is to wonder why this Barthes has been sidelined in favour of a more general strategy of cultural study in which commentary on the face of Greta Garbo stands in place of a response to the war in Algeria. This is also not to say that commentary on Greta Garbo cannot also be a response to Algeria, or that the urgency of Algeria leaves no place for filmic analysis; Barthes in fact does both. Rather, it is his English anthologisers who do one and not the other. My point here is that if one wished to formulate good reasons as to why the student of tomorrow should read the *Mythologies*, it is not because of the methodological schema of 'Myth Today', which is at best showing its age, but because Barthes' text has a relation to us today through the history it accounts for and passes on to us as text.[96]

The essay on 'The "Batory" Cruise', for example, offers a remarkably pointed summation of Gallic individualism: 'individualism is a bourgeois myth which allows us to vaccinate the order and tyranny of class with a harmless freedom' (Barthes, 1997, 97). Barthes makes this comment as a gloss on a *Le Figaro* journalist who takes umbrage when a Russian steward asks him to return his teaspoon after drinking tea (the point being that an interest in teaspoons is indicative of a faceless bureaucracy determined to make an inventory of the trivial). As anyone who has ever run a kitchen will know, teaspoons are one of the most important and easily misplaced items of cutlery and the Soviet steward's interest is not at all surprising – since the invention of the dishwasher the average home-owner is deeply concerned by the plight of the teaspoon. However, individualism remains the ideological preserve of the French journalist in the Soviet Union when faced with the proletarian multitude on the Moscow underground.[97] Barthes in his final paragraph produces a counter-example that gives the lie to the myth of French idiosyncrasy:

> No question but that 'individualism' is a luxury product for export only. In France, and applied to an object of a quite different importance, it has for *Le Figaro*, another name. When four hundred Air Force veterans, called up for North African service, refused to serve one Sunday, *Le Figaro* no longer spoke of the sympathetic anarchy and enviable individualism of the French: no longer any question here of museum or subway, but rather of colonial investments and big money; whereupon 'disorder' [*désorde*] was no longer the phenomenon of a glorious Gallic virtue, but the artificial product of a few 'agents' [*meneurs*]; it was no longer glamorous but lamentable, and the monumental lack of discipline of the French, formerly praised with so many waggish and self-satisfied winks, has become, on the road to Algeria, a shameful treason. *Le Figaro* knows its bourgeoisie: freedom [*liberté*] out front, on display, but Order back home, a constitutive necessity. (Barthes, 1997, 98)

The myth of individualism as invoked by Barthes here is perhaps the greatest ideological ruse of modern France, used to justify Gallic exceptionalism of every kind and one accepted by France's neighbours as indicative of true Gallic character. However, Barthes is clear, such so-called 'individualism' is really only a mask for class privilege in which the empowered are able to act in a sovereign manner and call it individualism, while disruptive action that threatens the state and the defence of bourgeois privilege is condemned as indiscipline orchestrated by a few ('*meneurs*' here means leaders as well as agents). Now, there is a thin line between collective disobedience and individual refusal of the Gallic type. The border between the two, if there is one, is porous and as such the valorisation or condemnation of such action moves according to the determining interests of such things as colonial priorities and the efficient run of capital. *Liberté* is said to be '*en vitrine, à titre décoratif*'; alongside Richard Howard's admirable but often reductive translation (Howard is a poetic master, translations as such are always necessarily reductive) we might say that personal freedom is in the shop window as a decorative heading (on a purely decorative basis), which justifies the repression of order in the back shop (*chez soi*). For Barthes, France is truly a nation of shopkeepers. The point is not to condemn *liberté* as an ideological ruse, it is one of the revolutionary virtues, but to point out the ways in which a term such as '*liberté*' that depends upon the idea of the sovereign and individual subject will be caught up in an unstable conceptual order that shifts meaning from left to right, from context to context. A term such as '*liberté*' or 'freedom' (but 'choice', 'rights' and 'virtue', say, might be other examples) is a term routinely abused by left and right because as a term in a conceptual order it has no fixed meaning beyond its link to the aberration of sovereign identity and as such is one of the most ambiguous and plastic of political terms even if its ideological and contextual implementation presents its meaning as set.

What gives Barthes the necessary critical leverage on this situation is the moment when the ambiguous Cold War pretensions of French bourgeois culture clash with the determining interests of the colonial moment. The admirable Gallic individualism that sets 'us' apart from communism is in another context precisely the sort of 'un-French' agitated indiscipline that will deliver us bound hand and foot to the communists. This, in short, is the story of the *Mythologies*: the way in which time and time again Barthes makes his critical cut at the moment when the ideological front of Cold War France is opened up by the imperatives of a dying colonialism, demonstrating the double standards in operation in the dominant ideology of mid-1950s France. Barthes never moves beyond the demonstration of this hypocrisy to an 'and so ...' moment in which he proposes an alternative model for social life in a post-colonial France. Rather, through the accretion of examples, his critique presents his readers with a necessary criteriology through which to interpret the world that the reader, the writer and the dominant ideology all inhabit, in order to make a judgement on that ideological moment. Barthes may later regret his inability to take this further step, and more generally lament writing's or theory's inability to do so. However, I would suggest in the spirit of another Roland Barthes that stating what should be done tomorrow is not the task of the textual activist, this is the preserve of the reader. Rather, to guide the reader to the point of judgement, having given them sufficient tools to understand why a judgement might be necessary, is the limit of what theory or philosophy might be able to do. If theory were ever to tip over into the constative declaration of what should be done then it would begin to pre-programme the moment of decision that it is there, in the first place, to render both necessary and undecidable.

Barthes' exposé of bourgeois culture does not result in the dissolution of that culture but rather renders it hopelessly compromised and forever problematic for those with the ears to read him. We might call this a transformative critique that changes the object it reads, exposing culture and rendering our understanding of it otherwise. Of course, one might criticise this formulation as the inevitable consequence of the bourgeois nature of Theory that is constitutively unable to render collective action; mere 'textual activism'. Such a retort would be a failure to recognise, as Barthes' example of the military reservists in North Africa demonstrates, the ways in which such a formulation of the so-called collective is dependent upon exactly the same conceptual order of sovereign individuality as that which it seeks to confront, and so merely repeats what it is said to oppose. I am interested not in preserving terms such as 'collective' or 'revolutionary' but in questioning them to the very bone as products of the same philosophical heritage that determines the vocabulary of bourgeois individualism. To have determined that collective revolutionary action is the appropriate response before the antagonistic moment has been read and diagnosed is precisely the sort of non-analysis and pre-programming that closes off the political from risk and any possible future. It is to end politics before politics has begun.[98] Allow me to offer a few more examples of the colonial–Cold War nexus in Barthes before suggesting how this operates in the text 'Myth Today'.

Some of the most brilliant and most neglected moments in the *Mythologies* are of this order. In the text 'The Great Family of Man' ('*La grande famille des hommes*'), Barthes turns his attention to an exhibition of photographs in Paris, transported from the United States, showing 'the universality of human actions in the daily life of all the countries of the world: birth, death, work, knowledge, play' (Barthes, 1972, 100). Barthes' critical eye, as ever, is wary of the gesture that projects a singularity into a universalism, eliding any difference in an ideological gesture that reduces all culture to the privileged perspective of the western bourgeois subject. The translation of the exhibition into French transforms the American exhibition from 'The Family of Man' to 'The Great Family of Man', introducing, says Barthes, a moralising and sentamentalisation of a zoological term; that is to say, the translation of science into ideology. In this way humanism asserts itself through the transformation of a biological category into the idea of community. The 'commune' in French, as Derrida notes many years later, suggests the elision of all particularity into the collective, '*comme une*', as one.[99] Thus, zoology becomes anthropology, and the western model of man and of family becomes the unacknowledged focus for the presentation of the photographs. It is a short step from here to the appreciation of the exhibition as a testament to the mythology and mystification of the 'human condition'. Barthes' 1957 response to this situation is interestingly plural. On the one hand, his retort to the universalising humanism of 'the human condition' is of an identifiable Marxist type when he offers the singularity of history and the relativity of institutional positions as a response to the gesture of the universal. On the other hand, the counter-examples that Barthes offers here are noticeable for what we have learned to call their 'post-colonial' character. Contra the exhibiting gesture he notes that the diversity of skin colour is not a superficial matter that can be elided by the humanist gesture: 'but why not ask the parents of Emmet Till, the young Negro [*nègre*] assassinated by the Whites [*des blancs*] what *they* think of *The Great Family of Man*?' (Barthes, 1972, 101). Again towards the end of the short text Barthes questions the universalisation of 'work' as an anthropological category, pointing out the historical and social specificity of class and race in relation to labour, 'because of its modes, its motivations, its ends and its benefits, which matter to such an extent that it will never be fair to confuse in a purely gestural identity the colonial and the Western worker (let us also ask the North African workers of the Goutte d'Or district in Paris what they think of *The Great Family of Man*)' (Barthes, 1972, 102).

Now, one does not wish to over-state the significance of Barthes' short text but the use of the example here is interestingly complex. On the one hand, Barthes has several other examples to hand, notably the

war in Algeria and the retreat from Indochina, to point out the difficulties of a universal and reductive humanism at this point. However, this
text, as with all of the *Mythologies*, is as interesting for what it leaves
out as what it actually says, and just as interesting for what Barthes'
Anglo-Saxon interlocutors chose to read in it and what they chose to
ignore. The example of Emmet Till is pointed. Emmet Louis 'Bobo' Till
was a fourteen-year-old black boy from Chicago who was murdered
in Money, Mississippi, on 28 August 1955. His murder and its subsequent fall-out was one of the defining moments in the mobilisation
of the nascent American Civil Rights movement. The main suspects
to the killing were acquitted by an all-white, all-male jury after only
sixty-seven minutes of deliberation, but later admitted to the crime.
Till's mother insisted on a public funeral with an open casket to demonstrate to the world the horrific nature of the attack on her son.
Photographs of Till at his funeral show a profoundly disfigured head
with his eyes gouged out. He had been beaten and shot through the
head before being thrown in the Tallahatchie River with a 75-pound
cotton gin fan tied to his neck with barbed wire. The Till case was considerably celebrated at the time and has been the subject of plays by
Toni Morrison and James Baldwin, poems by Langston Hughes and
Gwendolyn Brooks among others, and in 1962 a song by Bob Dylan.
The case was the subject of more recent documentary films and was
reopened as an active investigation in 2004, although no prosecution
has ever been made.[100]

It is perhaps then not so curious to find this example cited by Barthes,
although it is one of those occasions on which Barthes turns his critical gaze outside of France to North America. In a certain sense Barthes
himself might be accused of reinscribing the singularity of the Till case
into a more general axiomatic of injustice or suffering. Here he speaks
of what Till's parents would have to say to The Great Family of Man,
but while the insistence of Till's mother was well known, it was equally
well reported in the weeks before the trial that Till's father had been
executed while on service as a GI by the US Army in Pisa, Italy, in 1945
for double rape and attempted murder. This sorry story was widely dis-
seminated by the segregationist senator James Eastland in an attempt
to turn public opinion against Till's mother, Mamie Till Bradley, in
the weeks before the trial, the implication being that criminality ran
in the family. This might suggest that Barthes' interest in the case is
no more than journalistic, misciting an example in order to derive the
maximum effect as a counter-example. Thus, Barthes' text employs the

same universalising gesture it is said to oppose, in which the singular example of Till comes to stand for all examples of injustice, the counter-example metonymically standing as the universal example. In this way, Barthes' journalism is just another anthropology. However, one should not rush too quickly to close off a reading of the interest of Barthes' text in this way. Rather, the Till case (inaccurately cited as it is here by the Frenchman Barthes) comes to stand as one in a chain of substitutable examples that run like a red thread through the *Mythologies*, linking the ideological critique of humanism to a fear of communism and an anxiety about race. What links the death of a fourteen-year-old boy in a community of sharecroppers in Mississippi to the North African immigrants of the eighteenth arrondissement in the question of the '*l'ouvrier colonial*', the colonial worker. This is one of Barthes' neglected but privileged examples of ideological ex-appropriation by bourgeois culture in 1950s France.

In the text 'Wine and Milk' ('*Le vin et le lait*'), Barthes again connects the expansive culinary habits of bourgeois France to its colonial history. The mythology of wine and cheese is almost a definition of the exceptionism of Gallic culture. Barthes, of course, will have it otherwise, citing the myths of French wine consumption, in which inebriation is said to be an unfortunate but insignificant consequence, not an intention, as a 'coercive collective act' frequently presented in culture and literature (Barthes, 1972, 59). Camus has much to say on this topic as well in his stunning essay on the death sentence in France, in which he questions the influence of the wine lobby on policy-makers, suggesting that the murder rate in France might be more effectively controlled through more stringent licensing laws than through the alleged deterrent of the guillotine.[101] Nevertheless, the cultural inscription of French alcohol consumption as a question of pleasure rather than intoxication is profound and is as much projected onto French culture by Anglo-Saxon commentary as it is internalised by French bourgeois culture. Recent attempts by the United Kingdom's former Labour government to control so-called 'binge drinking' by deregulating licensing hours in pubs (regulations that date back to the First World War as a way of ensuring workers were in a fit state to offer their labour the following morning) have resulted not in the hoped-for 'continental café culture' but rather in all-night public, competitive intoxication in the city centres of Britain. If it was not clear at the time when the legislation was introduced, it certainly is now that such changes were the result of pressure from the alcohol industry's lobbyists offering the

French myth as a cure for the Anglo-Saxon disease. Barthes offers a similar pointed criticism to conclude his essay:

> The mythology of wine can in fact help us to understand the usual ambiguity of our daily life. For it is true that wine is a good and fine substance, but it is no less true that its production is deeply involved in French capitalism, whether it is that of the private distillers or that of the big settlers in Algeria who impose on the Muslims [*au musulman*], on the very land of which they have been dispossessed, a crop of which they have no need [*une culture dont il n'a que faire*], while they lack even bread. There are thus very engaging myths which are however not innocent. And the characteristic of our current alienation is precisely that wine cannot be an unalloyedly blissful substance, except if we wrongfully forget that it is also the product of an expropriation. (Barthes, 1972, 61)

Lavers' translation renders 'une culture' as a crop of which the Muslim population of Algeria have no need, but one could equally read '*sur la terre même dont on la dépossédé, une culture dont il n'a que faire, lui que manque de pain*' as 'on the same land of which one is dispossessed, a culture of which he can make nothing, he who lacks bread'. Equally one could say 'on the same land of which one is dispossessed, a cultivated land or agriculture of which he has no need, he who lacks bread'. 'Culture' here also resonates to take in the sense of an improving education, of which the breadless have no need or can do nothing with. Either way Barthes' comments strike a chord with the colonial condition of France, whose drinking habit was considerably threatened by the rise of Marxist decolonisation movements in North Africa. In the mid-1950s, along with Tunisia and Morocco, Algerian viticulture astonishingly accounted for two-thirds of all internationally traded wine. Algerian red wine was deeper in colour and higher in alcohol content than French wine, was produced from Aramon grapes and was used in blended wine for the French domestic market. Even though at the time of Algerian independence in 1962 more than a dozen Algerian vineyards had been granted VDQS (*Vin Délimité de Qualité Superieure*) status by the French, Algerian wine production collapsed with the repatriation of the pieds noirs. Despite a significant export market to the Soviet Union, the growing ascendancy of Islamic feeling in Algerian government eventually saw the vineyards turned to cereal farms, for making bread.

Barthes' text entitled 'African Grammar' is surely a playful and radicalising gesture to the 'Dictionary of Received Ideas' that Flaubert appends to his *Bouvard and Peuchet*, which is 'a book many people don't like, including Sartre' (Barthes 1985, 248). As with the dictionary, Barthes takes doxical terms and satirically opens them up to expose the lack of reflection and ideological nuances that accompany their quotidian use. Barthes' mini-dictionary treats the 'official vocabulary of African affairs' (Barthes, 1997, 103) with comic clarity. As with the ideological euphemisms of today, such as 'collateral damage' (meaning civilians killed by precision guided munitions) or 'friendly fire' (meaning allied soldiers killed by precision guided munitions), the terminology of African diplomacy of the mid-1950s 'is a language which functions essentially as a code, i.e. the words have no relation to their content, or else a contrary one' (Barthes, 1997, 103). Such terms are designed to name a thing without calling it by its name. It is an attempt to refer by mediating all of the literal or negative connotations of accepted or expected usage, somehow cleansing the act to which they refer by inventing a referential codification in which such acts are stripped of their conventional negative connotations and presented otherwise: what the linguist Deborah Cameron calls 'verbal hygiene'.[102] Such terminology of course deceives no one but their authors and this cynical use only calls attention to the ideological inflection rather than ensuring that the motivation is not drawn attention to, a necessary condition if the ideological operation is to be effective. Thus, the cynical glossing of violent colonialism with the veneer of civil discourse always draws attention to itself as trying to mean something else while still managing to say the thing that direct contact with is being avoided or obfuscated. Barthes offers numerous examples, among them 'war' (*guerre*):

> The goal is to deny the thing. For this, two means are available: either to name it as little as possible (most frequent procedure); or else to give it the meaning of its contrary (more cunning procedure, which is at the basis of almost all the mystifications of bourgeois discourse). War is then used in the sense of peace, and pacification in the sense of war.

> Phraseology: 'War does not keep measures of pacification from being taken' (General de Monsabert). By which we are to understand that (official) peace does not, fortunately, prevent (real) war. (Barthes, 1997, 105)

On the one hand this analysis and the situation it describes might seem to be the most obvious example through which the cultural archaeology we have been undertaking on Barthes' text from the 1950s connects his writing to our present condition. In fact, in a sense, this is his most 'dated' of texts, the one in which the meaning of terms has most significantly and irreversibly shifted. The 'war' described here, the War of Algerian independence, as a war of colonial liberation, bears little resemblance to the wars of our present moment.

Let me be quite clear that the so-called 'war on terror' is not a war in any rigorous sense of this word and it is certainly not a war of colonial liberation in the way that such a phrase accurately identifies the Algerian struggle for independence from France. First, the present moment is characterised not by a violent encounter between equal parties or between competing nation states over an issue of sovereignty or diplomatic significance, as a traditionally understood war might involve. Neither is the present moment identifiable as a partisan war or war of liberation or even a civil war, although traces of such structures can be found in non-rigorous ways in certain places today.[103] Rather, the war on terror is the invocation of the nomial effect of war in order to justify interventions and repressions of every kind, military, economic and ideological. There is no clear separation between one army and an identifiable enemy. The 'enemy' in this sense is non-specific. It is not a sovereign state nor even is it a paramilitary group, rather the enemy is 'terror' in general. This term covers not only precisely identifiable, religiously motivated attacks on American targets, but also the very idea of 'terror' as the name given to strategies and networks of cooperation used to direct violence against the United States for a range of competing and contradictory motives. Such an attack on attacks on the 'American way of life', or the American model or event of the western model of globalisation and capital, then comes to encapsulate a considerable range of targets and so justifies all anti-anti-American violence. Such a precedent having been set, other 'western' powers such as Israel, Russia and China can equally claim to be participating in the war on terror when they violently suppress challenges to their sovereign power. The war on terror is not a war as such because it sets the most powerful planetary entities in a repressive relation to small and radically unequal bodies. This is in no way to defend or sympathise with the political or theocratic objectives of a group (if that is what it is) such as Al-Qaeda – let us take that as read.[104] Rather, my point here concerns the way in which the term 'war' is invoked as if its traditional sense were presently identifiable in order to justify the sense of alarm, threat, sacrifice and intensity that this word carries in its classical sense. In fact the present use of repressive violence falls far short of being worthy of the name 'war' and is indicative of a global transformation in the conditions and possibility of armed confrontation. One might go as far as to say that under present conditions, the very idea of war as it has been traditionally understood is impossible. However, that would be to tempt fate and to ignore the very real possibility of, say, a future confrontation between Russia and the western democracies over energy supplies or between China and the United States over the sovereignty of Taiwan. Such things seem unlikely today but one should not attempt to prejudge the route by which the politically impossible can quickly become the politically inevitable.

I think the point to make here is that Barthes' identification of the ambiguous use of the word 'war' in the context of Algeria is precisely the sort of analysis that a critical appreciation of his legacy calls for today. However, one cannot conflate the two uses of 'war'; both are historically and rhetorically specific. In the case of Algeria, the French tactic was to deny that the conflict was in fact a 'war' because to do so would be to recognise the sovereignty of a colonised people and to admit to the scale of the event. Rather, the military repression in Algeria is identified as a policing, pacifying and 'normalising' (i.e. returning to the colonial status quo) operation, as exemplified by the cited quotation from General Monsabert, a hero of de Gaulle's French army, which assisted in the liberation of North Africa and later France itself from Nazi occupation (from 1951 to 1955, Monsabert served as a deputy in the Gaullist *Rassemblement de Peuple Français*). This is a familiar linguistic strategy for those who have to bear upon their consciences the public justification of repressive violence. In the case of the war on terror, the opposite is true. Here something that is not a war is given the name 'war' as frequently and forcefully as possible in order to inject an urgency and scale to a situation that has none. The end result is the same, but in the case of the present the name of war rather than peace is invoked to justify repressive violence. At the same time one should also say that the rhetoric of the war on terror is not stable even within its own limited use. When individuals were captured on the battlefield in Afghanistan and taken to the legal limbo of the military facility at Guantánemo Bay, they were not accorded the rights of prisoners of war but were spuriously classified as 'enemy combatants'. That is to say, they were not (so the logic goes) prisoners of a war but were illegally involved in combative activity against American interests. So, the question then has to be asked, if the captured combatants in this violent confrontation are not prisoners of war, how can this be a war in any meaningful sense? Further, according to which law is this 'illegality' to be judged, which US law has jurisdiction on the plains of Afghanistan? Equally, it should be noted that the war on terror has no end date, it justifies an open-ended war on any anti-Americanism. In the case of Algeria, to have called the struggle with the FLN a war would have been to presuppose the possibility of both an end date (requiring resolution) and a military solution to the political case for decolonisation. Hence, the denial of a war as such and the characterisation of the military activity as a pacification returns us to the normality of unquestioned colonial occupation. In both cases an obvious 'mythology' is in operation, and we will return to Barthes' essay 'Myth Today' momentarily. Let me then hold an account of how that mythology operates linguistically in abeyance for the moment.

However, it should also be noted here that a historical thread connects the Algerian War of Independence to the present, and connects Barthes' text to his readers today. I am thinking here not only of the systematic use of torture by General Massu's forces as a intelligence-gathering technique, but more significantly to the ongoing Islamic insurgency that has seen Algeria locked in a state of emergency for sixteen years, with over 120,000 dead in one of the most scandalously under-reported conflicts of the present day. In 1992 the Algerian army (closely aligned to the ruling FLN party) cancelled elections that were running in favour of Islamic parties and since then, in a brutal civil war, backed by the French and the Americans, has been engaged in a vicious conflict that has widened to include bomb attacks on the Paris metro, airline hijackings, car-bomb plots to attack Los Angeles International airport and the alignment of the Islamist cause with Al Queda and Al Queda-in-Iraq. Despite an armistice in 2005, this conflict is ongoing and draws a direct line from the present contest between a certain return of the religious and the western model of democracy and capital, through the withering of socialism and pan-Arab nationalism, to the wars of colonial independence that Barthes and his generation addressed. As Robert Young has pointed out, the history of what we call 'post-structuralism' is itself significantly marked by the situation of Algeria and more generally colonial North Africa, with almost every thinker of significance on the post-structuralist canon such as Althusser, Cixous and Derrida having either direct links to the region or, like Barthes, a considerable presence and cultural investment there.

Now, it might be said that so-called Islamic fundamentalism does not care for the distinction between semiology and deconstruction, and that there is a thin line, in this context, between critical alertness and liberal indignation. However, while the aporia of textual activism remains a consideration under such circumstances, I do not think that such analysis ever goes by without accumulating some value. I am thinking here of Albert Camus' texts on Algeria in which he argues for a post-colonial dispensation in which the French settlers and the Arab majority share a single sovereign independence from France based upon devolved government in confederations.[105] Camus' thought was dismissed at the time as colonial, notably by Sartre and Marxist thinkers. However, it might be argued that the repatriation of the '*pieds noirs*' after 1962 really only served to consolidate and confirm the politics of violent force in Algeria. It is precisely because of this effective partition, in which the settlers either through fear or through their own racist anxiety separated themselves from an Algerian inheritance, just as they had violently separated themselves from native Algerians during the occupation, that the model of political change through the will of the strongest became structurally ingrained in the post-colonial scene of Algeria. Had post-colonial Algerian independence been born according to the alternative vision offered by Camus the question of race, religion, national identity and relations with the west might be quite different in contemporary Algeria. This is not to excuse French colonialism; rather it is to seek an alternative model of sovereignty from that of partition, ethnic cleansing and repatriation, no matter which group holds the upper hand in any given situation.[106] Camus' suggestion seems to me to have much in common with Edward Said's later notion of a one-state solution to the Palestinian–Israeli conflict, whereby Said suggests that no partition of the country can guarantee secure borders for Israel and no delimitation of a Palestinian state can ever satisfy historical resentment.[107] Therefore, rather than through partition, true peace between the two ethnicities can only be achieved through a shared state with ethnic federation and a shared secular constitution. My point here about Camus and Said is that critical thought does offer a longer-term alternative to the limited, if powerful, response of violence. I am suggesting not that Camus and Said map onto each other or that their articulations of post-colonial sovereignty are reducible one to the other, but that they are connected through a historical relation (perhaps an alternative history of critical thought) and it is the patient uncovering of that historical link through critical investigation that will ultimately offer a greater understanding of the situation the authors describe and our relation to it.

Barthes' text on 'African Grammar' demonstrates the culpability between linguistic orders and economic-military violence. The

Flaubertian examples he cites in the first half of the mythology are all definitions of elastic vocabulary. He concludes:

> The predominance of substantives in the whole vocabulary, of which we have just provided a few samples, derives obviously from the huge [*grosse*] consumption of concepts necessary to the cover-up of reality. Though general and advanced to the last degree of decomposition, the exhaustion [*l'usure*] of this language does not attack verbs and substantives in the same way: it destroys the verb and inflates the noun. Here moral inflation bears on neither objects nor actions, but always on ideas, 'notions', whose assemblage obeys less a communication purpose than the necessity of a petrified code [*code figé*]. Codification of the official language and its substantivation thus go hand in hand, for the myth is fundamentally nominal, insofar as [*dans la mesure même où*] nomination is the first procedure of distraction [*détournement*]. (Barthes, 1997, 107)

Barthes goes on to address modal verbs and the ambiguity of adverbs and adjectives in colonial discourse, but the analysis of received ideas requires a theory of nouns as the carriers of concepts. In this sense, we can identify a frequent gesture in Barthes' work, namely the reduction of questions of thought to substantives. We see this continually throughout Barthes from the first book on Michelet to the book on Sade–Loyola–Fourier and in *A Lover's Discourse*, for example. This runs in conjunction with the importance of terms for Barthes such as '*neutre*' or the division of technical vocabulary such as '*lisible*'/'*scriptible*' and so on. This is significant, I think, when one considers Barthes' understanding of signification in this essay, where the meaning of a signified is borne by a nominated signifier, rather than, say, the play of signifiers within a wider scattering of meaning as a text is grammatically established. That is to say, the meaning of a noun is as much dependent upon its status in relation to other grammatical terms as it is upon its own signifying capability as a single term. Barthes states here that 'myth is fundamentally nominal' and thus its analysis is a matter of identifying terms rather than, say, appreciating the turn of meanings within the production of a wider textual grammar. I have already addressed in this essay the structural insufficiencies of Barthes' own idea of structure, so I will not labour a point. However, I am struck here by this example in which Barthes' nomial analysis of myth takes the reader only so far, to the very brink perhaps, but restrains itself or is incapable of taking us further into the wider realms of meaning.

One cute example of colonial vocabulary he quotes is that of the use of 'politics' itself as a term of abuse. Whenever a situation becomes difficult politicians will say that this issue is 'beyond politics' or 'beyond mere politics'. Rather 'politics' will be set aside and, for the good of the nation, politicians will take decisive action, which is of course in no way political. One witnesses the assigning of a limited domain on those occasions when the political antagonism has intensified to such a degree that it threatens to displace the status quo. In such 'emergencies' we are often told 'this is no time for politics'. Now, as the comedian Jeremy Hardy puts it, Christmas dinner is perhaps 'no time for politics' but these moments are surely the entire point of politics as such. However, it is here that a certain discourse seeks to distract us from looking at this antagonistic kernel, sweeping away the name and idea of 'politics' at the very moment when it is most political. However, while Barthes' identification of the ambiguous and unstable meaning of the word 'politics' in this context takes us to the edge of an insight into political textuality, it is unable to take us further. To say 'this is no time for politics' of course depends upon the ambivalence of the substantive 'politics' but it also depends upon a wider grammatical syntagmation that makes that ambivalence possible. The ambiguity of the phrase (that is, the double meaning and duplicity of the phrase) is only possible as a consequence of the grammatical chain and of the different variety of effects produced by that chain within a wider logos. That is to say, contra Barthes, ideological effects are not 'fundamentally nominal', they are on the contrary the product of a wider grammatical production that is at once more precise in its denomination and open to greater and more unstable plurality of meaning. The nominal is never the last word and it is the very duplicity of a phrase such as 'this is no time for politics' that makes it open to critical evaluation and reading, as well as producing its detierious effects as a sanitisation of political discourse. Now, Barthes seems to be aware of this: he entitles his text an 'African Grammar' rather than an 'African Semantics' after all, and his argument here is that the desire of colonialism is to fix the signifying code through the 'inflation' of nouns; verbs are not 'attacked' in this way. The verb, Barthes goes on to say, is 'reduced to the state of a simple copula, meant simply to posit the existence or the quality of the myth' (Barthes, 1997, 107–8). This would be a defining gesture of colonial logocentrism; Barthes' analysis is not wrong in any respect here.

However, what he does not do is to point out the ways in which the incalculable production of meaning through the syntagmatic chain of the predicate (as well as what precedes and succeeds it) is at the same time the means by which such nominalism is undone and critical reading (such as Barthes' own text) takes place. The issue is not just that there is a structural solidarity between discursive practices and economic, political and military violence but that the ways in which meaning and effect run between the two, 'actions' and 'notions', is complex, contradictory and often surprising or unpredictable. This is to say that the attempt to close-off meaning definitively by the colonialist should not be matched by the apparatus of the myth-hunter in their attempt to diagnose a problem because it is the very ambivalence of language that makes myth-hunting possible. If it were not so then the myth would never be identified as such because its mono-logic would always ensnare us. One can see this principle at work in Howard's translation of Barthes' own text here, when he translates '*détournement*' as 'distraction' rather than, say, 'diversion', where the emphasis of the substantive would be on its grammatical relation to a wider textual production (to get lost in a diversion) rather than on staying put but looking the other way. This is not mere nit-picking: the translation depends upon a fundamental assumption about the relation of the subject to the meaning, whereby the subject observes the production of meaning by colonial discourse, which distracts him or her from looking at real conditions. This is a different situation from a subject led astray and forced to go round the houses by language without there ever being a final destination to be reached. In this sense it is true to say that the idea of 'ideological production' that Barthes depends upon in the *Mythologies* is 'fundamentally nominal' but this does not mean that this is how ideology itself actually works.

The lion and the schoolboy

Now, at this point let me begin an account of 'Myth Today' proper. Having established the structural model of myth at the start of his essay, Barthes offers two examples of how myth works. These examples could be defined as 'the African' and 'Grammar', or by another index 'the African' and 'the grammatical animal'. Allow me to introduce this division and then to follow it for a while to see where it might take us. Barthes' first example of 'mythical speech' (*parole mythique*) is taken from Valéry:

> I am a pupil in the second form in a French lycée. I open my Latin grammar, and I read a sentence, borrowed from Aesop or Phaedrus: *quia ego nominor leo*. I stop and think. There is something ambiguous about this

statement: on the one hand, the words in it do have a simple meaning: *because my name is lion*. And on the other hand, the sentence is evidently there in order to signify something else to me. Inasmuch as it is addressed to me, a pupil in the second form, it tells me clearly: I am a grammatical example meant to illustrate the rule about the agreement of the predicate. I am even forced to realize that the sentence in no way *signifies* its meaning to me, that it tries very little to tell me something about the lion and what sort of name he has; its true and fundamental [*veritable et dernière*] signification is to impose itself on me as the presence of a certain predicate. (Barthes, 1973, 115–16)

I am reminded here of Derrida's comments in *The Post Card* concerning analytic philosophy's choice of examples.[108] Why, he asks, do such philosophers always choose dogs as their example? Is it because the dog is faithful and will always do what you ask it to do? That is to say, the example of the dog has been chosen because it proves the philosopher's point – it is an obedient example. However, Derrida's inference here is that a real dog might jump up and snatch or run away with the example. Barthes chooses the obedient pupil in the *lycée*, one who can read Latin, not a badly behaved one or one sitting in the corner with a dunce's cap. The lion here is equally placid, one who obligingly gives us their name: a well spoken, grammatical animal. This example then is said to have a true and fundamental (*dernière*, i.e. last or final) meaning. The exhaustion of meaning here will be important in an account of semiology. Barthes continues:

> I conclude that I am faced with a particular, greater [*agrandi*], semiological system, since it is co-extensive with the language: there is, indeed, a signifier, but this signifier is itself formed by a sum [*total*] of signs, it is in itself a first [*premier*] semiological system (*my name is lion*). Thereafter, the formal pattern is correctly unfolded: there is a signified (*I am a grammatical example*) and there is a global signification, which is none other than the correlation of the signifier and the signified; for neither the naming of the lion nor the grammatical example are given separately. (Barthes, 1973, 116)

There is an interesting point of confusion here. Barthes seems to be suggesting that while we are given the signifier '*quia ego nominor leo*' the ultimate meaning of this sentence is not 'because my name is lion' or 'because I am nominated lion' but rather 'I am a grammatical example'. Even though one cannot distinguish the given 'literal' meaning of the Latin from its operation as an example in a grammar textbook, the two meanings coexist and are both equally present and equally absent at once.

Barthes determines the 'mythical' meaning ('I am a grammatical example') to be fundamental if not final. This seems odd to me: if one meaning does not annul the other and both remain active possibilities then the model offered here of a 'first' meaning and a 'fundamental' or last meaning (even though presented together) seems to me to be a methodological convenience too far. One meaning does not take priority over the other, they are coterminous, and are not necessarily the point of exhaustion of this sentence either. First, the example is in Latin and Barthes' translation is in French (*car moi je m'appelle lion*) and Lavers' translation is in English. We have moved through several countries of meaning here, which the account of the example seems to elide. Why is the pupil studying Latin? Where is this *lycée*? Is it in Paris? Barthes' war-time *lycée* occupied by the Germans, where all the textbooks were destroyed? Is the *lycée* in Algeria, where Latin might be a crop for which they have no need, or it may be the very thing that is required for reasons beyond its grammatical exemplarity? And what of the lion here, who sits up and speaks its name. What if it were to turn on us or wander off through the pages of Barthes' text? What is the status of this example, which exemplifies an example itself? It also says to us, as readers of Barthes, I am a theoretical example. I exemplify the exemplary but I am no more exemplary than anything else. Is this to be the final meaning of this passage, or can the lion roar back and the schoolchild mistranslate? Will they take their jotter to the front of the class only to be told by the teacher that they have misunderstood, like the pupil in Kafka's letter who hears the teacher call his name (Leo, perhaps, rather than Abraham) and so walks to the front of the class to receive his prize only to find to his embarrassment that it was some other boy with the same name who was being called?[109] In this case the signified is not determined fundamentally, the boy still thinks he is the best pupil – otherwise he would not have (mis)heard his name. There is a meaning that imposes itself upon us (the boy's name) which is then shown to not be the meaning of the call (another pupil of the same name wins the prize) only for this second meaning not to be able to dominate the meaning of the call (our boy finally, or secretly, does think he is the brightest pupil, even if he is not). The lion is both a lion and a grammatical example and finally it is more than either a lion or a grammatical example and never fully a lion or ever fully an exercise in grammar.

Juxtaposed alongside the lion and the schoolchild is Barthes' second example, an African soldier photographed in *Paris-Match* saluting the French flag:

> I am at the barber's, and a copy of *Paris-Match* is offered to me. On the cover, a young Negro [*nègre*] in a French uniform is saluting, with his eyes uplifted, probably fixed on a fold of the tricolour. All this is the *meaning* of the picture [*l'image*]. But, whether naively or not, I see very well what it signifies to me: that France is a great Empire, that all her sons, without any colour discrimination, faithfully serve under her flag, and that there is no better answer to the detractors of an alleged [*prétendu*] colonialism than the zeal shown by this Negro [*ce noir*] in serving his so-called [*prétendus*] oppressors. I am therefore again faced with a greater [*majoré*] semiological system: there is a signifier, itself already formed with a previous system (*a black* [noir] *soldier is giving the French salute*); there is a signified (it is here a purposeful [*intentionnel*] mixture of Frenchness [*francité*] and militariness); finally, there is a [*il y a enfin*] presence of the signified through the signifier [*une présence du signifié à travers le signifiant*]. (Barthes, 1973, 116)

Barthes at the barber's reads *Paris-Match* and comes across the photograph. Is this example real? Did Barthes really open an edition

Paris-Match, front cover 25 June–2 July 1955. Reproduced courtesy of *Paris-Match*.

of *Paris-Match* at this page while waiting his turn to be clipped? This is not a flippant question, for it is really a question about the seemingly effortless and arbitrary nature of this example. The front cover of *Paris-Match* from 25 June to 2 July 1955 seems to match this description.

This is no soldier! It is a boy and one who ought to be in a *lycée*! It is impossible to confirm if Roland Barthes did indeed come across this image at the barber's, this part may or may not have been invented, nowhere else in this essay does Barthes tell us about his domestic and daily routine. The undecidability on this point is, finally, fundamental and this is important. Nevertheless, let us run with the notion that this is the front cover that Barthes refers to here. He is telling us a secret. He is telling us of a real event, his viewing of this image and his visit to the barber. The secret is presented in such a way that we are told what it is – there is no attempt to conceal it. And yet, we cannot be certain if Roland Barthes did go to the barber or whether his reading has been fictionalised. The fiction is irreducible even as it offers up its secrets to us, avowing what can never be avowed.[110] The meaning of this image is then doubly complicated. It is at once a photograph on the front of *Paris-Match* (edition number 326) and an example of a photograph on the front of *Paris-Match* (the sort of thing one might expect to find in a publication of this sort). It is, when read by a reader of Barthes today, once again a real front cover of *Paris-Match* and a secret, silent link to the life of Roland Barthes and a cultural archaeology of France in 1955. The scene of reading is complicated, mediated and remediated, from the biographical barber's to the autobiographical citation and reinvestment of the barber's as a reflection in a text, to the theoretical scene of reading where the barber's is one example among many of a haunt for the hunter of signs. The image oscillates between these three scenes and its two meanings and is saturated by none, because there is more to be said of this image than 'a black soldier is giving the French salute'.

First of all let us consider Barthes' description: 'a young Negro [*nègre*] in a French uniform is saluting, with his eyes uplifted, probably fixed on a fold of the tricolour'. What meaning does Barthes himself bring to this image? The boy is saluting but are his eyes uplifted? Is he really looking at a folding of the tricolour at the end of the day? He might well be but there is no evidence for this within the limited representation of the image itself. He may as well be saluting on a parade ground; as a boy almost everything and everyone would be above his line of vision. And those eyes, these (it seems to me) are not the eyes of one in awe at the majesty of France's great empire. They are infinitely ambivalent, so much fear there, so much unhappiness, they do not reflect back the greatness of the march of France's civilising mission, certainly not now when we look at them today. I do not wish to swap Barthes' fanciful assumptions regarding this image with my own. I am reminded here of the debate between Heidegger and Meyer Shapiro over the authentic ownership of Van Gogh's shoes.[111] Heidegger claims them, most eloquently, for the peasantry, Shapiro for the migrant artist. Derrida points out that finally one cannot determine their ownership one way or the other and the desire for attribution is really a desire for appropriation on the part of academics who align themselves to a particular ownership in their texts. I do not wish to appropriate this image for in this sense any questioning of Barthes on this point would become a matter of contested property. I think, clearly, this image speaks for itself concerning a certain contestation over ownership.

The text at the bottom right hand page of this cover entitled 'Les nuits de l'armée' explains that 'Le Petit Diouf' has come from Ouagagadougou with his comrades in the 'enfants de troupes d'A.O.F' for the opening spectacle of the military show at the Palais des Sports this week.

The title is ambiguous. 'Les nuits de l'armée' refers to what in English would be called a 'military tattoo', the sort of display of soldiering excellence that one might find at the Royal Tournament in London or nightly in the grounds of the castle at the Edinburgh Festival. 'Les nuits de l'armée' ran annually at the Palais des Sports in Paris between 1952 and 1955. However, read literally the headline could also be taken to mean 'the darkness of the army'. The pun is no doubt intentional and thus of considerable importance to the sign-hunter who is paying attention. How might one read such a headline? Surely, it means one thing to speak of, say, the mixed-race character of the victorious French World Cup side of 1998, and quite another to comment on the 'darkness' of the army in 1955. Our army is 'dark', not purely white 'French': what is one to make of this? This is a child 'soldier'; the future of the army is dark. Our future is black not white. No doubt the military tattoo held at the Palais des Sports (broadcast on the BBC in an early European transmission) was a celebration of Empire but the metonymical image of the boy 'soldier' is considerably ambiguous. The text states that the boy is one of a number of cadets from Ouagadougou who will be opening a presentation by the French Army at the Palais des Sports. The idea of 'l'enfant de troupes' is a peculiarly French notion: originally the children of enlisted soldiers who also trained for warfare during their fathers' enrolment, in 1884 the children were removed from the regiment and military preparatory schools (*l'enfant de troupes*) were founded to provide an education for the children of enlisted men, who would become wards of the state on the deaths of their fathers in action (like Roland Barthes himself). In 1982 these military academies changed their names to '*lycées de la defense*'. Little Diouf featured on the front cover of *Paris-Match* attended the military academy in Ougadougou, the capital of Upper Volta (*Haut Volta*), named Burkina Faso after independence. In 1955 the Upper Volta was one of eight colonies that made up the administrative block of French West Africa (AOF, *Afrique occidentale française*) designed to facilitate French colonial penetration into Africa. The 'French uniform' that Little Diouf is wearing is not then, in any easy sense, that of a French soldier, and his relationship to whatever or whoever he is saluting is not at all straightforward. It is, I would suggest, considerably misleading to reduce the meaning of this image to 'a black soldier is giving the French salute'. Diouf was a real boy of thirteen years old (just old enough to be studying Latin grammar) and one of three children from Ougadougou featured in the edition of *Paris-Match*. The other children were called Issa and Santoura. Three-quarters of this edition of the journal is dedicated to the question of colonialism in Indochina, the 'Belgian-Congo' and Mali. In the report on the three visiting children they are variously photographed but never quoted. In their silence they stare out from the pages of a journal to be found in a barber's shop in 1950s Paris but they hardly speak of the greatness of the French Empire; rather they speak of its appropriation of their voices as well as their image. If Diouf is saluting the folding of the French flag, perhaps those eyes are looking into the not so distant future, when in 1958 the tricolour was lowered over French West Africa for the last time, following the vote for autonomy from France.[112]

The location of the Army Nights tattoo, the Palais des Sports in Paris, is not an insignificant matter either in any attempt to ponder the meaning of this image. The Palais is another name for the Vel' d'hiv (Vélodrome d'hiver), the indoor cycling track where on 16 July 1942 over 13,000 Parisian Jews were rounded up by the Vichy police prior to transportation to Auschwitz. Hannah Arendt took shelter here on her way to the United States as German refugees were 'accommodated' in the Vel' d'hiv before the fall of France. It was also used three years after the publication of this image in 1958 as a 'detention centre' for Algerians in Paris, rounded up by Maurice Papon's police force in a precursor to the October 1961 massacre when the ex-Vichy official (and later recipient of the Legion of Honour under de Gaulle and minister in Valéry Giscard d'Estaing's government) ordered the violent suppression of a pro-FLN march protesting against the curfew he had imposed, killing up to 300 people. The Vel' d'hiv features elsewhere in the *Mythologies*, in the text '*Billy Graham au Vel' d'Hiv*', in which the McCarthyist 'conversion' of France takes place in the stadium where the deportation of the Jews of Paris began, 'the neophytes who this evening, at the Vel' d'Hiv, among the posters for Super Dissolution and Cognac Polignac, "received Christ" under the action of the magic Message, are led to a private hall, and even – if they are English-speaking – to a still more secret crypt: whatever it is that happens there, inscription on the conversion lists, new sermons, spiritual conferences with "counsellors," or collections, this new episode is an ersatz form of Initiation' (Barthes, 1997, 65). Here the Christian converts are taken away to a secret place for identification and ordering of a different kind. Barthes makes no mention of the history of the velodrome in his text. Any reading of the image of Diouf must pass through the historical sedimentation that accretes around this text as the play of differences. In this way it is the work of difference in this text that is truly historical, even if the idea of History, as associated with say a Michelet, might be synonymous with the very arrest and erasure of difference. What is striking about this front cover of *Paris-Match* is how, on any reasonable inspection, unlike Barthes' description it really is.

Barthes comments in the essay 'Introduction to the Structural Analysis of Narrative' that there is no structural difference between reading a novel and reading a bus ticket.[113] However, elsewhere Barthes is a careful reader of novels: his examinations of Poe and Proust and Sollers and Sade are justly famous (despite Barthes' frequent protestations of ambivalence: 'I must admit that I am not a great reader; I read very little…' [Barthes 1985, 188]). One must also read a bus ticket carefully lest one fail to arrive at one's destination, or worse still, board an entirely errant bus heading in quite a different direction. Similarly, we are called to read the front cover of a magazine with care and patience, even if we do so in a barber's on a warm day in June. It is critical vigilance that sets the sign-hunter apart from their contemporaries: many of us can decipher the denotation of our bus pass, few can read as closely, intently and imaginatively as Barthes does the nineteenth-century French novel. While there may be no difference between reading the bus ticket and the novel if both are done with care, care is itself the structure and 'institutional' setting by which the reading takes place. Within this act of reading, careful reading at that, there always remains the necessary structural possibility of errancy. The signified and signifier are not coterminous, a lacuna remains between them and it is in that space, where the entire sign system sits, that misreading begins and an opening is levered between signified and signifier, representation and meaning. The photograph of Diouf certainly imposes something upon us, it may even be the ideological baggage that Barthes suggests ('a black soldier is giving the French salute') but so much more is happening in this image that in fact this alleged signified constitutes only a fraction of the meaning of the picture. It is most typical of a literary scholar like Barthes to read an image as if it were a sentence; that is to say, as if it were in some way confined, efficiently disposable and saturable. Barthes of course is far too canny to imagine that sentences themselves work in this way. However, the implication of the analogy between the novel and the bus ticket is suggestive of just this sort of transience. It might in fact be the case that reading a bus ticket or reading the front cover of a magazine at the barber's is the most tricky and demanding thing imaginable, especially if the bus ticket were for the number 80 which connects to the 38 to run from the Panthéon to the Vélodrome d'Hiver. If there is one lesson to learn from Barthes, reading Barthes in a time of terror, it is not to read like Barthes does here, at pace and absent-mindedly. Barthes is too quick to utilise his example, working from its particularity to a universal theory of signification. 'Never universalise from local conditions' runs Gayatri Spivak's universalising dictum. The truth is more prosaic that one always experiences the universal and the particular in relation to one another; without this move philosophy and theory would just not be possible. The mistake is to believe in the obedience or containment of the example and that the universal is anything other than contingent, awaiting its immediate re-emersion in the particularity of examples. Consequently, it would do Barthes a great injustice if we were to halt our own reading of 'Myth Today' here, for the figure of Little Diouf runs away from the semiological apparatus, hiding behind and peeking out from the pillars that hold up Barthes' text.

It would seem that like Flaubert, Barthes; 'favourite book was not the novel but the dictionary' (Barthes 1985, 247). Before we follow Diouf around the architecture of Barthes' text I would like to pause a moment over the denomination '*nègre*'. This is obviously a contested term. In

French it implies the characterisation of sub-Saharan blacks suitable for or subject to slavery; in this sense the best translation for Barthes' use of the term would be 'negro'. In the francophone world of the 1950s the term is used by Jean Genet, in his still scandalously arresting play *Les Nègres* (the longest running off-Broadway show ever), as well as Franz Fanon, Aimé Cesaire and the 'nègritude' writers, as a term to be reinvested with positive meaning. Nevertheless, in colloquial French it does carry the pejorative meaning of 'nigger' as an abusive term. French delicacies of the time included '*tête de nègre*', which could refer either to a chocolate meringue (now known as a '*tête du coco*') or a stylised strip of liquorice in the shape of a black male face. '*Tête de nègre*' also refers to a dark brown colour, otherwise referred to as Moroccan brown. I recall, some time in the Glasgow of the 1970s, standing beside my mother in a shop that supplied school uniforms with her asking the Jewish owner if he had anything in 'nigger brown'. He knew exactly what she wanted and did not seem to bat an eyelid at the phrase; he was no doubt used too much worse. My much-loved and much-thumbed 1951 edition of Cassell's English–French dictionary directly translates '*tête de nègre*' as 'nigger brown'. In 1950s France the word also had two other meanings. First, one would refer to a 'ghost writer' as a '*nègre*' because this would be someone working for another and subordinate to them. Today the term '*écrivain privé*' is much preferred, although the phrase '*travailler comme un nègre*' is in frequent use to refer to an exploited worker. The *Petit-Robert* notes that this phrase now has 'no real racist connotation' although the demotic variants '*nègro*' and '*nègrou*' have a strong racist inflection. In the argot of the military academy, where the young Diouf hailed, '*nègre*' was also used to refer to the most brilliant student suitable for promotion. Etymologically this use is said to date from the nineteenth-century from its use at the Saint-Cyr military school by the French Governor of Algeria, of Irish extraction, Mac-Mahon (later President of the Republic), '*C'est vous le nègre? Eh bien, continuez!*' A colloquial use of this sense continues in an ironic way. Surely, all of these meanings are presented to us whenever Barthes attempts to deploy the term in a limited way. The word remains a point of concentration around which these meanings coalesce and pass through, naming a history of race and perhaps the very history of Modernity itself, certainly of the very idea of France. We might think of Diouf in all of these senses, as the 'ghost writer', the phantom absent in his presence and present through his absence in Barthes' text. He writes and rewrites the question of 'Myth Today' for Barthes, forever compelling us to reposition and rethink the 'Today' as well as exposing the 'myth' of Barthes. Second, he is an example exploited and worked hard by Barthes as he traverses the text of 'Myth Today' but he is also the brilliant student of the military academy, not only the one who has been chosen to visit Paris with his colleagues but the one whose brilliance leads us to rethink our own position as instructors. One must make way for Diouf and say '*eh bien continuez!*'

Barthes uses the term 'nègre' quite freely throughout the mythologies, notably in the text '*Bichon chez les Nègres*', which Richard Howard translates as 'Bichon and the Blacks'. The text concerns the reporting by *Paris-Match* of an academic couple (painters) who take their three-month-old baby with them on a tour of '*les pays de Cannibales*'. The magazine is concerned with the bravery of the teachers and their baby, Barthes is concerned with the thought that on the one hand if this trip is not really dangerous then it is disingenuous to speak of 'bravery', and on the other hand if it is truly dangerous then it is enormously stupid and irresponsible to impose such privations on a baby for the sake of painting. One immediately thinks here of contemporary 'explorer' or 'survivalist' reality television programmes where the imperilled presenters and crew spend their nights, off-camera, in luxury hotels. The achievements of baby Bichon and Steve Irwin (to name a stupidly and as it happens tragically visible example) are, says Barthes, 'demonstrations of an ethical order, which receive their final value only from the publicity they are given' (Barthes, 1997, 35). Barthes' text is an excoriating demolition of the colonial imaginary of the *Paris-Match* report and by extension the 'petit-bourgeois' imaginary of its one million readers. (Barthes is of course actually self-conscious here. As he would later say: 'Who will admit to being a petit bourgeois? Politically and historically, the petite bourgeoisie is the key to the century' [Barthes 1985, 267].) We will have to return to this particular universalising gesture in Barthes since he himself is a critical reader of *Paris-Match*, and it would seem not only when at the barber's, and one wonders whether such criticality might be extended to others who encounter this particular magazine.

I am often left uneasy by the young Barthes' undemocratic, homogenising 'class consciousness'. Ideology after all cannot ever be said to arrive finally 'in the last instance' in Althusser's famous formulation because if it did then we would all (without exception or possibility of escape) be walking somnambulantly through life fixed in a relation of false consciousness to our material circumstances. This might indeed be so and it might indeed be, like repression in a psychoanalytic sense, both unavoidable and necessary, but there must remain play (pliability) within the operation of ideology and in this opening reading takes place. Perhaps it is also true that there is no structural difference between reading a bus ticket, *Paris-Match* or a novel, but in that case one might offer that all reading is necessarily critical reading because all reading involves misreading; that is, the unavoidable encounter with the multiplicity of meaning as it passes through a unique signifier. However, Barthes here at once uses the term '*nègre*' as an untroubled designation (when used by himself) and mobilises it against colonial thinking:

> *Le voyage des parents de Bichon dans une contrée située d'ailleurs très vaguement, et donnée surtout comme le Pays des Nègres Rouges, sorte de lieu Romanesque dont on atténue, sans en avoir l'air, les caractères trop reels, mais dont le nom légendaire propose déjà une ambiguité terrifiante entre la couleur de leur teinture et le sang humain qu'on est cense y boire ...*

> The trip Bichon's parents made into a region situated quite vaguely and significantly labelled the Country of the Red Negroes, a kind of fictional site whose actual characteristics are skilfully attenuated but whose legendary name already proposes a terrifying ambiguity between the colour of their painted skins and the human blood they supposedly drink ... (Barthes, 1997, 36)

Howard's translation seems to me to miss several tricks here. The country of the Red Negroes is, according to Barthes, situated 'elsewhere, very vaguely'; the imagined non-place of 'elsewhere' is an important aspect of the Francophone colonial imaginary for this Romantic and novelistic ('*Romanesque*') space. As the French has it, the details of the country are attenuated without having given the appearance of so being (*sans en avoir l'air*), which Howard coherently renders as 'skilfully attenuated'. However, I think the force of Barthes' French is to suggest that a simulacrum of a country has been offered through the thinnest of sketches. That is, an idea of a country (*les caractères trop reels*) is suggested through a colonial ideological ruse: the ruse of language, as Cixous says of Joyce. This ruse is the naming of this suggestive non-place *le Pays des Nègres Rouges*, which Howard offers, translating Barthes, as 'a terrifying ambiguity between the colour of their painted skins ('*teinture*') and the human blood they supposedly drink'. I am not entirely sure that 'painted skins' is an appropriate translation of '*teinture*', which can mean a dye, dying or a colour or a hue. 'Tincture' might be a literal translation but 'complexion' may also be appropriate in this context; '*un tient pâle*' is often translated as a pale complexion. Painting is inserted here by the translator perhaps by the suggestive nature of the parents of baby Bichon, who are themselves painters, in *le Pays des Nègres Rouges* 'armed with palette and brush' as *Paris-Match* puts it. Barthes' text goes on to paint a vivid picture of the French colonial imaginary through his own mixing of terms and discussion of tones.

The blond baby Bichon is said to play the Parsifal role, 'contrasting his blondness [*sa blondeur*], innocence, curls and smile to the infernal world of black and red skins [*des peaux noires et rouges*], scarifications, and hideous masks'. Thus, he charms the natives, becoming their idol and god, fulfilling the civilising mission of Empire at an early age rather than being pushed in his pram around the Bois de Bologne. Now, the adventure of Bichon is not what interests me here. Rather, I am concerned with Barthes' use of the term '*nègre*'. In the paragraph that follows Barthes goes on to analyse the way in which this colonial simulacrum (my phrase not his) '*deviné l'image du Nègre*' and how this is played out through stereotype and reduction. However, the important thing here is the idea of the image or representation of the category '*nègre*'. In Franz Fanon's 1952 text *Peau Noire, Masques Blancs*,[115] for example, to cite Fanon as a touchstone of contemporary Francophone black consciousness rather than an authority, it is clear that Fanon's preferred term of self-identification is '*un Noir*' or '*un homme Noir*' or '*le Noir antillais*'. The term '*nègre*' is reserved as a classification and designation of French colonial discourse, '*il ne manquerait plus que ça, nous assimiler à des négres*'. One is assimilated as a '*négre*', one becomes a '*négre*' by being positioned as such by colonial attribution. Now, in French the term '*nègre*' is not reducible or translatable to 'nigger', in fact the word may be untranslatable as such. This is why one should be suspicious of the frequent translation of Fanon's famous reported speech at the start of Chapter 5 ('*L'expérience vécue du Noir*') of *Black Skin, White Masks*, '"Dirty Nigger!" or simply, "Look, a Negro!"'. The French here actually reads '"*Sale nègre!" ou simplement, "Tiens, un nègre!*"' The translation should read something like 'Dirty Negro!' or simply, 'Look, a Negro!': the first translation of '*nègre*' is an Americanisation of Fanon that does not necessarily (or only ambiguously) reflect the linguistic force of French in 1952. Given that the opening line of Fanon's study, in a chapter entitled '*Le Noir et le langage*', is '*nous attachons une importance fondamentale au phénomène du langage*', then one should take these distinctions seriously.

I am suggesting not that Barthes' ubiquitous use of the term is overtly racist, because it is not, but rather that this term is an appellation given to blacks by the white French which orientalises (to use a geographically inappropriate theoretical term) or authorises the othering of the black through the French language. Fanon is clear that his existence as a black Francophone is a dialectic between '*la conscience noire*' and '*la conscience nègre*'. The word itself then retains the resources for its own recovery when Fanon speaks of the '*la nouveau nègre*' or '*la nègre-a-venir*' or when Cesaire speaks of Negritude and so on, the play of the term is subtle and complex, and like any other signifier it is in principle not exhaustible. Its meaning is not reducible to its phonetic content. However, unlike Fanon's subtle interrogation and palyonymy, Barthes uses the word as his privileged term, moving between his own 'everyday' use and its colonial designation: '*le Nègre fait peur, il est cannibale*', as the ideology runs for Barthes. The following two sentences of the mythology are compelling here so allow me to lay them out in full:

> *Sans la présence implicite de ce risqué, l'histoire perdait toute vertu de choc, le lecteur n'aurait pas peur; aussi, les confrontations sont multipliées où l'enfant blanc est seul, abandonné, insouciant et exposé dans un cercle de Noirs potentiellement menaçants (le seule image pleinement rassurante du Nègre sera celle du boy, du barbare domestiqué, couple d'allieurs avec cet autre lieu commun de toutes les bonnes histoires d'Afrique: le boy voleur qui disparaît avec les affaires du maître).*

> Without the implicit presence of this risk [i.e. cannibalism], the story would lose all its shock value, the reader would not be scared; hence occasions are multiplied in which the white baby is alone, abandoned, carefree, and exposed in a circle of potentially threatening Blacks (the only entirely reassuring image of the Black is that of the *boy*, the domesticated barbarian, coupled, moreover, with that other commonplace of all good African stories: the *thieving boy* who vanishes with his master's things). (Barthes, 1997, 36–7)

The use of the word 'boy' in English by Barthes is intriguing, as he italicises it in the first instance but not the second, although Richard Howard emphasises both. However, what concerns us here is the move on Barthes' part between '*un cercle de Noirs potentiellement menaçants*' and the later reassuring image of the 'Nègre' as boy. This is a rare occasion in the mythologies when Barthes alters his vocabulary and deploys the noun '*Noirs*' rather than '*Nègres*'. As we can see here the distinction is not introduced in the manner of Fanon to distinguish between colonised subjectivity and self-awareness; rather the '*Noirs*' here are potentially menacing cannibals. The linguistic differentiation is not doing the same work for Barthes as it does for Fanon.

Between here and the end of the text on Bichon, Barthes returns to the preferred term '*Nègre*' when he speaks of the ideological operation of the text as '*donner à voir le monde nègre par les yeux de l'enfant blanc*' ('to display the world of the Blacks through the eyes of a white child', says Howard). Or again, when he comments critically on the article in *Paris-Match* that '*Au fond la Nègre n'a pas de vie pliene et autonome*' ('Ultimately the Black has no complete and autonomous life') and later of '*les efforts des ethnologues pour démystifier le fait nègre*' ('the ethnologists' efforts to demystify the Black phenomenon'). Barthes' final conclusion in this piece is that while the likes of Mauss and Lévi-Strauss have confronted 'the old racial terms in their various disguises' ('*vieux termes raciaux camouflés*') and so 'science' has moved on, 'collective representations' have not, '*elles sont des siècles en arrière, maintenues stagnantes dans l'erreur par le pouvoir, la grande presse et les valeurs d'ordre*' ('they are centuries behind, kept stagnant in their errors by power, the press and the values of order'). I quote Barthes' eloquent French here lest, after all that has been said, anyone is in doubt as to where Barthes' political sympathy and good intentions lie. His final line is poignant when he describes the attitude of *Paris-Match* as pre-Voltairean and suggests that Voltaire would in contrast '*il imaginerait plutôt quelque Bichon cannibale (ou coréen) aux prises avec le 'guignol' napalmisé de l'Occident*' ('he would imagine some cannibal (or Korean) Bichon contending with the napalmised *guignol* of the West'). This is just about Barthes' only mention of the Korean War in the whole of the mythologies, perhaps another remarkable omission. One wonders what would command the myth hunter's attention more at this point in history, the conflict on the Korean peninsula or an edition of *Paris-Match*? There is no doubt a structural solidarity between the two but any point Barthes might wish to make here is surely at best muted. It is not that the Bichon text is not worth addressing or that it does not provide critical access to the structures of western racism through a marginal case. Rather, my point of concern would be that given that this is the only occasion on which Barthes refers to the then largest global conflict (combining the twin problematic of race and communism) one wonders whether the critical leverage on Occidentalism afforded by the Bichon example is really adequate to the task of understanding the imaginary at work in western calculations in Korea.

The problem here that itches under the skin of Barthes' text is a subtle and difficult one. Just as it is correct to be critical of Fanon's translators who render '*nègre*' as both 'nigger' and 'negro', it is equally correct to worry over Howard's 1997 translation of '*nègre*' and '*noir*' as both simultaneously reducible to 'black'. No doubt in 1997 Howard discerns what we might provisionally and anachronistically call the 'politically correct' intention of Barthes' text and so chooses to translate Barthes' text in a 'politically correct' or least inoffensive way, as 'Bichon among the Blacks'. However, this is not the language that Barthes himself has used. Rather, he speaks in a seemingly undifferentiating way, as do Sartre, Camus, Genet and many others, of the classification '*nègre*', which might have been the accepted term but was not the 'politically correct' term, and this is why an anachronistic idea such as 'political correctness' will not get us very far in trying to understand this text, either to celebrate it or to condemn it. It would surely be a mistake to attempt to ideologise Barthes' writing on ideology. Neither attitude here is really an appropriate response. It is telling that the examples Barthes offers in contrast to the racism of *Paris-Match* are those of structural anthropology and Enlightenment thought. The complicity between the structures of western logocentrism and the anthropological gesture have been well documented elsewhere[115] and previously in this essay. The question for me concerning Barthes here is that in an economy of complicity there are modes by which one affirms or resists one's own complicit status. Barthes is clear in his attempt to operate critical leverage on the French colonial imaginary but at the same time falls back into that linguistic and cultural space at the level of his own signifiers. Thus, for reasons that his own text cannot understand (that is, cannot understand at a theoretical level) Barthes is complicit with the very colonial structures he wishes to criticise. His own theory of signification and of the model of myth works on the principle of a signified denotation coterminous with an ideological connotation, without taking into consideration the possibility of multiple and non-saturable meaning within any given articulation. Accordingly, while Barthes is able to read this article and its images against the grain of their ideological inscription, he does not see the ways in which the racial ideology he identifies in *Paris-Match* also permeates his own text and the history of this racist discourse draws itself through the play of difference in his own writing. Both critical and implicated, Barthes' text deals with a problematic of complicity in which he attempts to be more or less hospitable to the racial other while never escaping his own implicated status. Rather, there is here an exact and even imprudent blindness to the intellectual solidarity between a certain practice of structuralism and the conceptual orders of colonialism. Now, it is interesting to me that this conflict should arise at the level of the signifier because the point I would wish to affirm again and again about Barthes is that what interests me here is first and foremost Barthes as a theory-writer and only secondly Barthes as a 'theorist' as such. The complexity and complicity of Barthes' position derives from his use of language and thus from his status as a writer. It is here also that one can find the resources to read, reread, and recover Barthes. On the level of Barthes as a theorist in this respect, his model of signification will always remain insufficient and so is finally not worth recuperating. However, as a *scriptible* text, a writerly text that the creative and critical reader scrawls over and counter-signs its unspoken meanings, the Bichon text remains of interest even if it is not itself innocent.

Barthes écrivain

One might raise the objection at this point that to treat Barthes as a writer first and foremost is to depoliticise the Barthes of the *Mythologies*, just as it would be a depoliticisation of Marx, say, to affirm his credentials as a philosopher over his worth as a thinker of revolutionary action.[116] In the case of Marx this might well be true: there is a certain conservative gesture in reading Marx that says we are done with all this communist and revolutionary nonsense, now we can see Marx for what he truly is, a philosopher and an economist. In this way Marx is domesticated and allowed to enter the Pantheon of great thinkers.[117] I do not think that my reading of Barthes works in quite the same way. First, I have attempted to show that claims for the radical politics of Barthes must necessarily be complicated and conflicted. The idea of the literature of commitment best represented by Barthes is that of the Proustian writer committed to the sanatorium rather than to the barricades. This is not necessarily a difficulty for me; instead one should appreciate the 'greyness' of Barthes. Barthes' work allows us to think the problematic limits of writing and of theoretical endeavour in the humanities. It is certainly true that one should not universalise the situation of Barthes as a paradigm for the intellectual. On the contrary, one must always remain committed to the very idea of the humanities (at least in the Kantian sense) as the lungs of the university, whose paths have no proper course or limit as they irrigate all that must be thought in the name of truth and without which neither the university nor the socio-cultural space would be possible.

However, in the case of Barthes it is possible to discern a liminal case, where writing disseminates beyond the boundaries of its own imagined possibility not because its author wishes to impact upon the social but precisely because he imagined that it could not. While one can read 'Myth Today' as an enabling pedagogical text in the demystification of ideology it is equally implicated within the bourgeois culture it addresses. The significance of this essay and its attendant 'Mythologies' lies as much in what they do not say as what they do, or what they say without meaning to say, if you will. To raise this text of Barthes up as an example of political criticism is not a straightforward thing. Rather, we have here the inaugural problem of cultural studies. This is a text that has been read as political and politicising, and one should not underestimate its effects and the transitions it has enabled. However, as a piece of transformative critique it is compromised by both a structurally insufficient theoretical model and a critical object (the bourgeois media) that parochialises its political purpose. In this way, the fault lines that run through Barthes' text are ones that Barthes' own theory and method cannot recognise and so his text can never know itself. On the contrary, it is when Barthes is making his boldest political claims in this text that in fact he is falling back into a mode of thinking that his writing elsewhere does so much to displace, while it is when he attends to the complexity of writing and its effects that he as a writer is most successful at doubling and redoubling the unforeseen consequences of his work. What are significant in the *Mythologies*, as with the operation of cultural studies inaugurated by them, are not the moments of political programme, commentary or critique that attend them, but the shifting of ground and the breaking of moulds that gives rise to the possibility of thinking the political otherwise from a critical position.

We are heading towards a consideration of the impact of the French translation of Nietzsche on contemporary European thought. As Barthes says of Derrida: 'In addition to everything I owe to Derrida, and which others owe him too, there is something that brings us together, if I may say so: the feeling of participating (or wanting to participate) in a period of history Nietzsche calls "nihilism".'[118] It is when Barthes pushes at the limits of intelligibility that his work is of most consequence, not when he casually and occasionally slaps down the stupidity of petit-bourgeois culture. Thus, to wish to consider Barthes as a writer is in no way to depoliticise his writing in a 'post-political' age or to damn him with faint praise. Rather, it is to rethink fundamentally what it means to write, to write so-called 'theory' and to be a writer as such. Barthes is a liminal case because his writing life is lived at the frontier of a critical avant-garde that works at the porous edge between theoretical thought and the poetic. If Barthes grew to feel that the import of his work could never cross over into the realm of the social or have anything to offer the radical social movements of the sixties and seventies it is because there must, as with any pioneer, remain a certain loneliness felt at the frontier. On the one hand, the aporetic gulf of misunderstanding between Barthes and the student movement of 1968 is a testament to the significance of Barthes as a writer, his irreducible complexity that never allows his words to be appropriated. Lacan is quite correct, the events of 1968 do not demonstrate the irrelevance of Barthes' work but rather that structures do (clearly) take to the street. On the other hand, one continues to read Barthes but not Daniel Cohn-Bendit, say, to cite a metonymic and mediatic example, because Barthes is a writer whose subtle and suggestive text can be read and reread, not a didactic or professional revolutionary. As Barthes states in a 1977 interview: 'In my case, it would be demagogic to speak of revolution, but I would willingly speak for subversion. I find it a clearer word than revolution. It means: to come up from underneath so as to cheat with things, to divert them from their assigned paths, from their intended destinations.'[119] In this sense, Barthes' work might be said to be 'untimely', to borrow a term of Heidegger's used by Derrida apropos of Marx.[120]

It is untimely, not necessarily because it was not recognised at the moment it was most needed (Barthes has been well recognised in other places and other times). Rather, it might be said to be untimely because it both disrupts a moment through its critical acuity and speaks to another moment beyond itself. This is the nature of the avant-garde: Barthes is an evangelist for another kind of writing and another kind of thinking. Barthes' relation to cultural studies is one of misprision. If one chooses to arrest the play of Barthes' text and to channel his writing into a critical method (as with the *Mythologies* as an application of a model of ideological demystification based upon a theory of signification targeted at popular culture) then one is surrendering the text of Barthes to its own insecurities and fears. For his own

part, Barthes was in a insistent process of moving beyond the quag-
mire of his own imagined aporias through the constant reinvention
of his object. He will outflank the analysis of petit-bourgeois culture
through an affirmation of literature, he will sidestep the dead-end of
structuralism through a reinvestment in desire and reading, he will
confound the sclerosis of his own body of work through an engagement with something that might be called 'autobiography' but that is
in fact an alertness to the frontier of writing that he has always trod-
den. Every time one finds the act of invention in Barthes that moves his
writing beyond its own insecurity by actively forgetting its theoretical
shortcomings and rearranging its political desires. To say that Barthes
is a writer is to pay Barthes the highest compliment that I can because
so few theorists know how to make their prose live off the page. That is
to say, Barthes, like the poets, articulates what it means to live in this
world (politically, culturally, animally, as a human being). A singular
and queer human being no doubt but one who might be said to join a
select group of poet-theorists: Nietzsche, Benjamin, Adorno, Arendt,
Derrida. This is an alternative history of cultural studies as the practice
of 'theory-writing'.

   One might raise an eyebrow at this list: Paul de Man is a better theorist than Barthes, Cixous is a better writer than all of them, there are
more significant philosophers than those listed here. However, what
this in many ways disparate and conflicting group of names have in
common is an ability to bend discourse to allow the everyday to speak
in an enabling and ennobling way. They are all part of a tradition of critique that can inflect itself with the present and open thought to a new
idiom that advances readership. For such poet-theorists the critique
is always, as Nietzsche puts it, a question of style and style is always
plural.[121] Style in this sense is a question of inventing an idiom of writing that weaves between plural voices and positions, avoiding closures
while complicating, and never giving in to reduction while advanc-
ing towards a reader in the most hospitable way possible, even at the
expense of any simple notion of 'clarity' or 'openness'. These writers
address the social by raising the tone of discourse on the social, not
by rushing headlong into the cul-de-sac of common denominators.
Such writing takes the reader with it, moving and removing the reader,
taking them along the experience of the frontier of writing as critical
thought. It is by such mobility that the inertia of institutions and the
pitfalls of rehearsed arguments take their place in the landscape of
thought while the reader is carried forward on a journey without set

destination. The task of rewriting the social text would be analogous to Barthes' recovery of things past: 'Proust's novel, which seems to us so "positive", so liberating, is born explicitly of a book impossible to write' (Barthes 1985, 27).

This *of course* does not mean that there is no relation between Barthes the writer and the political positions he avows in his texts.[122] As we saw with his text on the African grammar he is frequently at his most writerly when he is most significantly engaged. One might think here of his sharp texts on the populist neo-fascism of Pierre Poujade, '*Quelques paroles de M. Poujade*' and '*Poujade et les intellectuels*'. A supporter of the Vichy regime, Poujade rose to prominence at the end of the Fourth Republic as the leader of the *Union de Defense Commercants et Artisans* (UDCA), which emerged from a tax protest he coordinated to prevent tax inspectors verifying the income of shopkeepers. By the time of the 1956 general election his unique brand of anti-Semitism, anti-Americanism, anti-urbanisation, anti-industrialisation and pro-colonialism had won his party fifty-three seats in the National Assembly, including the youngest member of parliament, Jean-Marie Le Pen. This was the high-water mark of Poujadism as the fourth largest party in the Assembly with 12.6 per cent of the popular vote. As his party's fortunes declined Poujade distanced himself from Le Pen's later incarnation and was in fact appointed by François Mitterrand to the *Conseil économique et social* where he used his position to promote bio-fuels. However, in the early 1950s he was the epitome of the petit-bourgeois ideology at which Barthes directed his cultural critique.

The significance of the 1956 general election in France should not be underestimated today, it was a defining moment in France's own 'war on terror'. After the rout at Dien Bien Phu in June 1954 the government of Pierre Mendès-France brought an end to the war in Indochina and subsequently began independence talks with the representatives of Tunisia and Morocco. His cabinet fell in 1955 as he attempted concessions to Algerian nationalists in the face of *pieds noirs* and 'patriotic' disapproval. Edgar Faure, from the right of Mendès-France's Radical Party, replaced him as Prime Minister on the promise of a more repressive response to the Algerian War. Elections followed within the year when Faure lost a crucial vote in the National Assembly. The election that took place on 2 January 1956, the last of the Fourth Republic, was then dominated by the colonial question. The election was won by a coalition of Mendès-France's Radical Party and Guy Mollet's socialists.

The Communist Party was the single biggest group with 25 per cent of the vote and although excluded from government they supported Mollet and Mendès-France's attempt at peaceful resolution in Algeria. However, Mollet's government was soon pushed towards further repression and by May 1956 Mendès-France had resigned as his deputy, citing the failure of Mollet to address the economic and social needs of poor Muslims in Algeria as part of the 'pacification' process. Mollet's government floundered through the Suez crisis of September 1956 and the events of January to March 1957, now known as the Battle of Algiers, when General Massau operated outside legal frameworks, including the use of torture, to clear the FLN out of Algiers. His government fell in June 1957 after losing a debate on taxation to fund the Algerian counter-insurgency. Three further iterations of a left-wing cabinet followed, each lasting a few months before the military *coup d'état* in Algeria led by Generals Massau and Salan, following the invasion of Corsica and the mobilisation of troops on the mainland, demanded de Gaulle's unelected return to power, leading to the dissolution of the Fourth Republic and ultimately de Gaulle's own negotiated withdrawal from Algeria as the first President of the Fifth Republic. All of this is serious and significant historic upheaval but does not feature anywhere in the text of Barthes even though it may have come to his attention while reading *Paris-Match* at the barber's.

The *Mythologies* were all completed by the end of 1956 but nonetheless the political scene into which they make their articulation was clearly one of intense ideological consequence. One cannot criticise Barthes for not foreseeing, in this book, how brutal the repression in Algeria would become, one could even argue that it was the relatively benign atmosphere of the Mendès-France government that informs Barthes' writing; however, I think it is legitimate to question the idea that the *Mythologies* constitutes a searing political critique of its age when so much goes uncommented upon and the objects of Barthes' 'myth-busting' appear so parochial within the wider sweep of the cultural history of France. In this sense Barthes' concerns are at least as petit-bourgeois as the culture he criticises. This of course is why he can write of these objects so evocatively and fondly. In 1958 Barthes was working on a temporary contract as a researcher at the CNRS in Paris, spending his time between editing his theatre journal and reading Marx's *Critique of the Gotha Programme* and the novels of Alain Robbe-Grillet, rather than dedicating himself to his report on the vocabulary of the social question in 1830. His uncertain situation at this time, despite the publication of the Michelet book, *Critique et Vérité* and the *Mythologies* is I think indicative of the ways in which Barthes owes his place in contemporary thought much more to the post-Libertaion, Marxist counter-culture than to any academic preferment. In this sense, he is a much more institutionally maverick figure than say Derrida at this time. This in part explains Barthes' commitment to social criticism as an avant-garde of writing. The difference between Barthes and Derrida in these terms is that Barthes' career was ultimately recuperated by the academy and he was elected to the Collège de France; Derrida in contrast never held a professorial chair in France and was never appointed above the level of *répéteur*. One could say of this that, contrary to received wisdom that tells us cultural studies has never made inroads within the French academy, this period was the 'cultural studies moment' in France. It is intimately linked to the historical conjuncture of this particular 'war on terror' and emerges at the interstices of academic and public discourse as the articulation of a resistance to inherited modes of intelligibility. It is surprising then that Barthes seems to have nothing to say publicly about the military coup that gripped France at this time.

His position on Poujade, at the time of writing an unelected populist, is perceptive if curiously focused. While Barthes has the discrimination to see in Poujade a form of aggressive populism around which the nationalist, colonialist, racist and anti-Semitic elements of the French right were beginning to coalesce and which ultimately abandon him in favour of the generals and de Gaulle's 'strong leadership', the particular reason Barthes dislikes the Poujadists is their 'anti-intellectualism'. 'France is stricken with an overproduction of men with diplomas, polytechnicians, economists, philosophers and other dreamers who have lost all contact with the real world', says Poujade (Barthes, 1997, 52). In this respect Poujade sounds very similar to the perennial critics of the academy and more particularly the theoretical. I have argued elsewhere that this key aspect of Poujadism is shared by both the impatience of a certain type of 'activist' and those 'culture warriors' such as Roger Kimball who express their contempt for the humanities because they feel threatened by the intellectual and political implications of Theory.[123] What such people share with Poujade is a resolutely binary understanding of the so-called 'real world' and the supposedly abstract and 'Ivory Tower' character of the theoretical or thought as such. While the boundary between the two is never transparent or simple, I think it has been sufficiently demonstrated in this

book and throughout the oeuvre of Roland Barthes that such a mode
of thinking is little more than a blinkered metaphysics romantically
infatuated with the ideology of unmediated practicality as an insula-
tion against the challenge of complex thought. Barthes comments that
Poujade's real enemy is the dialectic: 'Will the rue de Rivoli be stronger
than Parliament?', asks Pierre Poujade, 'the dialectic more valid than
Reason?' (Barthes, 1997, 52). Here the dialectic stands metonymically
for complex thinking (a form of disreputable and discredited soph-
istry) and 'Reason' (raison, 'rightness') means the innate 'common
sense' of the ordinary man. It is the universalisation of such 'common sense' that weaves the ideological cloak of the petit-bourgeois
mythologies that Barthes relentlessly critiques. Poujade's attacks on
the intellectual are, for Barthes, his worst crime because this reductionism is an assault on culture itself, 'the specific symptom of all fascisms' (Barthes, 1997, 53). Barthes then names Poujade as a 'fascist'.
There is a piece of work to do on another occasion that follows from
this not necessarily unjust appellation of Poujade, through Barthes'
insistence in 1968 that the term must be used accurately in order for
it to carry any meaning, to his late inaugural lecture at the Collège de
France in which he declared, reportedly to the dismay of his audience,
that all language is fascist.

However, on this occasion the naming of Poujade is a defence of critique and complexity in a moment of political tumult that calls for serious and considered thinking rather than popular and brutal responses.
The difficulties that France faced at this moment during a period of
colonial war, violent threat and the rise of dark and undemocratic
practices require that the intellectual do justice to this scene and to
his or her vocation by thinking through the complexity of the moment.
The tension comes between the urgency of the moment, the need to
respond now, and the time required to undertake the necessary analysis of this complexity. I have suggested in my reading of Barthes that
to my mind the Mythologies too often miss that urgency by displacing an understanding of the present scene into a series of readings of
popular cultural objects, which may appear superficially 'radical' but
which frequently miss their mark. Ultimately, these readings appear
to be subversive because their object is margarine or Citroën cars but
in fact they are only ever readings of texts in the most traditional of
scholarly exegesis. We might not remember Barthes' book so readily
but he may as well be reading Shakespeare and Racine at those points
when exposition and the unmasking of ideology are his concern. In

this respect the *Mythologies* play out an inaugural problem of cultural studies itself, namely, that the substitution of objects of analysis without the disarticulation of the model of reading and scholarly activity itself does nothing to transform the academic activity; rather, it is to fall back on the most conservative and expected of academic protocols while imagining oneself to have moved elsewhere. However, the texts on Poujade are a good example of the ways in which the text of the *Mythologies* and the process of reading it sets in place continue to resist any such final designation of Barthes (or even cultural studies). There remains for Barthes a commitment to the transformative critique of the present through a practice of writing and intellectual investigation that not only must be defended in times of trouble but must also be engaged to say all that must be said in the name of truth at such moments. This is why for Barthes the intellectual is one of a chain of abject figures for fascism, along with the non-European and the Jew. Often for fascisms there is no difference between the Jew and the intellectual. As Poujade declares of Mendès-France, 'You're the racist! Of the two of us, he's the one who can be a racist, he's the one who has a race' (Barthes, 1997, 132). For Poujade and his young disciple Le Pen (sufficiently advanced as a political character even in 1954 for Barthes to mention him by name) the 'aesthetes of the New Left' and the Jewish threat and the Algerian terrorists are all syntagmatically linked in their lack of 'Frenchness'. One way to read Barthes' book is as a nascent text in the tradition of the theorisation of national identity. In part I have employed here what we might call provisionally a contemporary 'post-colonial' appreciation of Barthes in this reading. However, to persist in a reading that made significant claims concerning Barthes' own attitude to race and nation would be to entirely miss the point of Barthes' own demystification of the bourgeois culture he reads and to use as an objection against Barthes a series of complications that his own text first identifies. Let us do Barthes the justice of reading him more patiently than this.

The text on Baby Bichon suggests that the child is an effective agent of the colonial mission because the photographs that accompany the narrative of his jungle visit depend 'upon the pathetic collusion of white flesh and black skin, of innocence and cruelty, of spirituality and magic; Beauty subjugates [*enchaîne*] the Beast, Daniel is nuzzled [*se fait lécher*] by lions, and a civilisation of the soul triumphs over the barbarism of instinct' (Barthes, 1997, 37). Here the lion of 'Myth Today' appears out of the undergrowth of Bichon's camp to step forward to lick the face of this young Daniel. The lion here ('my name is lion') is the native face in the 'black and white' photographs of 1950s *Paris-Match*. The lion is an African who is not making the French salute, rather he is an 'enchained' beast, subjugated as Howard translates it, enslaved as the suggestion might be, by the innocent Christian spirituality of the civilising soul. The lion escapes Barthes' grammatical example, refusing its role as the faithful dog – it is after all a big cat – only to be brought to heal elsewhere in the *Mythologies*. Similarly, just as Barthes wishes to appropriate the appropriation of Diouf as his theoretical example, he discovers that the boy will not sit still as he has his hair cut. Diouf's mobility is a concern to Barthes, one he is keen to 'flag up' as it were, given Barthes' own invention of the parade ground scene. Allow me to follow the lion and the boy through the remainder of Barthes' text and this will lead us to the conclusion of this present reading.

These two examples become entwined, chained together (*enchaîne*) as Barthes attempts to lay out the different aspects of his general theory of Myth. For Barthes the signifier can be understood in two ways, as either the final term of the linguistic system of reference or the first moment in the 'mythical system'. Accordingly, he seeks to name this doubleness through the terminology '"meaning" (my name is lion, a Negro is giving the French salute)' as the last point of reference, and 'form' as the ideological import of the signifier. Barthes wishes to continue to separate the signified as a point outside this moment of ambiguity ('in the case of the signified, no ambiguity is possible: we shall retain the name concept'). While in terms of reference the signifier and signified produce a third term 'the sign', the 'chief peculiarity' of myth is that the signifier 'is already formed by the signs of language' and the third term of myth that combines meaning and form Barthes calls 'signification'. Now, Barthes seems to be in something of a muddle here. If the signified is inseparable from the 'sign' and the sign is already the signifier of myth, then how can he continue to insist on the non-ambiguous and separate 'concept' of the signified? Barthes is keen to attempt to retain some of the methodological clarity that informs his source material in Saussure's *Course in General Linguistics*; however, the proposition he is setting up around myth is one that will return to undermine any such set of distinctions, provisional and methodological as they might be. In this sense, perhaps the fault line in Barthes' theory of Myth lies in the very methodological principles he uses to elaborate the theory.

He continues that myth then is necessarily ambiguous, simultaneously meaning and form:

> As meaning, the signifier already postulates a reading, I grasp it through
> my eyes [*je le saisis des yeux*], it has a sensory reality (unlike the linguis-
> tic signifier, which is purely mental [*psychique*]), there is a richness in it:
> the naming of the lion, the Negro's salute are credible wholes [*ensembles
> plausibles*], they have at their disposal a sufficient rationality. As a total
> of linguistic signs, the meaning of the myth has its own value [*une valeur
> proper*], it belongs to a history [*il fait partie d'une histoire*], that of the
> lion or that of the Negro: in the meaning, a signification is already built,
> and could very well be self-sufficient if myth did not take hold of it [*ne
> la saisissait*] and did not turn it [*faisait tout d'un coup*] suddenly into an
> empty parasitical form. The meaning is already complete, it postulates a
> kind of knowledge, a past, a memory, a comparative order of facts, ideas,
> decisions. (Barthes, 1972, 117)

On the one hand, Barthes may at this point be assumed to be in agreement with my own restoration of the story of Diouf and the historical
circumstances surrounding the writing of Barthes' text. He seems to
suggest that the referential meaning of the photograph that precedes
its appropriation by myth is a complete and true history of the boy. It is
only the use of the image by myth that deprives the photograph of this
meaning and puts it to use in the ideological service of French colonialism. I do not think that this position is defensible either from the
point of view of 'interpretation' of this image or from a methodological
or theoretical point of view. In the case of the latter, I am concerned by
the idea that there remains a 'signified' (the true history of Diouf) that
is anterior to or preliminary to the operation of the ideological function of myth. That is to say, it would be possible to extract this photograph from its iterative history (its appearance in *Paris-Match*, its
citation by Barthes, his rereading here) and in a state of neutrality or
innocence understand the pure image prior to ideological inscription.
I am not convinced that any such originary meaning exists. Rather,
while Barthes is correct to say that the image belongs to the history
of the boy, the history of the boy is always already that of his appropriation by colonial ideology. There is no prelapsarian state in which
this image of the young Diouf exists prior to his representation as a
subject of Empire. Chronologically speaking the photograph was taken
on the occasion of his visit to Paris, for the purpose of reporting the
event in *Paris-Match*. Through the editorial practice of the newsroom
it is chosen to represent by metonymy the story that the magazine

wishes to report; one might say as Barthes does of Bichon, to 'narrate'. From the very beginning the photograph is a material product of the material processes of Empire. Its meaning is irreducibly conceptual but in its singularity and concentration it collapses all of the distinctions between the conceptual and non-conceptual orders of western Occidentalism, between the logos and the machine gun.

The history that it tells of Diouf is that of a colonial appropriation without limit, in terms of both its material practices and the way that Barthes himself appropriates the image as an example in his essay. Diouf is a '*Nègre*' from the very beginning, positioned by the French colonial system, the army that dresses and educates him, *Paris-Match* which photographs him and Barthes who recognises him and names him repeatedly as '*un Nègre*' in the same way as he identifies Bichon's friends. There is no final moment of reference in which a meaning is held back from myth. The photograph is ambiguous, Barthes is correct here, because it does not know and can never in principle know anything other than its initial and immediate appropriation by ideology. The ambiguity arises not because there is a true meaning overlayed by a false one but because its meaning as such depends upon the possibility of an at least double understanding of the image as it arrives. The picture is a colonial appropriation but there remains within the image itself sufficient and unsaturable resources for it to be understood otherwise. In the presentation of the 'Negro giving the French salute' there is reasonable doubt and sufficient pliability for us to resist the ideological insistence. However, this pliability is the structuring principle of all meaning, not the consequence of a primordial or orginary truth that predates signification at the level of an unmediated and unsigned 'concept'. There is no 'pre' or 'alternative' history of Diouf that both comes before this image and can be deduced from this image. Rather, this image is the concentrated history of Diouf and it is the play of meaning within the image that is itself historical. History in this sense is the simultaneous play of difference and its repression. This history, it might be said, is not a happy one, but to my mind there is sufficient ambiguity in this image to enable a resistance to determination that at once undoes a final appropriation by colonialism and every subsequent attempt to rename and recover the meaning of the image. There is obviously a history of Diouf the person that might be told but only through a syntagm of other signs, themselves always already mediated and always already inflected and inverted by both ideology and the resistance to it. Barthes says that myth empties out this true meaning in a parasitic way; my counter suggestion would be that there can only ever by something like myth and that the parasitic form is endemic to the signifying process, which if it is truly 'empty' then is always already empty and achieves the fullness of its meaning in this emptiness. I am not sure here either why Barthes imagines that the naming of the lion has a 'sensory reality' and that the linguistic signifier ('which is purely mental') does not: as if the complexity of meaning involved in writing 'my name is lion' on a page is any different from saying it to oneself, assuming one ever would outside of the institutional mediation of Latin classes.

The objection might be raised here, what do Barthes' shortcomings as a theorist or his complicity in the racist discourse of 1950s France matter if both this present reader and Barthes come to the same conclusion regarding colonialism and the necessity to reinvest in the history of Diouf? Up to a point this is a valid objection, I am not hammering Barthes for his insensitive vocabulary and we are all in one way or another complicit with the systems we oppose, giving ourselves up to that complicity in different ways. However, I would like to suggest that Barthes' position here arises in spite of his theoretical model not because of it, and that the reason such a position emerges is that Barthes is too much of a writer to be held back by his own theoretical exposition. Barthes suggests of signification that 'when it becomes form [myth], the meaning leaves its contingency behind, it empties itself, it becomes impoverished, history evaporates, only the letter remains'. I find this a curious idea, namely that whenever meaning is carried away by ideology, contingency and history are lost. On the contrary, surely ideology installs a history, perhaps a certain idea of History is synonymous with ideology as such, while it is contingency that ensures that the final determination of ideology never exhausts or empties meaning. Barthes describes it as 'a paradoxical permutation in the reading operations, an abnormal regression from meaning to form', from the linguistic sign full of meaning to the empty mythical signifier:

> If one encloses *quia ego nominor leo* in a purely linguistic system, the clause finds again there a fullness, a richness, a history [*histoire*]: I am an animal, a lion, I live in a certain country, I have just been hunting, they would have me share my prey with a heifer, a cow and a goat; but being the stronger, I award myself all the shares for various reasons, the last of which is quite simply that *my name is lion*. But as the form of the myth, the clause hardly retains anything of this long story [*histoire*].

> The meaning contained a whole system of values: a history, a geography, a morality, a zoology, a Literature. The form has put all this richness at a distance [*éloigné*]: its newly acquired penury calls for a signification to fill it. The story [*l'histoire*] of the lion must recede [*reculer*] a great deal in order to make room for the grammatical example, one must put the biography of the Negro [*nègre*] in parentheses if one wants to free the picture, and prepare it to receive its signified. (Barthes, 1972, 117–18)

This methodological distinction between 'form' as the first moment of myth and 'meaning' as the last moment of pure linguistic signification is going to be difficult to sustain. At the limit point when will it be possible to decide we have crossed over into myth and how, when we are in myth, will it be possible to hold off the structure of the pure signifier? And in what way can this purity continue? Not to labour a point but my position would be that this meaning is always already impure, implicated, hybrid and complex.

Insofar as the signifier, as Barthes suggests, is historical then this history is always already ideologically inscribed ('a whole system of values'). All the histories, geographies, moralities, zoologies and literatures of the world are ideological. There can be no point of signification, and no history as the play of its consequences can therefore be prior to myth. Equally, although the biography of Diouf or the story of the lion is said to 'recede a great deal' there must remain traces of it legible in the presentation of myth and so contingency, ambiguity and reading are possible beyond the determination of 'form'. While Barthes suggests the history must be put in parentheses in order for the ideological signified to take precedence, he goes on to qualify this in a significant way:

> But the essential point in all this is that the form does not suppress the meaning, it only impoverishes it, it puts it at a distance [*éloigner*] , it holds it at one's disposal. One believes that the meaning is going to die, but it is a death with reprieve [*une mort en sursis*]; the meaning loses its value, but keeps its life, from which the form of the myth will draw its nourishment. The meaning will be for the form an instantaneous reserve of history [*histoire*], a tamed richness, which it is possible to call and dismiss [*éloigner*] in a sort of rapid alternation: the form must constantly be able to be rooted again [*puisse reprendre racine*] in the meaning and to get there what nature it needs for its nutriment [*s'y alimenter en nature*]; above all, it must be able to hide there. It is this constant game of hide-and-seek between the meaning and the form which defines myth. (Barthes, 1972, 118)

We might describe this relationship between 'form' and 'meaning' in Barthes' essay then as dialectical. The myth is parasitic on the pure signification that both sits in reserve as the myth articulates its ideological operation and is what disguises that ideological operation within the articulation of myth. This situation is seductive but still I am not satisfied with the separation of parts here. Insofar as myth is a question of an always already impure language then as a matter of writing beyond semiology it calls for a thinking about 'the dialecticity of dialectics that is itself fundamentally not dialectic', as Derrida puts it one of the interviews with Maurizio Ferraris.[124] As Barthes' own characterisation of the biography of the lion and Diouf demonstrates, what we might call his writerly apprehension of the silences that must be addressed, within any dialectical situation there remains an element that does not allow itself to be integrated into the systematicity of the dialectic but that presents non-oppositional difference that exceeds the dialectic, which is itself always oppositional. This is what Derrida means by the supplement and is here represented by that which can be contained by neither the form of myth nor the purity of signification but which moves between the two, being mastered by neither, and outflanking the necessity of the binary structure. Here we have the biography, literature and zoology of the lion, the story of Diouf. This history does not allow itself to be dialectised and, as that which is not dialectical, is necessarily then recuperated by the dialectic that it relaunches. 'Thus the dialectic consists', says Derrida, 'precisely in dialectizing the non-dialectizable'.[125] This scenario is not recognisable as the dialectic in any easy sense of synthesis, totalisation, identification and transcendence. Rather this non-dialectical dialecticity of the dialectic is a form of synthesis without synthesis, what Derrida frequently terms 'ex-appropriation', which is both an essentially anti-dialectical concept and the necessary condition of dialectics as such. It is the non-dialectical dialecticity of the story of Diouf that both provides the nourishment for myth and is the place where myth hides, although there is neither myth nor story outside of the image itself. The biography or history is synthesised by the image but despite its singular articulation, it exceeds the image. The biography is interiorised within the image, keeping the otherness of Diouf present within the ideological presentation. The doubleness of language allows meaning to be faithful to Diouf but this faithful interiorisation is unfaithful at the same time as the ideological inscription of the image effaces the radical otherness of Diouf (holding him at a distance as Barthes puts it).

The image is obliged to harbour something that is greater and other than itself, both appropriating and singularising Diouf and ex-appropriating itself. Thus meaning carries the image beyond its own ideological determination, escaping itself into the fullness of its non-saturable meaning. Diouf resists his appropriation; as Barthes puts it, 'The form of myth is not a symbol: the Negro who salutes is not the symbol of the French Empire: he has too much presence, he appears as a rich, fully experienced, spontaneous, innocent *indisputable* image'. To an extent this is true, although one might question the idea of what is meant by 'fully experienced' and 'spontaneous' in the context of this deferral of meaning, as well as the notion of an 'innocent' image in the context of the economy of implication suggested by the picture. It is certainly not indisputable, the 'true story' of Diouf is no more indisputable than the myth. Barthes qualifies this again in relation to the dialectical hide-and-seek he proposes: 'but at the same time this presence is tamed, put at a distance, made almost transparent; it recedes a little, it becomes the accomplice of a concept which comes to it fully armed, French imperiality: once made use of, it becomes artificial'. The 'presence', if this is what it is, and not in some complex way a discernible absence, is both put at a distance (a sort of tele-phonic image) and rendered artificially transparent when deployed by myth. The confusion here and the methodological cumbersomeness in Barthes seems to me to come from his use of a metaphorics of inside and outside to attempt to portion off true meaning from ideology while recognising, quite rightly, their coterminous presentation in the image.

As an alternative one might turn here to what deconstruction much later terms 'the secret', the notion that the image or the sentence might present itself and in so doing also present the impossibility of its final interpretation. The image of Diouf presents all that there is to know about him but at the same time we cannot read this image to exhaustion. Right under our very noses or eyes the image avows all that can be said but simultaneously as a condition of this saying a secret is disavowed. There is no hidden meaning, no buried treasure to dig up, the secret is all on the surface, we know what it is but still it eludes us and we cannot master it finally. Thus, the image of Diouf presents all of its meaning, ideological and historical, at the same time. All meaning is avowed in the image at the same time as escaping from us. Accordingly one might say that the one thing that the image would like us to understand is the ideological inscription of Diouf but the resistance of the image to such determination leads to the undoing of any such resolve by the history or narrative, if you prefer, of Diouf; only for the attempted imposition of any notion of purity and authority in that narrative to be rendered equally impossible as the image insists structurally on its failed attempt at denotation. However, Barthes' model of signification through myth works on a dialectical principle and scrambles for a vocabulary and conceptual model to describe this endless escape of language. His interest is at once in using a certain model of the ideological that lies barely half-submerged in his essay while turning that model around to take account of something as complex as the signification of cultural texts. Insofar as the *Mythologies* become a foundation stone for the enterprise of cultural studies, the entire apparatus of the study of popular culture is grounded on a defective corner stone. This does not render such study or cultural studies per se obsolete or misguided, it is simply that the model of ideology-critique that forms the theoretical predicate for the exercise needs to be opened up to further scrutiny.

For Barthes here 'history' is a problematic term. He would like to use it in a double way, as both the content of the pure signifier of 'meaning' and an agency that lies beyond this dialectic but that equally contributes to its determination. He begins the next paragraph of this section of the essay 'Let us now look at the signified: this history which drains out of the form will be wholly absorbed by the concept.' The concept here refers not to the unambiguous 'signified' that Barthes has previously, after Saussure, named 'concept' but the intention of the myth, in the case of Diouf 'French imperiality'. Hence the true history of Diouf made transparent (drained) by myth is absorbed by the mythical concept, the determination of which Barthes goes on to say 'is at once historical and intentional'. So, history sits both inside and outside of myth, constructing myth as much as it is appropriated by myth. And as Barthes' argument continues to unfold one notes that the mythic concept is in turn also an initiator of history. Grammatical exemplarity and French imperiality are 'the very drives behind the myth'; their concepts are said to reconstitute 'a chain of causes and effects, motives and intentions'. These concepts are, according to Barthes, 'in no way abstract' like 'form' but rather 'filled with a situation. Through the concept, it is a whole new history which is implanted in the myth'. Now, as with the case of the purely mental linguistic signifier versus the 'sensory reality' of 'meaning', once again we have the introduction of a division between a somehow abstract mythical form and a historical concept. Bearing in mind that 'meaning' is the last moment of language before it becomes the first moment of form and in so doing seems to cross over or cross back from sensory reality into the abstract only to be claimed again by the mythical concept. This back and forward is becoming difficult to track and one finds it hard to imagine how this might all work in practice beyond an experience of instantaneous switching or the simultaneous presentation of all meaning at the same time in such a way that neither myth nor signified can ever truly dominate the other. Once Barthes' model is put into play against the examples of the lion and the boy soldier, he is once again forced to give ground on the permeability of his method.

He begins with a lyrical outline of the condition of the pupil in the *lycée* that leads through a revolving door to Diouf:

> In the name of the lion, first drained of its contingency, the grammatical example will attract my whole existence: Time, which caused me to be born at a certain period when Latin grammar is taught; History, which sets me apart, through a whole mechanism of social segregation, from the children who do not learn Latin; pedagogic tradition, which caused this example to be chosen from Aesop or Phaedrus; my own linguistic habits, which see the agreement of the predicate as a fact worthy of notice and illustration. The same goes for the Negro-giving-the-salute: as form, its meaning is shallow, isolated, impoverished; as the concept of French imperiality, here it is again tied to the totality of the world: to the general History of France, to its colonial adventures, to its present difficulties. (Barthes, 1972, 119)

Everything we have been saying about Barthes in this essay finds its way into this concentrated passage. Barthes the writer overspills Barthes the structuralist theorist to provide a more complete and reasoned estimation of his problematic. The schoolchild who learns Latin in the France of the 1950s where no Latin is spoken is not a simple or innocent case. The '*Nègre*' on the front cover of *Paris-Match* overruns the limits of this page, he is connected to the whole history of France and to her 'present difficulties', by which I take Barthes to mean the War in Algeria and the rise of popular right-wing sentiment. The inscription and determination of Diouf by what Barthes calls 'Myth' cannot hold for long:

> Truth to tell, what is invested in the concept is less reality than a certain knowledge of reality; in passing from the meaning to the form, the image loses some knowledge: the better to receive the knowledge in the concept. In actual fact, the knowledge contained in a mythical concept is confused, made of yielding, shapeless associations. One must firmly

stress this open character of the concept; it is not at all an abstract, purified essence; it is a formless, unstable, nebulous condensation, whose unity and coherence are above all due to its function. (Barthes, 1972, 119)

The mythological concept is historical precisely because it draws together an endless chain of associations ('my whole existence', 'the general History of France', there can be nothing outside of this in these cases) only for Myth's failed attempt at denotation to show that such histories are not some unshakeable concrete reality but 'a certain knowledge of reality' that is confused, yielding and shapeless. This suggests an outpouring of meaning that goes far in excess of any delimited dialectic. It is only the function of Myth, what we might call its textual character or its linguistic nature, that somehow ensures the appearance of 'unity and coherence' through a centrifugal force of reference, an illusion that is undone by the openness of the text that spills the contents of this concept over the pages of meaning. Barthes goes on to liken this condensed openness to latent content in Freud. The parallel is acute because while Barthes makes the concession of appealing to authority to demonstrate the validity of his paradox, he happens to appeal to an authority whose writing is frequently wracked by the same contortions as we find in Barthes; namely, the difficulty of having correctly identified the impossibility of closure in meaning and metaphysics only to continue to attempt to use a vocabulary that is metaphysical through and through in order to describe this radical alterity. Such tension leads to all the wonderful black holes in the text of Freud, where his method is incommensurate with the implications of his insights and only his skill as a narrator and writer carries his text beyond logical aporia. We find the same situation in Barthes as his writing that obeys its own laws of disseminative possibility wriggles free of the theoretical model that structures it. In this way, Barthes' own text is itself a demonstration of the inadequacies of the very thing it seeks to promote.

I will call a halt to this reading of 'Myth Today' at this point, even though the figures of Diouf and the lion run ahead of us for several pages yet. To do justice to the pair I would be required to follow Barthes' texts to the level of the sense-eme and to work forensically, in the style of the Barthes of *S/Z* or the essay on Poe's 'Valdemar', in order to present the galaxy of possible meanings these two generate. However, my point has been amply made and the resources within Barthes' own writing duly identified to suggest the ways in which the essay 'Myth Today' overspills its own ideological limits. It is simultaneously the most compelling index of the *Mythologies* and not part of them, an afterthought indeed, to create coherence that is itself as inchoate and conflictual as the texts they describe. It is simultaneously writerly and theoretical and at its most theoretical when writing takes over and most writerly when theorising. It is a remarkable text that continues to overspill its contents and context, running all the way to us today through historical resonance and its resonating of history itself. It deserves today to be read and reread with all the resources and rigour of the theoretical endeavour it gave rise to. Its richness and permeability in this respect are testament to the strength of both its writing and its theory, as if we have ever managed to separate out the two or would ever want to. As Barthes says of his own writing career, 'I differ perhaps from colleagues who are close to me in other ways, [in] that my concern is not to show the relationships between semiology and ideology or anti-ideology, in short between semiology and the political, but rather to pursue a general and systematic enterprise, polyvalent, multidimensional, the fissuration of the symbolic and its discourse in the West.'[126] Having considered the writing and life of Roland Barthes as an example of the aporias of the public realm, I am reminded of his own description of André Gide, 'He was a Protestant. He played the piano. He talked about desire. He wrote. (Barthes 1985, 261.) Like Heidegger's description of Aristotle (that he was born, he worked, he died) what remains of Barthes today is that he wrote.

When I began writing this text on Barthes, the question that led me was how one might read Barthes today, in a time of terror and during another long-running foreign war. Behind this thought lay another more utilitarian question: how might the text of Barthes help us to understand this moment? While it may not be possible to provide an answer to either of these questions directly, the case of Barthes has, for me, demonstrated a particular problematic in the relation between academic life, critical thinking, published writing, teaching and leverage within the public space of citizenship. This network of relations is always complicated and contradictory and, as the phrase goes, overdetermined. As this study draws to a close, the issue that confronts the critical thinker like a toothache is not so much the war in Iraq or the occupation of Afghanistan by western forces, although neither has gone away. Rather, it is the rapid acceleration of the so-called 'credit crunch' into a potentially apocalyptic moment for the western model of capitalism. Such a situation calls for a sustained and sober analysis, a deconstruction of capital and its mythologies if you will. One cannot point to a moment in the text of Barthes that will help us understand what is happening to global markets at this time (as Barthes himself felt insecure in 1977 in the movement from the oil crisis to the epoch of neoliberalism: 'What seems new to me in the current situation [1977] is that I can't find any touchstone for guidance' [Barthes 1985, 269]). This is a new materiality that has arrived in the here and now and for which we as yet have no philosophical or theoretical frame of reference by which to explain it. However, I think the point of this study has not been to attempt to recover from the Barthes under-used or neglected theoretical tools to apply to present conditions. On the contrary, I have been at pains to point out the structural inadequacy of Barthes' methodology even as it reinvents the Marxist heritage of Ideology for his own contemporary moment. Instead this study has sought to recognise a certain spirit of Barthes, one that places Barthes in a line of critical inheritance within Modernity, that includes Benjamin and Adorno as exemplars of transformative critique of the present conditions of thinking and critical engagement. In that spirit of Barthes then, how might one begin to read (as displacement) the situation of the credit crunch that has witnessed the nationalisation of the American banking system and the wholesale collapse of the ideological creditability an entire model of so-called globalisation and economics? I cannot answer that question here but I suspect that the answer might lie in the Nietzsche of the later Barthes. As he says in a 1972 interview, 'I believe that nihilism is the only possible philosophy for our current situation. But I must immediately add that I do not confuse nihilism with violent, radically destructive behaviour, or – on a deeper level – with behaviour that is more or less neurotic or hysterical. Nihilism is a type of reflection and utterance (because problems must always be framed in terms of language) which demands an effort of intelligence and a certain mastery of language.'[127] I cannot answer that question here. This particular adventure in writing must now come to a close. I put a marker down here as a promissory note to the reader. We will return to it later, *always a return*.

To answer one of the initial questions with which we began, what remains for us today of Roland Barthes, once we have stripped away the scientificity and the dream of structure and questioned his model of the sign and his faith in an unalienable and transparent reality? Perhaps you might say 'very little, almost nothing'. However, one does not have to be a true believer in Barthes to continue to wish to return to Barthes again and again for intellectual nourishment. This book in truth has yet to really begin the task of reading Barthes anew in a sustained and systematic way, we have yet to move beyond a fascination with the *Mythologies* and the disavowed moment of cultural studies in France. So much remains to be read and to be reckoned with. How then shall we read Barthes tomorrow or read after Barthes, in the manner of Barthes or at least a certain Barthes? I will conclude this present scene of reading by borrowing from one of my favourite moments in Barthes. In *Roland Barthes par Roland Barthes* he discusses an important image for his writing, 'that of the ship *Argo* (luminous and white), each piece of which the Argonauts gradually replaced, so that they ended with an entirely new ship, without having to alter either its name or form'.[128] On this principle surely it is possible to continue to write social critique today in the manner of Barthes? Through substitution, combination, correction, repair and an insistence on nomination one can continue while very little, almost nothing, remains of the origin. What matters here is the cause of the *Argo* not its essence or component parts. Thus as Argonauts on an interminable voyage we must return to our desks where sentences are adventures.[129]

3   An Answer to the Question: What Is Cultural Studies?

To hear Barbara Engh tell it, it all begins with Kant.[1] I have stated elsewhere that if cultural studies, troubled by its own rapid institutionalisation, wishes to reorientate itself it ought to do so with a turn, if not a return, to Kant, rather than, say, to Birmingham or even Derrida.[2] This will now require a little justification in the light of the extended commentary on Roland Barthes and the origins of a French cultural studies in the previous chapter. I think that there are three 'strong' theoretical claims made with regard to Barthes in the text that you will have just read. First, what we call cultural studies has a much longer provenance than one might expect and one that places Barthes, as the logothete of contemporary cultural study, in an extended tradition of philosophical reflection on the present that can be traced through the likes of Benjamin and Adorno to Kant and the Enlightenment tradition. Second, an alternative history of ideology and demystification as a concept and operation can be traced coterminous with this and according to the same indices. Third, something like a method of critical inquiry that followed the historical play of différance in a text, tangentially referred to here as 'cultural archaeology', emerges from this rereading of Barthes today. I will have to postpone a fuller examination of these last two points until another occasion. However, what follows is an attempt to make good on the first leg of this theoretical tripos, to properly place both Barthes and cultural studies in relation to its philosophical heritage and to determine how such a relation might function under the institutional circumstances of today. The significant difference between the cultural studies that pervades the humanities today and the 'cultural studies' of Barthes is that while Barthes' inquiry is the product of a literate media and counter-culture that had a space not only outside of the university but in some important respects in reaction to the university structures of its time, the cultural studies of today is not only comfortable within the university but importantly antithetical to a reductive mediatic sphere, which simultaneously disavows it as not rigorous enough to be a true humanity and too abstruse for media consumption. It is the institutionalisation of cultural studies across the Anglophone academy that marks the intervening years between Barthes' early critical practice and what we call cultural studies today. We must therefore attend to this problem first.

Classifying culture

Given that, literally speaking, 'cultural studies' is that which studies culture, I will begin by paying a visit to Raymond Williams' unsurpassed contribution to theoretical precision, *Keywords*, a book written in 1976 some two decades after the work of Barthes' *Mythologies*.[3] Under the entry for 'culture' Williams states that 'culture is one of the two or three most complicated words in the English language'.[4] The etymology of 'culture' as an English word is complex, derived from the Latin *cultura*, which has at its root *colore*, meaning to inhabit, cultivate, protect, honour and worship. From the beginning then, in understanding the meaning of culture, we are faced with problems of architectonics, colonialism, politics and the religious. *Colore* is the root of *colonus* and so 'colony', and of *cultus* and so 'cult'. Agriculture and cultivation are thus etymologically linked to the colonialism of the Roman Empire and to the aura of Roman deities, but the significance of this genealogy of culture is that in its earliest expression culture was a noun of process. The key moment in Williams' definition is the figural shift from Humanism on into the eighteenth century, in which the metaphorical significance of cultivation is transferred from husbandry to human development in general, and so 'an extension of particular process to a general process, which the word could abstractly carry'.[5] This is as much to say that it is at this point in the archaeology of culture that a certain metaphoric transference takes place through the principle of metonymy (husbandry standing for human development in general), and thus what we might call, after de Man, the rhetoric of culture is initiated and the conceptualisation of culture begins (i.e. the category of culture as a concept in the western tradition).

Culture as a category will present certain difficulties for philosophy, while it will be philosophy's task as the transcendental discipline to explain culture, and philosophy cannot be held accountable to a thing called culture (of which it is undoubtedly a part) because culture is now a philosophical concept. It becomes a philosophical concept by its inclusion, examination and expansion in the texts of Enlightenment philosophy, of which the work of Rousseau, Kant, Herder, Hegel and Hobbes would be only the most obvious touchstones. In this way, the question of culture in its modern genealogy is inextricably linked to the development of the aesthetic and to the project of critique and ultimately to the long history of Modernity itself. Williams points out, as Bourdieu will later on,[6] that it is in this figural shift to culture as a general process that, through the cognate terms 'cultivation' and 'cultivated', the idea of culture 'acquired definite class associations'.[7] The development of the word in English is related, says Williams, to its progress through French and especially German. In particular, Williams points to Herder's use of the term in *Ideas on the Philosophy of the History of Mankind*, in which he, as Williams reads him, posits, as a challenge to the idea of 'civilisation' or 'culture' as the historical development of humanity in line with an ideal of European identity, the notion of '"cultures" in the plural: the specific and variable cultures of different nations and periods, but also the specific and variable cultures of social and economic groups within a nation'.[8] That is to say, for good or ill, in Herder's text one can find an inflection of the term 'culture' that is not only popularised in nineteenth- and twentieth-century anthropology but is the understanding of the term upon which cultural studies as a disciplinary event is predicated. Williams proposes that under the influence of Herder European Romanticism provided an alternative to the idea of human development based on progress and civilisation. This is quite a claim and would require a book-length study to interrogate. Williams does go on to qualify this assertion by noting that the development of plural 'cultures' as a concept was used in the early nineteenth century in England, Germany and France to emphasise the idea of national and traditional cultures, including the emerging notion of a 'folk-culture'. In this way, says Williams, politically the term 'veered between radicalism and reaction and very often, in the confusion of major social change, fused elements of both'.[9] The etymology of a word is no doubt frequently over-determined but in the case of 'culture' one can trace a certain inchoateness that would seem to be structural to the concept itself and that goes some way to explaining the elasticity with which the category is used today.

What we might call here the reactionary use of 'culture' is linked, Williams continues, to criticism of the abstract rationalism of the Enlightenment and the inhuman industrialisation of Modernity. Deployed in this way, 'culture' comes to name something like spiritual progress in contrast to the material development of Modernity (once again 'culture' is clearly marked by the structure of the religious). To add to the complexity of its flexible and contradictory development, Humboldt reverses this distinction, rendering culture as material and civilisation as spiritual development. In Chapter 2 of *The Phenomenology of Spirit* Hegel describes culture as 'the world of self-alienated Spirit', implicating both spirituality and materiality in a single formulation. Culture as materiality can be read as a continuation of the association of culture with the material process of agriculture and has its residual trace when one speaks today of bacterial or germ cultures. Culture as spirituality, on the other hand, coming from *cultus* and early religious associations, defines the development of the category in the texts of the Enlightenment as an independent and abstract noun describing a general process of intellectual, aesthetic and spiritual development. This usage is in contrast to and coterminous with its development as an independent noun signifying the way of life of particular groups at particular times. Both of these senses are then combined in what Williams suggests is a much later usage, which he dates to the late nineteenth century, citing Matthew Arnold as an example, whereby culture describes the works and practices of intellectual and artistic activity. In this way, a further rhetorical drift occurs in which the meaning of the intellectual and spiritual process of culture is transferred to the works that represent and sustain it. This metaphorico-metonymic transition is now all but indistinguishable in something like cultural studies, the adjective 'cultural' itself dating, according to Williams, from the 1870s and established by the 1890s only after the anthropological and artistic-intellectual sense of culture had become dominant.

The point here is not necessarily the desire for conceptual clarity within cultural studies, but to point out that the contradictions of cultural studies might be explained by the structural complexity of the concept of culture itself. As Williams puts it, the complexity 'is not finally in the word but in the problems which its variations of use significantly indicate'.[10] In this respect Williams' text is doubly interesting in that it does not name the emergent discipline of 'cultural studies' as such, of which it is a founding text. Rather, in the concluding sentences of the entry Williams points to the initial impetus of cultural studies as a challenge to claims of dominant culture, noting that any Anglo-Saxon hostility towards the term culture can usually be traced (with the temporary exception of anti-German feeling during the Great War to propaganda concerning *Kultur*) to 'claims to superior knowledge, refinement and distinctions between "high" art and popular art and entertainment'.[11] What is revealing here is that even at the end of Williams' brilliant elucidation of the difficult genealogy of this word, he gestures towards adopting the anthropological use of the term in a not necessarily complicated way in order to obtain political leverage within the academy. He concludes, 'It is interesting that the steadily extending social and anthropological use of culture and cultural and such formations as sub-culture (the culture of a distinguishable smaller group) has, except in certain areas (notably popular entertainment), either by-passed or effectively diminished the hostility and its associated unease and embarrassment.'[12] The meaning of 'culture', then, remains to be contested, for Williams, around the popular and the sub-culture of the working class. Thus, British contemporary cultural studies was born.

However, there remains a use of the term 'culture' in Williams' book which resists explaination, namely the subtitle to *Keywords: A Vocabulary of Culture and Society*. The book defines 'a vocabulary of culture' (let us leave 'society' here for another day) and in so doing is compelled to define 'culture' itself, it being 'one of the two or three most complicated words'. In this way, 'culture', for Williams, is both the universal set and an element of that set. It is both the object of definition and beyond definition, inside and outside of his project of conceptual clarity, demonstrating the impossibility of a definition of culture that would be anything other than an exact map and repetition of the thing it represents. Culture, one might say, is the supplementary term in Williams' text that undoes the suggested logocentrism of 'keywords' to demonstrate that any complete index of 'culture and society' would necessarily be the inexhaustible history of all culture and society. 'Culture' here is an aberration in de Man's sense, being one element of a series used transcendentally with respect to that series in order to totalise, dominate or explain it.[13] In this way, the invaginated architectonics of the category of culture are considerably complicated and the work of cultural studies (as that which studies 'culture') is potentially endless. However, in this sense cultural studies is precisely that which does not study 'culture' (i.e. the philosophical category, the limits of which we have been trying to establish), but rather like Williams at the end of his definition, cultural studies slips out of this category into the study of the sub-set 'cultural' (i.e. the anthropological practices of sub-cultural groups), replacing the one with the other in a rhetorical legerdemain, in which the metonymic sub-set stands in the place of the wider metaphoric concept. The consequence of this slippage for cultural studies is that while it offers the illusion of a firm promise of radicality, cultural studies in fact falls into the most metaphysical of gestures in which a stable notion of culture is substituted for a more problematic and endlessly open appreciation of the term. In fact, cultural studies relies for its understanding of culture on the same metaphysical concept used to justify nineteenth-century nationalisms and the construction of '*volk-kultur*'. This classification of 'culture' is at least as reactionary as it was empowering for 'British cultural studies', in that while the valorisation of working-class culture as a sub-group provided a point of theoretical departure for this work, the work of cultural studies itself does nothing to interrogate the one concept upon which it depends but which it can never adequately explain, i.e. 'culture' itself. An emphasis on 'popular culture', as Williams points to at the end of his definition, is entirely historically specific, given that today a significant number of the woes of cultural studies can be traced to a too easy assertion of the importance of the 'popular' as a de facto radical gesture, when in truth much of what might constitute the 'popular' today is a construct of global capital and anything but radical. This tricky situation for cultural studies arises from a reliance on an essentially metaphysical understanding of the category of culture, which leaves the discipline beholden to a reactionary conceptual framework (at least as reactionary as it is radical) and structured by the trace of the religious, which it so often piously dismisses. The 'cult' in cultural studies might go some way to explaining the discipline's desire to found alternative canons of popular culture, which imagines itself as a challenge to high culture, while doing nothing to displace the very idea of canon formation, which is the founding principle of the metaphysical illusion that substitutes 'cultural objects' for the 'cultural process' itself.

Now, I am not proposing to correct this genealogical misprision by insisting on an idea of culture as the progress of civilisation; this would be to repeat the metaphysical gesture by choosing an alternative dead-end for the concept. Rather, it is necessary to be aware of what is truly radical in cultural studies, namely the divisible instability of the conceptual category it studies. It is, as Williams says earlier on in his text, 'the range and overlap of meanings that is significant',[14] not the service-ability of the term. In fact, it ought to be the business of cultural studies to render the term 'culture' unemployable in any useful context given its immanent heterogeneity and conceptual difficulty. To this end, it will be necessary for cultural studies to concentrate on the other term that it adopts so blithely but pays so little attention to, namely 'studies'. In order to achieve something like a meaningful understanding of the first term, 'culture', cultural studies will have to undertake some study and for the moment forgo the sort of 'representational readings' that leave it open to Tom Cohen's accurate attack when he speaks of 'the relapse of cultural studies into mimetic modes' and 'the strategies of historicism, or identity politics, or cultural studies that evade the problematic and programming of inscription'.[15] While Cohen is taking a pop at an easy if pervasive target (the representations-of-Scotsmen-on-film mode of cultural studies), if the discipline wishes to resist such accusations there needs to be more study and less culture. One might propose a course of study for the discipline in which it sought to understand why 'culture' might be a problematic term for philosophy, which both defines it and is part of it, sitting outside of it and subsumed by it. This exercise would pass from the architectonics of *civilis*, the foundation of the city state and *demos*, *eikos* and *nomos*, *mimesis*, *poesis*, *technē*, *physis* and *khora*, through the formalisation of critique under the hegemony of aesthetics, to Hegel's histories of Spirit, Nietzsche's genealogies and Heidegger's assertion that 'the business of culture' understood as technology is 'the basic form of appearance in which the will to will arranges and calculates itself in the unhistorical element of the world of completed metaphysics'.[16] Such a syllabus obviously names only a fraction of the potential scene of reading for cultural studies. This is a task that cannot be completed within the confines of this chapter, even if this chapter begins the labour hinted at here, namely to reclaim a tradition of thought that studied culture before the formal appellation of cultural studies was adopted as part of the myth of the autochthonous origins of the Birmingham School. This book points towards Barthes as one such signpost in a longer history.

Cultural studies in deconstruction

Having set up what we might call a 'deconstructive' endeavour (to decentre the palaeonymic name of Cultural Studies) let me momentarily postpone that work to interrogate the place of cultural studies in deconstruction, or more specifically the texts of the late Jacques Derrida, who unlike Barthes was a member of the French Grandes Écoles who lived through the dissemination of modern French thought through the Anglophone humanities as cultural studies. I have suggested throughout this book a proximity between Barthes and Derrida that has hitherto been underplayed by most commentary on both thinkers. However, I would like to emphasise here the relation between the heterodox analysis of Barthes from outside the university and the allergen of Derrida's deconstruction from within the academy. The intellectual positions of the two men are not necessarily compatible but I would like to suggest that they are both part of a critical philosophical inquiry into the very idea of 'today'. In this sense, Derrida's writing is close to the spirit of Barthes that I have been seeking to reclaim throughout this present study and so it will be productive to examine the way in which Derrida carries on this tradition for Barthes and why ultimately the idea of an institutional cultural studies is so problematic for such a tradition of enquiry. Derrida is a philosopher, even if the deconstruction of phallogocentrism as philosophy is always more than philosophy itself. He does not do cultural studies as such, although he has written extensively on the perennial concerns of cultural studies, such as television or contemporary politics. However, Derrida was an academic employed in the North American higher education system and thus could not fail to be familiar with the work of cultural studies in that context. I will resist the temptation to speak from another country of meaning and comment on something as distant to me as the protocols of the Napoleonic code that govern the space of philosophy in the French university system. However, it should be noted that the transplanting and rapid spread of cultural studies in the North American humanities has not been without its difficulties. The history of theory in the North American academy, and deconstruction's part in it, is somewhat over-determined (sadly, recovering and clarifying this narrative will also need to be postponed). The importation of a certain variety of cultural studies[17] into the North American scene has allowed a number of weeds to flower and obscured much indigenous growth, as well as producing productive hybrid varieties. Just as Derrida rarely refers to so-called 'theory' or 'postmodernism' (if he does so at all it is usually to distance himself from such terms), so too his citation of 'cultural studies' is usually brief and dismissive. I would like now to turn to a text by Derrida published

in 2001, when it would seem that Derrida felt unable to ignore the institutional fog of cultural studies, the essay 'The Future of the Profession
or the University without Condition (Thanks to the 'Humanities', What
Could Take Place, Tomorrow)'.[18]

In this text Derrida revisits his longstanding interest in the state of
the university.[19] He does so in relation to the themes mobilised in his
later writing, notably the notion of democracy-to-come as a *raison
d'être* for the humanities: 'I will call the unconditional university or
the university without condition: the principal right to say everything,
whether it be under the heading of fiction and the experimentation of
knowledge, and the right to say it publicly, to publish it'.[20] In this sense
the humanities are a space of the 'as if': 'this reference to public space
will remain the link that affiliates the new Humanities to the Age of
Enlightenment … it is also what fundamentally links the university,
and above all the Humanities, to what is called literature … as the right
to say everything publicly, or to keep it secret, if only in the form of
fiction'.[21] Of course, for Derrida this is not a future humanities but the
task of the humanities in the here and now. The point of the 'humanities to come' is to reaffirm a '"more-than-critical" (deconstructive)
unconditionality … in the university'.[22] The profession of the title then
refers to this affirmative deconstruction as a profession of faith, with all
the due complications Derrida renders around the idea of 'faith'. This
then, from a deconstructive point of view, is all very straightforward, if
not without complex consequences we do not have space to visit here.
My interest in this essay today lies in a comment made by Derrida (one
made in passing) towards the end of his text. After some reflections on
the privileged place afforded to philosophy by Kant in his architecture
of the university, Derrida notes: 'These Humanities to come will cross
disciplinary borders without, all the same, dissolving the specificity of
each discipline into what is called, often in a very confused way, indisciplinarity or into what is lumped with another good-for-everything
concept, "cultural studies"'.[23] Heaven – if there is such a thing – forbid
that the 'humanities to come' might be cultural studies but at the same
time cultural studies seems to be singled out here in a way no other
'discipline' is in the essay. Literary study, philosophy, theology, juris-
prudence and so on are all signalled as playing a role in the humanities
to come, while we are asked not to confuse 'cultural studies' with the
'humanities to come' as if 'cultural studies' were equivalent to inter-
disciplinarity, which is a structural relation between disciplines and
not a thing in itself. Certainly, cultural studies likes to think of itself as

interdisciplinary but now that the institution lays claim to the term as a distinct entity it is definitely a thing in its own right, with its own disciplinary knowledges and protocols. Cultural studies has now emerged from within closed disciplinary boundaries to occupy its own space in the humanities, enriching those disciplines it left behind, but I think it disingenuous to continue to claim that the practice of cultural studies today involves a dialogue between disciplines in any meaningful way. Furthermore, the space now afforded to cultural studies for its own practice simply is not contested any more. However, even if cultural studies may be interdisciplinary, interdisciplinarity is definitely not reducible to cultural studies. Derrida's comment here is the equivalent of confusing a verb (a process) with a noun (a thing), repeating the rhetorical misprision of culture identified by Williams.

Derrida's withering invocation of the name of 'cultural studies' no doubt points to a frustration with woolly thinking, whose looseness is mitigated by its supposed claim to radicality, the claim and the thinking in fact disguising a profoundly regressive modus vivendi. This is the characterisation of a certain cultural studies with which I am total agreement with Derrida and Tom Cohen – I suspect the irremediable literary critic Roland Barthes would have agreed with such exasperation. However, given my commentary above and my attempt to salvage something of cultural studies in this book, I would like to reply to Derrida's uncharacteristically reductive gesture here to open up what is designated by the nomial effect 'cultural studies'. It would be as suspicious to dismiss philosophy as such on the grounds of one's dissatisfaction with some of its institutional manifestations (and one can think of many so-called philosophical spaces that would find an accommodation of Derrida unconscionable). Similarly, it would be a mistake to belittle the idea of 'cultural studies' on the grounds of certain institutional excesses. What I am suggesting here is that cultural studies has a much older provenance than some of the late arrivals in the humanities such as English literature or art history. In this sense the space in which cultural studies has traditionally taken place is from within philosophy itself. Hence, philosophy has such a complex relation to cultural studies, one that is played out in the ambiguity of Derrida's passing comment. On the one hand, this might be read as a cursory dismissal of cultural studies as indicative of the failings of thought characteristic of the technocratic university. On the other hand, a less defensive reading of the sentence might suggest that there is nothing here to indicate that Derrida is actually dismissive of cultural studies as such. Rather, what he criticises is the confused thinking that equates cultural studies (or 'interdisciplinarity' as it is often invoked) with the necessary practice of crossing disciplinary boundaries without dissolving the specificity of disciplines. In this sense, an over-sensitive reading of this sentence in fact accuses Derrida of making the very error he is highlighting, namely confusing cultural studies with the traversing of disciplines.

It is interesting to note here that Derrida refers to cultural studies as a 'good-for-everything concept'. In this sense, what Derrida dismisses is not the quasi-disciplinary thing cultural studies but the idea of cultural studies as the interdisciplinary practice of the humanities. This is in marked contrast to, say, a Mieke Bal who positively endorses so-called 'cultural analysis' as both a remedy for cultural studies and a paradigm for all humanist enquiry.[24] Rather, what is at stake here is the very idea of cultural studies. Cultural studies is of little interest as (depending on the participant) a weak or quick version of media and film studies. Nor, is it of much relevance to the rest of the humanities as a sub-set of sociological or anthropological methodology. Cultural studies is only interesting when its immanent divisibility can catch out a thinker like Derrida. This sentence demonstrates the same rhetorical confusion we found in Williams' definition, namely the simultaneous reduction and invocation of the heterogeneity of the double operation of the conceptual material that 'culture' names. In Derrida there is the simultaneous dismissal of cultural studies as a bland ('good-for-everything') institutional platitude (in the case of Williams this is precisely what he felt necessary to valorise, historically and strategically, in his acceptance of the anthropological designation of 'cultural') and the recognition that the name of cultural studies cites a performative transformation of the university across disciplines. In this way, philosophy enacts its traditional problematic relationship with 'culture', in that it determines culture as a concept and in so doing sees itself subsumed in the very thing it defines. Similarly, Derrida's text calls for a crossing of disciplines as a transformative gesture and in so doing is caught in a 'call' that is characteristic of cultural studies. The philosophical text then feels it necessary to qualify that this transformative gesture is not equivalent to cultural studies but is in fact beyond the transformations already effected by cultural studies. Thus, in its desire to be philosophical and not 'cultural' the text must out 'cultural studies' cultural studies in order not to relapse into the 'mimetic modes' that the previous transformations of cultural studies qua institutional banality had already relapsed into. In the meanwhile, as the text dismisses a certain idea of cultural studies, it valorises a crossing of disciplines in the humanities, leaving open the question: according to which index is cultural studies actually being audited here? When is a work of literary studies that crosses boundaries still literary studies and not cultural studies? What is the relationship between a 'theoretically informed' cultural studies and the philosophical gesture that is in excess of philosophy as it attends to the exemplary or the political? This difficulty arises from the elastic ambiguity of the term 'cultural studies', which in a certain institutional context names a regressive mimetic appeal to representational modes of analysis of popular culture but which residually also names a general impulse to transformation and cross-disciplinary work within the humanities. Both impulses of cultural studies (what it can be and what it might be, its 'here and now' and 'what could take place tomorrow') are implied by Derrida's statement and so a certain manifestation of cultural studies is rebuked while a certain idea of cultural studies is simultaneously salvaged. One might refer to this situation as the quasi-transcendental nature of the idea of cultural studies, in which the work of the concept lies somewhere between the constant shuttling between its aspiration and its expression and mastered by neither. In this sense one might call cultural studies a 'quasi-discipline': it has departments and degree courses that take its name but in so doing must manifest themselves as something other than cultural studies, an allegory of a discipline.

While I may seem to be correcting Derrida I am obviously in agreement with his commentary on the humanities in general, namely the need for a 'more-than-critical (deconstructive) unconditionality' in the university. Once upon a time in the Anglophone academy this work was done by cultural studies, which transformed the space of the humanities by refusing to confine a mode of thought to the limits of traditional disciplines. In its initial phase cultural studies did this in a parasitic way, living within a host discipline to decentre and open out that discipline without dissipating the particularity of that discipline. One might think of Williams' work in English studies or Stuart Hall's in sociology, both following Barthes. In this way, cultural studies in its post-Barthes phase was an exemplary deconstruction of the humanities before we were ever familiar with the term deconstruction. In its nascent and contingent form one might even say that 'cultural studies', as a performative transformation of the academy, which was present in its absence and disappeared in its appearance, was a nonequal name equivalent to what we understand by 'deconstruction' or 'supplementarity'. Now, Derrida is correct when he points out that 'cross-disciplinarity' or 'inter-disciplinarity' cannot take place without the specificity of disciplines, and thus the institutional sclerosis of cultural studies is due not so much to the belief that an indisciplinary cultural studies can exist in isolation to the rest of the humanities as an end in itself but to the transformation of the initial decentring impulse of cultural studies into a discipline of its own. What remains interesting about cultural studies is the conceptual residue of its nomial effect, namely the task of a deconstructive unconditionality in the university. If this work does not reside in cultural studies as such any more then fine, let us make different interventions in the institution under another name or none at all.

However, the difficulty for cultural studies as such is then the task of living with the inheritance of the concept 'culture' and making good on the sorts of protocols of analysis it requires. Given that 'culture' as a concept subsumes every discipline in the humanities (including philosophy) it stands in a curious relation to all those other disciplines, at once crossing disciplines, falling between disciplines, immanent to disciplines and transcending disciplines. Cultural studies is the one discipline that draws on every other discipline while attempting to explain the object of those disciplines. Simultaneously, in deriving its protocols and methods from those disciplines, and in particular taking a philosophical notion of culture as its rationale, cultural studies struggles to lay claim to a distinctive disciplinarity as such and so in its institutional manifestation takes the form of a weak anthropology of the popular. The fog surrounding cultural studies in the academy, this 'good-for-everything concept', is then a consequence of the lack of clarity over the operation of the term 'cultural', a divisibility that is basic to the concept itself. As soon as there is cultural studies there is confusion because cultural studies is both a discipline (a thing in its own right) and in no way disciplinary, both inside the humanities and transcendent of the humanities, both beholden to philosophy and beyond philosophy.

Before turning to other citations of 'cultural studies' in the text of deconstruction, I would like to push this relationship between philosophy and cultural studies a little. On the one hand, the very serious project I have suggested above regarding the conceptual history of 'culture' may alarm many practitioners of cultural studies. From the point of view of cultural studies qua weak anthropology, this project looks like an attempt to recuperate the 'radical' impulses of cultural studies back into a study of dominant or high culture, namely the tradition of western philosophy, and on this reading 'cultural studies' becomes just another sub-set of philosophy like aesthetics or logic. If this is the impression I give then I do not apologise for it, with the caveat that one appreciate that if cultural studies is that strand of philosophy that attends to the formation of the concept 'culture' and deals with the place of the exemplary in philosophy, then philosophy itself is absolutely altered by cultural studies. That is to say, philosophy does not exist in transcendental isolation but all philosophy is in fact 'applied' philosophy, inseparable from historical and political conditions and functioning within the institutions that determine the parameters of the possibility of thought. Cultural studies, in this sense, may be the very opening of philosophy onto non-philosophy, which makes philosophy as such possible. Certainly, this idea of cultural studies is very far removed from the version of cultural studies attacked by Tom Cohen and the one close to the hearts of many people who work under the appellation of 'cultural studies', but it is one that has its roots in the philosophical tradition.

In his essay 'An Answer to the Question: What Is Enlightenment?' Kant writes that:

> *Enlightenment is the human being's emergence from his self-incurred minority. Minority* is inability to make use of one's own understanding without direction from another. This minority is self-incurred when its cause lies not in lack of understanding but in lack of resolution and courage to use it without direction from another. *Sapere aude*! [Dare to be wise!] … For this enlightenment … nothing is required but freedom, and indeed the least harmful of anything that could even be called freedom: namely, freedom to make public use of one's reason in all matters.[25]

I am less concerned here, in this instance, although it would be the sort of work that cultural studies might do, with an analysis of Kant's political accommodation of Fredrick William II. Rather, I turn to this essay in response to Derrida's affirmation of the university without condition, 'the principal right to say everything … and the right to say it publicly, to publish it', which remains for Derrida 'the link that affiliates the new Humanities to the Age of Enlightenment'. Foucault has already commented on this essay by Kant for us, suggesting that while the text does not provide an adequate explanation of Enlightenment or an account of the social, political and cultural transformations of the late eighteenth century, it is nevertheless an important essay in that it is exemplary of a turn in philosophical thought that sought to reflect critically on its own present.[26] This leads Foucault to the observation that one should not think of modernity as a period of history but as an '"attitude" … a mode of relating to contemporary reality; a voluntary choice made by certain people; in the end, a way of thinking and feeling; a way, too, of acting and behaving that at one and the same time marks a relation of belonging and presents itself as a task … [which] ever since its formation, has found itself struggling with attitudes of "countermodernity"'.[27] I find Foucault's analysis extremely suggestive in this context. There is a clear connection between Kant's description of the Enlightenment as the moment when reason is to be put to use in a public space without subjecting itself to authority and the development of critique as a philosophical method. Equally, there is a link between the intellectual endeavour of critique and the critical attitude to the present represented by the Enlightenment outlook of '*Sapere aude*!' It is significant, it seems to me, that also at this time 'culture' becomes a concern for philosophy. I would suggest that with this adoption of 'culture' as a philosophical concern (although in no way limited to the Enlightenment) comes a critical interrogation on the present and on ourselves, which as a way of philosophising characterises the long history of modernity. It is no doubt under such circumstances that the quasi-discipline, or sub-discipline, of 'cultural studies' emerges, even if it is not named, and develops its three defining traits: its concern with the present, its assumed worldly vocation and its desire to make an intervention in the institution that plays host to it. The latter two characteristics might be thought of as a manifestation of Kant's weak messianism, which wishes 'to make use of one's own understanding without direction from another'. While, as I have argued, the considerable conceptual complexity of 'culture' itself makes no systematic pronouncement on cultural studies possible, it needs to be said, in addition to my request that cultural studies pay attention to its conceptual history, that cultural studies studies nothing if it does not attend to the present. If we wished to complete the formal definition offered above, one might say that cultural studies (when it studies) is the branch of philosophy that critically reflects on the present. In this way, it is a considerably older enterprise than one might have been led to believe up to now, and is in fact as old as modernity itself. That is modernity qua attitude in the Foucauldian sense; the sort of attitude that Barthes demonstrates on a daily basis from the confines of his study, where, as Flaubert puts it, sentences are adventures.

The deconstruction of cultural studies

While Derrida appears to dismiss the loose thinking that surrounds cultural studies, there have been other more hospitable responses to cultural studies within the expanded text of deconstruction – among them Gary Hall's excellent *Culture in Bits* but also notable texts by J. Hillis Miller and Gayatri Spivak.[28] They are significant for us here because such appreciations of cultural studies are true to the rigorous literary inheritance of Barthes as well as the critical ethos of his engagement with culture. Miller begins with the conceptual difficulties of cultural studies, noting correctly that 'the universalizing idea of culture in cultural studies may be so all-inclusive as to be virtually empty, may be a place of exchange where the other turns into the same'.[29] This is a point well made concerning the recuperative power of the logos, which cultural studies in general persists in remaining wilfully blind too. However, Miller's concern in his writings on cultural studies is really with the perceived crisis in literary studies, remarking on 'the way many young scholars trained in literary study now feel so great a call to study popular culture that they more or less abandon canonical literature'.[30] I will continue to resist the temptation to comment unadvisedly on the American scene or even to plead guilty to being one of the generation abandoning literature, for I feel I still have much to say regarding the canonical, even if so-called 'literary studies' now affords less and less space for such comment, while within cultural studies it is less of a struggle to exercise 'the principal right to say everything … and the right to say it publicly, to publish it'. Rather, I am interested and concerned by the link Miller makes between the transformation of literary studies into cultural studies and 'the replacement of the Humboldtian university by the new technologized transnational university that serves the global economy'.[31]

As Miller usefully, if only strategically, redefines it for a cultural studies engaged with a critical reflection on the present, 'culture names the media part of a global consumerist economy'.[32] This then provides a *raison d'être* for cultural studies, namely that if one wishes to understand and challenge the ways in which power operates in the world today one must attend to the mediatic space and its images. Charged with this important task, Miller's complaint regarding cultural studies is that it falls back on 'thematic' modes of reading and so 'university administrators unconsciously view the introduction of cultural studies as a nonthreatening change that leaves old institutional structures

more or less intact'.[33] What is lost in the transformation of literary studies into cultural studies, for Miller, is the more-than-critical, deconstructive, unconditionality of reading. While anti-theoretism disables
cultural studies as a recuperation by the conservative gesture of ideological mimetism, reading should not be confused with 'theory'. For
Miller, deconstruction is 'good reading', which ought to be able to
transform and then transcribe the conditions of reading in an inaugural founding gesture that is without ground or precedent, which would
constantly reinvent the institution with every act of reading and posit
a new culture while being faithful to the tradition of culture. A critically lively, alert, deconstructive cultural studies would take this sort of
performative praxis as its inaugural responsibility, with the good reading of a text transforming the culture into which that reading enters on
each singular occasion without predicting or programming the future.
This prescription leads Miller to the startlingly bold assertion that 'the
reading itself, recorded in an essay or lecture, may become a new event
and thus help to bring about what Jacques Derrida calls the democracy to come, which is, or ought to be, the goal of cultural studies'.[34]
Elsewhere in *Illustration*, Miller notes that cultural critics, 'act in the
name of a universal justice'.[35] This is not a million miles away from the
Barthes of the closing section of 'Myth Today'.

    Now, this is just the sort of thing Miller used to say about 'the lin-
guistics of literariness',[36] and it is no surprise that Miller should have
recently revisited the text of de Man in the light of his post-cultural
studies significance for the academy, in the *Material Events* book. What
is important for Miller, as it was for Barthes, is not cultural studies per
se but 'good reading' or deconstruction. Gayatri Spivak also sees a role
for a deconstructive cultural studies in the age of globalisation. Going
even further than either myself or Miller, she says of the conceptual
difficulty that names cultural studies, 'the very concept of culture may
seem to be synonymous with the culture of death, as if the expression
"culture of death" were ultimately a pleonasm or tautology',[37] stating
that cultural studies lacks rigour and now only provides foregone conclusions to in-house debates. She would like to see cultural studies
ponder questions of economics in response to the challenge of globalisation, and is open to the possibility of freeing deconstruction from its
North American institutional tie to comparative literature to let it loose
in cultural studies 'to reveal the saturnalia of an imagined counter-
globalization'.[38] Finally for Spivak, deconstruction and cultural studies
have a strong allegiance: 'we must remain open to the scrutiny of the

improper ... the last lesson of deconstruction for the proper investigation of culture'.[39] What both Spivak's and Miller's engagements with
cultural studies suggest is that: (1) With regard to cultural studies' ori-
entation towards the present and its assumed worldly vocation, there is
certainly work for it to do. (2) If this work is to be in any way successful
cultural studies will have to smarten up its act and take on board some
serious thinking. (3) Deconstruction cannot be applied to cultural
studies; instead cultural studies must be turned around from within,
auto-critiquing itself and its institutional spaces just as it decon-
structs the question of culture. (4) While cultural studies provides an
opportunity for this work, none of this work is necessarily specific to
cultural studies and it is more important to allow the dual tasks of critique and deconstruction to take place in newly invented spaces rather
than defending the propriety of disciplines. (5) Just as cultural studies
needs to attend to the philosophical so it must also look to the spirit of
its Marxist inheritance as a performative critique that transforms the
thing it critiques, the 'generation by a joint and simultaneous grafting,
without proper body, of the performative and the constative'.[40]

   While all this may be extremely therapeutic for great swaths of those
who work under the nomenclature of 'cultural studies', I fear it will
ultimately fall on deaf ears. The basic problem of cultural studies (the
problem that names cultural studies as well as the problem that ruins
cultural studies) is the diremption between the idea of the task it is
engaged in (transformative critique) and its institutional form. There
is a chasm between the inaugural reading and teleopoesis imagined by
Miller and Spivak and the vast majority of work undertaken by cultural
studies. The institutional fate of cultural studies is indicative of a failure of the very logic of newness. There is nothing older in the western
tradition than the claim for radical newness and breaks with the past.
The most certain way to ensure that one repeats the errors of the past is
to claim to have broken with it. The recuperative powers of revolution
are obvious for all to see. Cultural studies robbed of the auto-critique
of theoretical vigilance becomes just another disciplinary endeavour
(the term 'studies' gives it away), while without the risk and corruption
that goes with the founding of institutional spaces the aspirations of
cultural studies remain as a pure negation of the very thing they would
wish to affirm. In a sense the question 'what is cultural studies?' misses
the point of this quasi-transcendental and catachrestic name by ontol-
ogising a linguistic trap, seeking to name by the aberrant of nomial
effect that which it cannot possibly signify. 'Cultural studies', the sort

of work one would like to do, the sort of intervention one would like to make, does not happen in either the abstraction of pronouncement or the edifice of achieved institutionalisation. Rather, it exists always, if it remains alert to its own interminable practice, in the chasm of making between affirmation and position. For those who have chosen (or have been chosen by) the path of this sort of work, it is not out of disrespect for the specificity of disciplines (one cannot or should not be trained in just cultural studies); rather it is an acceptance of the constant reinvention of the conditions under which thinking can take place. Rather than ask 'what is cultural studies?' one might well ask 'why, when, or even how, cultural studies?'

Let me conclude with a reference to a second text by Derrida, which demonstrates more forbearance with the question of culture. In the essay '*Un ver à soie: Points de vue piqués sur l'autre voile*', brilliantly translated by Geoffrey Bennington as, 'A Silkworm of One's Own: Points of View Stitched on the Other Veil', Derrida deploys the intersexed figure of the silkworm as a metaphor for the patient deconstruction of phallogocentrism in the writing of Hélène Cixous, 'the invisible progress of the weaving, a little as though I were about to stumble on the secret of a marvel … so foreign yet so close in its incalculable distance'.[41] Derrida reminds us that the work of the silkworm is known as 'sericulture' (again that reference to cultivation and process). I find this a resonant image for the work of cultural studies: sericultural studies, which would follow the patient weaving of a critical philosophy with the long history of modernity, to spin an account of the present, stitched into the web of the institution, embroidering it anew with each secretion. 'Sericulture', writes Derrida, recalling his own husbandry of silkworms as a boy, 'was not man's thing, not a thing belonging to the man raising his silkworms. It was the culture of the silkworm *qua* silkworm'.[42] A patient, reflective, critical, engaged, interminable and endlessly open sericultural studies would not belong to those who farmed its name; rather it would be the marvellous and surprising work that was impossible to designate or appropriate but that nevertheless progressed, 'so foreign yet so close in its incalculable distance'.

Barthes, an alternative ending for cultural studies

Allow me to offer a coda after this coda. Rather than the work of Derrida's patient silkworms, an alternative ending awaits cultural studies. Barthes' favourite novel, Flaubert's *Bouvard and Pécuchet*, remained unfinished at Flaubert's death, although according to notes he had planned a conclusion that might serve as an allegory for the possible fate of cultural studies. The novel concerns two Parisian copy-clerks, the eponymous Bouvard and Pécuchet, one of whom inherits a large fortune, allowing the clerks to buy a property in Normandy. Here they combine and confuse leisure and learning (etymologically the same thing in Greek, *schole*, as the state of being free from the necessity of labour), 'working' their way through almost every discipline (including agriculture, chemistry, anatomy, biology, medicine, archaeology, architecture, history, literature, drama, aesthetics, politics, religion and education). As amateurs they flounder through the episteme, abandoning one subject as quickly as they take up another. The comedy of this picaresque study is derived as much from the constitutive lack of the disciplines as from the misadventures of the scholars. Running in parallel to the clerks' inter-disciplinary practice is the story of their ever-deteriorating relations with the local community, who in the notes left to the incomplete manuscript eventually try to run the pair out of town or have them committed to an asylum for the insane. Flaubert's notes propose that a disillusioned Bouvard and Pécuchet retreat from intellectual endeavour and the world in order to return to copying. The book would have ended with their keen preparations for the construction of a two-seated desk on which to write. The suggestion is that Flaubert would have concluded the work with a sample of their copy, such as 'The Dictionary of Received Ideas', an encyclopedia of commonplace ideas or what Barthes would call 'doxa'. Such might be the fate of a cultural studies that untied itself from philosophy and critical intervention, or, to paraphrase Stuart Hall, turned back from the theoretical limits before it. The significance of cultural studies as an articulation in the humanities in the late twentieth century is not its commitment to the inter-disciplinary approach or its interest in new forms of media. On the contrary, inter-disciplinarity is often a scene for the justification of Bouvard and Pécuchet type academic amateurism. The idea of inter-disciplinarity itself often erases the correctly elastic nature of disciplines themselves, which as expanded and complex fields of knowledge are more regularly marked by epistemological heterogeneity than one might suppose. Rather, the significance of cultural studies after Barthes is the way in which it creates a space for philosophising beyond philosophy at a time when the professionalisation of philosophy as a university subject, according to the ossifying principles of set traditions of what has the right to be called 'philosophy', required the displacement of the tasks of thinking elsewhere. That is to say, cultural studies after Barthes should not abandon the questioning and productive direction of Barthes in favour of an ontologisation of its own history and tropes. If this happens (and there is every evidence that it is happening, with considerable fallout for the rest of the humanities) then the professor of cultural studies will be reduced to the status of the copyist, content to reiterate the doxa of the day as commentary on the popular. In this case, cultural studies like the late Bouvard and Pécuchet will have retreated from the world and from any attempt to engage with thought. The significance of cultural studies after Barthes is the way in which it both returns to and turns around a certain idea of philosophising as an activity that happens across disciplines and in response to the present. It may at times be faintly comic in its textual activism and outflanked by the speed of 'current affairs' (there are no doubt good reasons to run it out of town or to have it committed to its own institution) but this is surely preferable to the double desk of copying, in which cultural studies receives doxa and then reinscribes it as scholarship that is little more than academically approved journalism. Philosophy is a question posed to the academy beyond the contested institutional accreditation of professional philosophers. If it is to have a future, beyond the commemoration of a name and a project that may have already been annulled before its inception, then it will need to continue to open spaces of deterritorialisation beyond its own exteriority. Cultural studies, after Barthes, is such a space. The challenge for cultural studies is to accept this inheritance and to continue to expand the possibilities of thinking in the present rather than settling for disciplinary recognition as an anthropology of the popular and a taxonomy of media practices. Flaubert's 'Dictionary of Received Ideas' says of philosophy, 'always snigger at it'. The task for cultural studies after Barthes is never to snigger at philosophy.

Notes

1 R.B.: Bio-bibliography

1. Louis-Jean Calvet, *Roland Barthes: A Biography*, trans. Sara Wykes (Bloomington: Indiana University Press, 1994), p. 88.

2 Reading Roland Barthes in a Time of Terror

1. Roland Barthes, 'Politics', in 'Twenty Key Words for Roland Barthes', *Le Magazine littéraire*, February 1975.
2. For a particularly inventive reading of Barthes as a queer sort of narratologist see Judith Roof, *Come As You Are: Sexuality and Narrative* (New York: Columbia University Press, 1996).
3. Antony Easthope, *Privileging Difference* (Basingstoke: Macmillan, 2000), p. 23.
4. See *Roland Barthes*, catalogue de l'exposition, Centre Pompidou, 2002, coédition Centre Pompidou/IMEC/Le Seuil, Paris. A version of some of the exhibition content can be found at http://www.centrepompidou.fr/education/ressources/ENS-barthes/ENS-barthes.html
5. Allow me to gloss this comment with some notable Anglophone exceptions: the section on Barthes in Carol Mavor's *Reading Boyishly* (Durham, NC: Duke University Press, 2008) and Timothy Scheie's *Peformance Degree Zero: Roand Barthes and Theatre* (Toronto: University of Toronto Press, 2006). Some recent translations into English include Andy Stafford's edition of the collection of essays *The Language of Fashion* (Berg, 2006) and the lecture course at the Collège de France, translated by Rosalind Krauss and Denis Hollier, *The Neutral* (New York: Columbia University Press, 2007). Neil Badmington has edited a substantial set of volumes of commentary on Barthes over the past thirty years: see his *Roland Barthes: Critical Evaluations in Cultural Theory*, Vols 1–4 (London: Routledge, 2009).
6. Roland Barthes, *Michelet*, trans. Richard Howard (New York: Hill and Wang, 1987).
7. This text was first written in 2007–8. The text deliberately has little to say on the specifics of the so-called 'war on terror'. Rather, it is concerned with what it might mean to read and write as a scholar in a time of crisis.
8. Paul de Man, 'Roland Barthes and the Limits of Structuralism', in *Romanticism and Contemporary Criticism: the Gauss Seminar and Other Papers*, eds E. S. Burt, Kevin Newmark and Andrzej Warminski (Baltimore: Johns Hopkins University Press, 1993), p. 175.

9. I am thinking here of the lasting legacy of structuralism and semiotics in linguistics and literary study in Scandinavia, notably in Denmark following the institutional influence of Louis Hjelmslev. Equally, narratology as a science continues to hold sway in certain pockets of European literary study.

10. See Martin McQuillan, *Deconstruction after 9/11* (New York: Routledge, 2008).

11. Jacques Derrida, 'Force and Signification', in *Writing and Difference*, trans. Alan Bass (London: Routledge, 1978), p. 3. For a greater commentary on the gloss that follows see Derrida's essay.

12. Jacques Derrida, 'Structure, Sign and Play in the Discourse of the Human Sciences', in *Writing and Difference*, p. 280–1.

13. Paul de Man, 'Interview with Stefano Rosso', *The Resistance to Theory* (Minneapolis: University of Minnesota Press, 1986): 'I have always maintained that one could approach the problems of ideology and by extension the problems of politics only on the basis of critical-linguistic analysis, which had to be done in its own terms, in the medium of language, and I felt I could approach those problems only after having achieved certain control over those questions. It seems pretentious to say so, but it is not the case. I have the feeling I have achieved some control over technical problems of language … It was on working on Rousseau that I felt I was able to progress from purely linguistic analysis to questions which are really already of a political and ideological nature'.

14. Roland Barthes, *Le Plaisir du Texte* (Paris: Editions du Seuil, 1973).

15. See Paul de Man, *Blindness and Insight: Essays in the Rhetoric of Contemporary Criticism*, 2nd edn (London: Routledge, 1983).

16. Interview with Claude Jannoud, *Le Figaro*, 27 July 1974.

17. Interview with Edgar Tripet, *La Gazette de Lausanne*, 6 February 1971.

18. See Roland Barthes, 'An Introduction to the Structural Analysis of Narrative', in Susan Sontag, ed., *Roland Barthes: A Reader* (New York: Hill & Wang, 1983).

19. Roland Barthes, *Writing Degree Zero*, trans. Richard Howard (New York: Hill and Wang, 1968).

20. *Les Lettres Françaises*, ed. J. Ristat, 29 March to 4 April 1972, p. 3.

21. Barthes had a changing and ambiguous public feint around reading literature as demonstrated by two contrasting utterances: 'I read very little, and rather casually… If a book bores meand I'm easily bored by booksI drop it' (Barthes 1985, 199); 'Only literature should be taught, because all knowledge could be approached within it' (Barthes 1985, 237).

22. The second contradictory corollary to note here is that as theory and indisciplinarity have become the dominant idiom for humanist study, the 'disconnect' between the complexity of that study and public discourse, marked by mediatic reductionism, has never been so clearly marked. 'Today the avant-garde object is essentially *theoretical*: the double pressure of politics and intellectuals ensures that it is now *theoretical positions* (and their exposition) which are avant-garde, and not necessarily creative works themselves' (Barthes, 1985, 191). Attempts by 'media dons' to make an 'impact' beyond the academy by framing their work for the media is to miss the point of the relation between complexity and reduction that distinguishes academic discourse from other channels of communication. The whole notion of 'knowledge transfer' popular with western governments and university managers (whereupon the value of academic research is measured by its 'transfer' into the public realm or

its 'economic impact') is premised on a one-way reductionism in which academic discourse is diluted for easy understanding and utility. It is a ludicrous and insulting idea as if the humanities has had nothing to say on the internal problematic of resistance within transference. Knowledge is created in the relation, which as a relation has no presence, not by transfer from equal mode A to B, and knowledge as such always already implies an unequal relationship. There is little consideration given at a policy level to the ways in which the complexity of thought as practised in humanities departments might overspill and transform the public space and the use of mediatic technologies. Above all the irreducible assumption is that the transfer of episteme will produce economic and social benefits based on a virtuous circle of innovation and creativity. But what happens when 'impact' within your academic discipline (cultural studies, say, or philosophical critique more generally) is 'measured' by the most effective and innovative critical leverage on the system? What if this social critique implied an elite critical caste or even a pedagogical mission? The supposition in the west is that the arts and humanities research paid for by the capitalist state should benefit the capitalist state. However, I am certain that a similar model predominated in Communist Europe and elsewhere. The problem is not necessarily that of capital but of the national economy or even the global economy insofar as the national sponsor benefits as part of that global schema. It might be the case, however, that as a humanist my work may not only refuse affiliation with the state, benefit those living outside it and even do active harm to the national economy. The paths of dissemination are long and complex and what seems avant-garde or even useless today is more often than not quickly caught up in a dialectic of recuperation, which is not the same as transference. The very real difficulty for institutional managers in the arts and humanities is: how do you protect the arts budget from the treasury without engaging with the vocabulary and presuppositions of the treasury? The answer is that you can't but there are ways of living with that structural complicity that are intelligent and do justice to the complexity as two-way advocacy, or are merely surrender to compliance. The episteme is not a client of any sponsor and is under no obligation to justify itself. It cannot be defended on anything other than its own excessive terms. This is not to say that any social critic worthy of the name does not dream of producing writing that makes an impact. This is because it is the very idea of the university that it 'transfer' knowledge. It does so through teaching and published research. The reason so many in the arts and humanities are non-plussed by this discourse is because they consider the transfer of knowledge to be the worn out faces of the coins of their profession. It is what they do: why is a metalanguage of pseudo-sociology required to justify it? If the greatest minds of philosophy cannot explain the path of the episteme from an inside to an outside and the whole of the domain of comparative literature is yet to determine a viable model for translation, what makes us think the advocates for our research councils can? However, the difficulty here is a supposed choice between banalisation and elitism. Theory as a practice of critique rejects both. A 'publicly engaged intellectual' is not the same thing as a 'media intellectual'. Third, this scenario is a peculiarly Anglo-American difficulty (this odd conjunction includes Australia and New Zealand). On the one hand, cultural studies remains a spectre yet to arrive for national education systems across the world. For the post-socialist countries of the former Soviet Union, say, or China, Theory holds out a promise of reforming a moribund academy. It is telling now that in many of these instances the opportunities of Theory or cultural studies are contemporaneous with free market reforms in national higher education systems. The former is subversive of the latter but equally their speculative value would not be possible without the latter. It has been suggested that liberal economics cannot survive without liberal democracy. Only time and a global economic downturn of significant proportions will tell if China continues to buck this prediction. However, one wonders how long totalitarian relations can survive in a state where something like cultural studies or Theory is introduced to its universities. Enlightenment values and Enlightenment critique are coterminous. The relationship between the 'inside' and 'outside' of Theory today is not straightforward but is, as one might imagine, surprising, unpredictable and complex. However, the predicament of globalised cultural studies is not the one addressed by Barthes in his riposte to Picard.

23. See Paul de Man, 'Roland Barthes and the Limits of Structuralism', in *Romanticism and Contemporary Criticism*, eds Ellen Burt, Kevin Newmark and Andrzej Warminski (Baltimore: Johns Hopkins University Press, 1993).

24. Robert J. C. Young, *White Mytholgies: Writing, History and the West* (London: Routledge, 1990).

25. Robert Eaglestone, *The Holocaust and the Postmodern* (Oxford: Oxford University Press, 2008).

26. See Martin McQuillan and Ika Willis, eds, *The Origins of Deconstruction* (Basingstoke: Macmillan, 2009).

27. Barthes outlines his relation to the post-war milieu in a 1975 interview: 'When I began to write, after the war, Sartre was the avant-garde. The encounter with Sartre was very important to me. I have always been, not fascinated, the word is absurd, but changed, carried away, almost set on fire by his writing as an essayist. He truly created a new language of the essay, which impressed me very much. Sartre's distrust of science, however, came from the standpoint of phenomenological philosophy, a philosophy of the existential subject, whereas mine is rooted in a psychoanalytic language, at least at present.' Roland Barthes, 'The Three Arrogances', in 'Twenty Key Words for Roland Barthes', *Le Magazine littéraire*, February 1975.

28. Roland Barthes, *Criticism and Truth*, trans. Katrine Pilcher Keuneman (London: Athlone Press, 1987), p. 29.

29. Jacques Derrida, *Specters of Marx: the Work of Mourning, State of the Debt, and the New International*, trans. Peggy Kamuf (London and New York: Routledge, 1994).

30. Roland Barthes, *Criticism and Truth*, p. 29.

31. Ibid., p. 30.

32. Ibid., p. 31.

33. A significant history of Theory has yet to be written. However, for useful sources of documentation see See Antony Easthope, *British Post-Structuralism since 1968* (London: Routledge, 1991) and more recently Francois Cusset's *French Theory: How Foucault, Derrida, Deleuze & Co. Transformed the Intellectual Life of the United States* (Minnesota: University of Minnesota Press, 2008).

34. See Jonathan Culler and Kevin Lamb, eds, *Just Being Difficult? Academic Writing in the Public Arena* (Stanford, CA: Stanford University Press, 2003). See also texts by Jacques Derrida such as 'Above All no Journalists!' in *Religion and Media*, eds Hent de Vries and Samuel Weber (Stanford, CA: Stanford University Press, 2001) and 'The Work of Intellectuals and the Press (The Bad Example: How the *New York Review of Books* and Company Do Business)', in *Points: Interviews 1974–1994* (Stanford, CA: Stanford University Press, 1995).

35. See Roland Barthes, 'The Death of the Author', in *Image, Music, Text*, trans. Stephen Heath (New York: Hill and Wang, 1977).

36. Much of what is at stake in this book and in the career of Barthes is the question of the relation between the avant garde and the public realm. This is why Brecht is such an important figure in Barthes' writing, as he states in a 1975 interview: 'Avant-garde literature is no longer the pride of the bourgeoisie, and it isn't read by the general public. It is the prerogative of a mandarin caste, an intellectual elite. Couldn't that form the basis for new alienation? That is an objection often made against avant-garde literature, which is accused of both revolutionary pretensions and social impotence. This objection usually comes from the bourgeoisie, and their idea of revolution is, paradoxically, more sovereign than that of the revolutionaries themselves; this might be true in politics, where the event can be sudden and brutal, but in the field of culture, no revolution can avoid passing through a long period of contradictions. One of these contradictions, inevitably, is that in our nonrevolutionary society the avant-garde writer's role is not to please the vast majority of the public, which by the way should not be purely and simply equated to the proletarian class, because in order to please this public the artist would often have to adopt the art and shibboleths of a petit-bourgeois ideology, which are not revolutionary at all (and that's another of the contradictions which must be worked through). Brecht himself tried to construct a theatre that was both popular and critical; let's admit that he failed.' Interview with Claude Jannoud, *Le Figaro*, 27 July 1974.

37. Barthes describes his own vexed and changing political identity in an interview with Bernard-Henry Lévi: 'It would be up to the left to say whether it considers me to be among its intellectuals. As for myself, it's fine with me, providing that the left is understood not as an idea but as an obstinate sensibility, a way of perceiving reality. In my case an inalterable foundation of anarchism, in the most etymological sense of the word.' Interview with Bernard-Henri Lévy, *Le Nouvel Observateur*, 10 January 1977.

38. See Martin McQuillan, 'Karl Marx and the Philosopher's Stone', in *The Politics of Deconstruction: Jacques Derrida and the Other of Philosophy* (London: Pluto Press, 2007).

39. Roland Barthes, *Criticism and Truth*, p. 34.

40. Ibid., p. 33.

41. Ibid., p. 51. See my comments on the nouveau roman and forms of intelligibility in *Theorizing Muriel Spark: Gender, Race, Deconstruction* (Basingstoke: Macmillan, 2000).

42. I treat this at length in 'Karl Marx and the Philosopher's Stone'.

43. Roland Barthes, *Criticism and Truth*, p. 49.

44. Ibid.

45. Ibid., pp. 51–2.

46. See Paul de Man, 'Roland Barthes and the Limits of Structuralism'.

47. Edward Said, 'Critical Essays, Mythologies' *New York Review of Books*, 30 July 1972: 'At least four of his books do little more than articulate sets of analytic rules for the study of verbal objects, yet I am convinced that no matter how useful these are to Barthes and to other critics, the rules are more valuable for the fact of their articulation than for what they enable one to do with them. The overcoming of a senseless "thereness" in things by a method that shows what put them there, and how and why they are there, this matters more than whether the method's rules are universally applicable'.

48. Roland Barthes, *Sade, Fourier, Loyola*, new edn (Baltimore: Johns Hopkins University Press, 1997), p. 7.

49. Interview with Jean-Jacques Brochier, *Le Magazine littéraire*, January 1976.

50. Barthes twice makes reference to '*Sininess*' in the *Mythologies*, as a neologism for the orientalist view 'a French petit-bourgeois could have of [China] not so long ago is another: for this peculiar mixture of bells, rickshaws and opium-dens', pp. 84, 119. Or, as he puts it in footnote 5 to 'Myth Today', 'perhaps *Sinity*? Just as if Latin/latinity = Basque/x, x = Basquity'.Barthes was to later take a famously sterile trip to China with Kristeva and Sollers among others.

51. On the problem of examples see my 'Emergency on Planet X', *parallax*, 5(2), 1999, pp. 82–92.

52. For further discussion of this problematic see Derrida's discussion of the mediatic in *Specters of Marx*.

53. Roland Barthes, *Michelet*, p. 35.

54. On the very difficult question of 'relevance' see me, jd.

55. I elaborate a fuller appreciation of cultural studies in Paul Bowan, ed., *Interrogating Cultural Studies: Theory, Politics and Practice* (London: Pluto Press, 2003).

56. On the issue of structuralism and history see Derek Attridge, Geoffrey Bennington and Robert Young, eds, *Post-Structuralism and the Question of History* (Cambridge: Cambridge University Press, 1989).

57. On Ideology see Tom Cohen, *Ideology and Inscription: 'Cultural Studies' after Benjamin, de Man, and Bakhtin* (Cambridge: Cambridge University Press, 1998) and Andrzej Warminski, ed., Paul de Man, *Aesthetic Ideology* (Minnesota: University of Minnesota Press, 1996).

58. See Barthes' use of the term in *The Pleasure of the Text*.

59. See 'The Same Informed Air', in *Theorizing Muriel Spark: Gender, Race, Deconstruction*, ed. M. McQuillan (Basingstoke: Macmillan Press, 2002).

60. See *Roland Barthes: oeuvres completes*, vol. 1, ed. Eric Marty.

61. Louis-Jean Calvet, *Roland Barthes*, p. 117.

62. A phrase I borrow from Martin Stannard; see his review of my own *Theorizing Muriel Spark* in *The Modern Language Review*, 99(3), 2004, pp. 762–4.

63. Calvet, *Roland Barthes*, p. 246.

64. Ibid., p. 215.

65. Interview with Bernard-Henri Lévy, *Le Nouvel Observateur*, 10 January 1977.

66. Paul de Man, 'Roland Barthes and the Limits of Structuralism', in *Romanticism and Contemporary Criticism*, eds E. S. Burt, Kevin Newmark and Andrzej Warminski (Baltimore: Johns Hopkins University Press, 1993), p. 164.

67. See Fred Orton's 'Reflexio Lucis: On Reading Paul de Man Reading Marx and Marxism', forthcoming.

68. At 'The Languages of Criticism and the Sciences of Man' conference in Baltimore (18–21 October 1966), Barthes, an invited speaker from Europe (along with Georges Poulet, Tzvetan Todorov, Jean Hyppolite, Jacques Lacan and Jacques Derrida), has just delivered his lecture 'To Write: an intransitive verb'. We are in the middle of the question and answer session. Paul de Man stands up. 'I would like to speak a moment of Roland Barthes' treatment of history. I find that you have an optimistic historical myth (the same one I saw in Danato) which is linked to the abandonment of the last form of traditional philosophy that we know, phenomenology, and the replacement of phenomenology with psychoanalysis, etc. That represents historical progress and

extremely optimistic possibilities for the history of thought. However, you must show us that the results you have obtained in the stylistic analyses that you make are superior to those of your predecessors, thanks to this optimistic change, which is linked to a certain historic renewal. I must admit, I have been somewhat disappointed by the specific analyses that you give us. I don't believe they show any progress over those of the Formalists, Russia or American, who used empirical methods, though neither the vocabulary nor the conceptual frame that you use. But more seriously, when I hear you refer to facts of literary history, you say things that are false within a typically French myth. I find in your work a false conception of classicism and romanticism. When, for example, concerning the question of the narrator or the 'double ego', you speak of writing since Mallarmé and of the new novel etc., and you oppose them to what happens in the romantic novel or story or autobiographyyou are simply wrong. In the romantic autobiography, or, well before that, in the seventeenth-century story, this same complication of the ego (*moi*) is found, not only, unconsciously, but explicitly and thematically treated, in a much more complex way than in the contemporary novel. I don't want to continue this development; it is simply to indicate that you distort history because you need a historical myth of progress to justify a method which is not yet able to justify itself by its results. It is in the notion of temporality rather than in that of history that I see you making consciousness undergo a reification, which is linked to this same optimism which troubles me.' Thanks to an early tape recording of conference interchange we have a record of Barthes' shocked and unconvincing reply, for what is there to say when one has been accused of making no progress beyond formalism (the full exchange can be found in *The Structuralist Controversy*, ed. R. Macksey (Baltimore: Johns Hopkins University Press, 1972), pp. 150–1). No doubt de Man, a keen reader of *The German Ideology*, is thinking even in 1966 that Barthes has failed to displace the inherited model that distinguishes between false and true consciousness. His comment that Barthes relies on a myth of historical progress his own making that cannot know itself prefigures his criticism of the Mythologies in the *NYRB* piece. Derrida intervenes here and supports Barthes with a constructive comment. Barthes' English is imperfect, he has only ever learned enough to allow him to read certain works of literature. At this stage Derrida's English is also shaky, it will not be until several years into his tenure at UC Irvine that he will master the idiom. De Man is playing at home, strangely enough. I love the expository power of de Man but my inclination here is always to support the underdog.

69. Paul de Man, 'Roland Barthes and the Limits of Structuralism', p. 170.

70. Myth in this sense can be contrasted to Theory as a figure in Barthes' thought: 'We must remember that "theory", which is the decisive practice of the avant-garde, does not have a progressive role in itself; its active role is to reveal as past what we still believe to be present: theory mortifies, and that is what makes it avant-garde.' Interview with Claude Jannoud, *Le Figaro*, 27 July 1974.

71. Ibid., pp. 173–4.

72. Interview with Stephen Heath, *Signs of the Times*, 1971.

73. Paul de Man, *Allegories of Reading* (New Haven, CT: Yale University Press,).

74. 'Marx is one of those rare thinkers of the past to have taken seriously, at least in its principle, the originary indissociability of technics and language, and thus of tele-technics (for every Language is a tele-technics)', Jacques Derrida, *Specters of Marx*, p. 53.

75. Tom Cohen, *Ideology and Inscription*, p. 18.

76. When considering Barthe's linguistic approach to ideology, it is helpful to recall Paul de Man's gnomic statement in 'The Resistance to Theory': 'It would be unfortunate … to confuse the materiality of the signifier with the materiality of what it signifies … What we call ideology is precisely the confusion of linguistic with natural reality, or reference with phenomenalism. It follows that, more than any other mode of inquiry, including economics, the linguistics of literariness is a powerful and indispensable tool in the unmasking of ideological aberrations, as well as a determining factor in accounting for their occurrence. Those who reproach literary theory for being oblivious to social and historical (that is to say ideological) reality are merely stating their fear at having their own ideological mystifications exposed by the tool they are trying to discredit. They are, in short, very poor readers of Marx's *German Ideology*.' Paul de Man, 'The Resistance to Theory', in *The Resistance to Theory* (Minneapolis: University of Minnesota Press, 1986), p. 11.

77. Louis Althusser, 'Ideology and Ideological State Apparatus', trans. Ben Brewster, in *Lenin and Philosophy and Other Essays* (London: Monthly Review Press, 1971).

78. On this point see Derrida's essay 'Marx & Sons', in *Ghostly Demarcations: A Symposium on Jacques Derrida's Specters of Marx*, ed. Michael Sprinkner (London: Verso: 199X).

79. Sarah Kofman, *Camera Obscura: of Ideology* (1998), p. 19.

80. See Willy Maley, 'Spectres of Engels', in *Deconstruction: A Reader*, ed. M. McQuillan (New York: Routledge, 2001).

81. See, for example, two classic examples: Richard Hoggart, *The Uses of Literacy: Aspects of Working Class Life* (London: Chatto and Windus, 1957) and Dick Hebdige, *Subculture: The Meaning of Style* (London: Routledge, 1981).

82. See Thomas Docherty, 'Deconstruction not Reading Politics', in *Deconstruction Reading Politics*, ed. M. McQuillan (Basingstoke: Macmillan, 2008).

83. See Marx and Engels, *The German Ideology*, ed. C. J. Arthur (London: Lawrence and Wishart, 1970), p. 62.

84. 'Edward Fuchs, Collector and Historian', in *Walter Benjamin Selected Writings, Volume 3, 1935–1938* (Cambridge, MA: Harvard University Press, 2002), pp. 260–302.

85. See Stuart Hall, 'Old and New Identities, Old and New Ethnicities', *Culture, Globalisation and the World-System: Contemporary Conditions for the Representation of Identity*, ed. Anthony King. (Minneapolis: University of Minnesota Press, 1997), pp. 31–68.

86. Interview with Jean Duflot, *Politique-Hebdo*, 13 January 1971.

87. An additional note to Marx, not discussed here, follows from the category 'Identification. The petit-bourgeois is a man unable to imagine the Other' and reads 'Marx: '… what makes them representative of the petit-bourgeois class, is that their minds, their consciousness do not extend beyond the limits which this class has set to its activities. (*The Eighteenth Brumaire*). And Gorki: 'the petit-bourgeois is the man who has preferred himself to all else'.

88. See Paul de Man, 'Roland Barthes and the Limits of Structuralism'.

89. See my 'Karl Marx and the Philosopher's Stone'.

90. Roland Barthes, 'Writers, Intellectuals, Teachers', *Image, Music, Text*, trans. Stephen Heath (New York: Hill and Wang, 1977), p. 194.

91. See John Banville, *Shroud* (New York, Knopf, 2003), Gilbert Adair, *Death of the Author* (New York: Melville House, 2008) and Bernhard Schlink, *Homecoming* (London: Vintage, 2009).

92. Roland Barthes, *Roland Barthes*, trans. Richard Howard (Basingstoke: Macmillan, 1977), pp. 80–1.

93. Roland Barthes, 'Marx', in 'Twenty Key Words for Roland Barthes', *Le Magazine littéraire*, February 1975.

94. Interview with Guy Scarpetta, *Promesse*, 29, Spring 1971.

95. Louis Calvet, *Roland Barthes*, p. 139.

96. Barthes proposed a research project to Stephen Heath in a 1971 interview: 'There is in fact a real problem, a practical, human, social problem, which is the question of whether one can change actual, practical reading in relation to social groups, whether one can learn to read or to not read or to reread texts outside of academic and cultural conditioning. I'm convinced that all these things haven't been studied or even considered as problems.' Interview with Stephen Heath, *Signs of the Times*, 1971. This remains an enormous set of questions that have taken on a new urgency in an epoch of a newly and differently mediatised public realm.

97. One is reminded here of another experience of individualism on the Paris Metro that Barthes cites in a 1979 interview: 'The most literally scandalous thing I ever saw in my life… was a young man seated in a subway car in Paris who pulled some knitting out of his bag and openly began to knit.' Interview with Christine Eff, *Le Monde-Dimanche*, 16 September 1979.

98. In a 1971 interview Barthes describes the responsibility of Theory as a counter-culture of intelligence: 'Now, in our present society, theory is the subversive weapon par excellence. I'm not saying that this holds true in other countries, in other historical states … I feel that, in our case, theoretical work is still vital. So I take these countercultural movements seriously when they take a stab at intelligence, when they accept the responsibility of producing an intelligent discourse regarding their goals and actions.' Interview with Jean Duflot, *Politique-Hebdo*, 13 January 1971.

99. See J. Hillis Miller's '"Don't Count Me In": Derrida's Refraining', in *For Derrida* (Fordham: Fordham University Press, 2008).

100. See the autobiography of Till's mother, Mariane Till Mobely, *Death of Innocence: The Story of the Hate Crime that Changed America* (One World Books, 2003).

101. See Albert Camus, 'Reflections on the Guillotine', in *Resistance, Rebellion and Death*.

102. Deborah Cameron, *Verbal Hygiene: The Politics of Language*, (London: Routledge, 1995).

103. See Jacques Derrida, *Rogues: Two Essays on Reason*, trans. Pascale Brault and Michael Naas (Stanford, CA: Stanford University Press, 2004).

104. I discuss these matters at some length in my *Deconstruction after 9/11* (New York: Routledge, 2008).

105. See Albert Camus, *Resistance, Rebellion and Death*.

106. Despite his obvious sympathies Barthes always refused to be co-opted into the cause of political violence, as he stated in a late interview in 1978: 'A particularly thorny problem is presented by violence claiming to be in the service of a cause or an idea. For my part, I find it difficult to accept giving doctrinal alibis to violent and destructive behaviour. I agree with these simple words of Castellion, a Calvinist of the sixteenth century: "Killing a man is not defending a doctrine, it is killing a man."' Interview with Jacqueline Sers, *Réforme*, 2 September 1978.

107. See also Virginia Q Tilley, *The One State Solution* (Manchester: Manchester University Press, 2005). See also my 'The Last Jewish Intellectual', in *Deconstruction after 9/11*.

108. See Jacques Derrida, *The Post Card: from Socrates to Freud and Beyond*, trans. Alan Bass (Chicago: Chicago University Press, 1984).
109. See Franz Kafka, Letter to Robert Klopstock, in Kafka's *Briefe 1902–1924*, ed. Max Brod (New York: Schocken Books, 1958), pp. 332–4: 'An Abraham who should come unsummoned! It is as if, at the end of the year, when the best student was solemnly about to receive a prize, the worst student rose in the expectant stillness and came forward from his dirty desk in the last row because he had made a mistake of hearing, and the whole class burst out laughing. And perhaps he had made no mistake at all, his name really was called, it having been the teacher's intention to make the rewarding of the best student at the same time a punishment for the worst.'
110. On secrets, see J Hillis Miller, 'Derrida's Topographies', in *South Atlantic Review*, 59(1), 1994, pp. 1–25.
111. See Jacques Derrida, *The Truth in Painting*, trans. Geoffrey Bennington and Ian MacLoed (Chicago: Chicago University Press, 1987).
112. The Belgian-American film director Victor Meessen attempted to find Diouf and his comrades in 2006 in order to make a film of their experiences at the military festival in 1955 and in order to restore their voices to them on film in a reflection on the events. See '*Restitution de l'histoire: à la recherche de Diouf, Issa et Santoura, enfants de troupe en 1955*', Sidwaya, 12 August 2008. It is not clear whether the film maker found the children, now in their sixties, or whether they are even still alive. www.africatime.com/burkina/nouvelle.asp?no_nouvelle=274412&no_categorie=4
113. Roland Barthes, 'Introduction to the Structural Analysis of Narratives'.
114. Franz Fanon, *Black Skin, White Masks* (New York: Avalon Travel Publishing, 2000).
115. See Derrida's discussion of *Triste Tropiques* in *Of Grammatology*, trans. Gayatri Spivak (Baltimore: Johns Hopkins University Press, 1977).
116. See Derrida, *Specters of Marx*, p. 31.
117. Marx was voted the 'greatest philosopher of all time' on the BBC website: http://www.bbc.co.uk/radio4/history/inourtime/greatest_philosopher.shtml
118. Interview with Stephen Heath, *Signs of the Times*, 1971.
119. Interview with Bernard-Henri Lévy, *Le Nouvel Observateur*, 10 January 1977.
120. Derrida, *Specters of Marx*.
121. See Jacques Derrida, *Spurs: Nietzsche's Styles*, trans. Barbara Harlow (Chicago: University of Chicago Press, 1981).
122. Barthes, ever the post-doc of the CNRS, once again offers us an as yet unfulfilled research project: I don't know if literature *should* be taught. If one thinks that it should, then one should accept, shall we say, a reformist perspective, and in that case one becomes a 'joiner': one joins the university to change things, one joins the schools to change the way literature is taught. In the main, I would be more or less inclined, by personal temperament, to this provisional localized reformism. In this case, teaching would be directed toward exploding the literary text as much as possible. The pedagogical problem would be to shake up the notion of the literary text and to make adolescents understand that there is text everywhere, but that not everything is text; I mean that there is text everywhere, but repetition, stereotype, and *doxa* are also everywhere. That's the goal: the distinction between this textuality, which is not to be found only in literature, and society's neurotic, repetitive activity. People should be made to realize that we have a right of access to texts that are not printed as texts, as I did with Japan, for example, by learning to read the text and fabric of life, of the street. We should perhaps even redo biographies as writings of life,

no longer based on real or historical referents. There would be a whole spectrum of projects, tasks that would be directed roughly toward a *disappropriation* of the text. Interview with Stephen Heath, *Signs of the Times*, 1971.

123. See my 'Spectres of Poujade' in *Deconstruction after 9/11*.

124. Jacques Derrida, *A Taste for the Secret* (Cambridge: Polity Press, 2001), p. 32.

125. Ibid.

126. Interview with Stephen Heath, *Signs of the Times*, 1971.

127. Interview with Jean Duflot, *Politique-Hebdo*, 13 January 1972.

128. Roland Barthes, *Roland Barthes by Roland Barthes*, trans. Richard Howard (Basingstoke: Macmillan, 1989), p. 46.

129. Let me conclude this text with a note from Derrida's memorial text for Barthes which speaks eloquently to the responsibilities of reading the life and writing of Barthes: 'I shall not make of this an allegory, even less a metaphor, but I recall that it was while travelling that I spent the most time alone with Barthes. Sometimes head to head, I mean face to face (for example on the train from Paris to Lille or Paris to Bordeaux), and sometimes side by side, separated by an aisle (for example on the trip from Paris to New York to Baltimore in 1966). The time of our travels was surely not the same, and yet it was also the same, and it is necessary to accept these two absolute certainties. Even if I wanted or was able to give an account, to speak of him as he was for me (the voice, the timbre, the forms of his attention and distraction, his polite way of being there or elsewhere, his face, hands clothing, smile, his cigar, so many features that I name without describing, since this is impossible here), even if I tried to reproduce what took place, what place would be reserved for the reserve? What place for the long periods of silence, for what was left unsaid out of discretion, for what was of no use bringing up, either because it was too well known by both of us or else infinitely unknown on either side? To go on speaking of this all alone, after the death of the other, to sketch out the least conjecture or risk the least interpretation, feels to me like an endless insult or wound – and yet also a duty, a duty towards him. Yet I will not be able to carry it out, at least not right here. Always, the promise of return.' Jacques Derrida, 'The Deaths of Roland Barthes', in *The Work of Mourning*, trans. Pascale-Anne Brault and Michael Naas (Chicago: University of Chicago Press, 2001), p. 55.

3   An Answer to the Question: What Is Cultural Studies?

1. Barbara Engh is the Director of the Centre for Cultural Studies at the University of Leeds. She is to my mind the most interesting scholar of cultural studies working in the United Kingdom today. This chapter is dedicated to her in gratitude for all she has revealed to me about cultural studies.

2. See 'Editor's Introduction', in *The Year's Work in Critical and Cultural Theory*, vol. 12 (Oxford: Oxford University Press, 2004).

3. Raymond Williams, *Keywords: A Vocabulary of Culture and Society* (Glasgow: Fontana, 1976). Some of the motifs in this chapter, including this reading of Williams, were first articulated in the interview with Paul Bowman, 'The Projection of Cultural Studies', in *Interrogating Cultural Studies: Theory, Politics and Practice*, ed. Paul Bowman (London: Pluto Press, 2003).

4. Williams, *Keywords*, p. 76.
5. Ibid., p. 77.
6. See Pierre Bourdieu, *Distinction* (Cambridge, MA: Harvard University Press, 1984).
7. Williams, *Keywords*, p. 78.
8. Ibid., p. 79.
9. Ibid., p. 79.
10. Ibid., p. 81.
11. Ibid., p. 82.
12. Ibid.
13. See Geoffrey Bennington, 'Aberrations: de Man (and) the Machine', in *Reading de Man Reading*, eds Wlad Godzich and Lindsay Waters (Minneapolis: University of Minnesota Press, 1989), p. 216.
14. Williams, *Keywords*, p. 80.
15. See Tom Cohen, J. Hillis Miller and Barbara Cohen, 'A "Materiality without Matter"' and Tom Cohen, 'Political Thrillers: Hitchcock, de Man, and Secret Agency in the "Aesthetic State"', in Tom Cohen, Barbara Cohen, J. Hillis Miller and Andrzej Warminski, eds, *Material Events: Paul de Man and the Afterlife of Theory* (Minneapolis: University of Minnesota Press, 2001), pp. 115 and xi.
16. Martin Heidegger, *The End of Philosophy*, trans. Joan Stambaugh (Oxford: Blackwell), p. 93.
17. Just as I have suggested there might be a longer genealogy of cultural studies before the institutional emergence of the Birmingham School, similarly one could identify an American tradition that studied 'culture' prior to the advent of the nomenclature of cultural studies.
18. Jacques Derrida, 'The Future of the Profession or the University without Condition (Thanks to the "Humanities", What *Could Take Place*, Tomorrow)', in *Jacques Derrida and the Humanities: A Critical Reader*, ed. Tom Cohen (Cambridge: Cambridge University Press, 2001).
19. See, for example, Jacques Derrida, 'The Principal of Reason: The University in the Eyes of Its Pupils', trans. Catherine Porter and Edward Morris, *Diacritics*, 13(3), 1983, pp. 3–20; 'Languages and Institutions of Philosophy', *Recherches Semiotiques/Semiotic Inquiry*, 4(2), 1984, pp. 91–155; *Who's Afraid of Philosophy? Right to Philosophy I*, trans. Jan Plug (Stanford, CA: Stanford University Press, 2002).
20. Jacques Derrida, 'The Future of the Profession', p. 26.
21. Ibid., pp. 26–7.
22. Ibid., p. 39.
23. Ibid., p. 50.
24. 'I suggest reconfiguring and reconceiving "cultural studies" as "cultural analysis"', Mieke Bal, *Travelling Concepts in the Humanities: A Rough Guide* (Toronto: University of Toronto Press, 2002), p. 45. For a full review of Bal see my 'Editor's Introduction', in *The Year's Work in Critical and Cultural Theory*, vol. 12 (Oxford: Oxford University Press, 2004).
25. Immanuel Kant, 'An Answer to the Question: What Is Enlightenment?', in *Practical Philosophy*, trans. Mary J. Gregor (Cambridge: Cambridge University Press, 1996), pp. 17–18.
26. Michel Foucault, 'What Is Enlightenment?', trans. Catherine Porter, in *The Foucault Reader: An Introduction to Foucault's Thought*, ed. Paul Rabinow (London: Penguin, 1984).

27. Ibid., p. 39.
28. Gary Hall, *Culture in Bits: the Monstrous Future of Theory* (London: Continuum, 2002); J. Hillis Miller, 'Cultural Studies and Reading', *ADE Bulletin*, 117, Fall 1997, pp. 15–18, reproduced in *Literary Theories: A Reader and Guide*, ed. Julian Wolfreys (Edinburgh: Edinburgh University Press, 1999), pp. 604–10; J. Hillis Miller, *Illustration* (London: Reaktion Books, 1992); Gayatri Spivak, 'Deconstruction and Cultural Studies', in *Deconstructions: A User's Guide*, ed. Nicholas Royle (Basingstoke: Palgrave, 2000), pp. 14–44.
29. J. Hillis Miller, 'Cultural Studies and Reading', p. 607.
30. Ibid., p. 605.
31. Ibid., p. 606.
32. Ibid., p. 605.
33. Ibid., p. 608.
34. Ibid., p. 610.
35. J. Hillis Miller, *Illustration*, p. 54.
36. 'The millennium of universal justice and peace among men … would come if all men and women became good readers in de Man's sense', J. Hillis Miller, *The Ethics of Reading: Kant, de Man, Eliot, Trollope, James, and Benjamin* (New York: Columbia University Press, 1987), p. 58. While it is true that if everyone read as well as Paul de Man the world would be a richer and more sophisticated place, unfortunately good reading did not stop de Man making the misjudgements in his public and private lives with which his name is now too readily associated. Miller's comments were written before the 'de Man affair' broke in August 1987.
37. Gayatri Spivak, 'Deconstruction and Cultural Studies', p. 15.
38. Ibid., p. 35.
39. Ibid., p. 36.
40. Ibid., p. 33.
41. Jacques Derrida, 'A Silkworm of One's Own: Points of View Stitched on the Other Veil', trans. Geoffrey Bennington, in *Veils* (Stanford, CA: Stanford University Press, 2001), p. 89.
42. Ibid.

Annotated Bibliography

The complete text of Roland Barthes can be found in: *ŒUVRES COMPLÈTES, 1942–80,* vols 1–5, (Paris: Éditions du Seuil), ed. Eric Marty, nouv. éd. rev., corr. et présentée (22 octobre 2002).

This does not include the posthumous publication of Barthes' seminar; where English language translation has occurred this is included below. All French publication is with Éditions du Seuil unless otherwise stated. I have attempted, where possible, to list the original edition of the English language translation to give a sense of Barthes' entry into the Anglophone academy although multiple e ditions now exist for several texts.

LE DEGRÉ ZÉRO DE L'ÉCRITURE, 1953. *Writing Degree Zero,* trans. Annette Lavers and Colin Smith (London: Jonathan Cape, 1967); edition with preface by Susan Sontag published by Hill and Wang, New York, 1968.

Barthes' first book, part published by Camus in his journal *Combat.* It takes up the large themes of existentialism and literature, attempting with audacious ambition to offer general theories of 'What Is Writing?' and what makes for the best model of political writing. Clearly influenced by Sartre's *What Is Literature?,* the text outlines a thesis that proposes the decline of bourgeois literature (after its triumph in the modern period) and its replacement by a new avant-garde of writing. The book works on a level of some generality and gives little clue to Barthes' considerable powers as a reader. However, it is a seminal text in the way that it ties Barthes' formation to a particular historical moment in French culture.

MICHELET PAR LUI MÊME, 1954 (edited by Roland Barthes). *Michelet,* trans. Richard Howard (New York: Hill and Wang, 1987).

An early research project from Barthes' time in Saint-Hilaire sanitorium, which establishes his interest in history and textuality, as well as his biographical and fragmentary method. Barthes attempts to squeeze his inauguration of a theoretical discourse into the requirements of an illustrated 'writers and their work' series to considerable effect. The book combines selected quotation from Michelet with fragments of commentary from Barthes, who sees in Michelet a modern figure who speaks to his own concerns: a critic of Empire, an interest in historiography over history, a concern for the history of the people rather than the *dramatis personae* of History and someone who was displaced from the academy. Unlike Barthes, Michelet never retrieved his seat at the Collège de France.

MYTHOLOGIES, 1957. *Mythologies,* selection trans. Annette Lavers London: Jonathan Cape, 1972) and *The Eiffel Tower and Other Mythologies,* trans. Richard Howard (New York: Hill and Wang, 1979).

A collection of journalistic texts first published monthly between 1954 and 1956, and later brought to coherence by the extended methodological essay 'Myth Today'. The 'mythologies' treat all aspects of French popular, literary, political and juridicial culture, offering a decisive ideology-critique of the dominance of 'petty-bourgeoise' taste in the last days of the Fourth Republic. The concluding essay sets out a project of semiological analysis based upon an adaptation of structuralism's understanding of signification. Translated into English in 1972, this book provided considerable resources for the development of an Anglophone cultural studies.

SUR RACINE, 1963. *On Racine*, trans. Richard Howard (New York: Hill and Wang, 1964).

A collection of essays on Racine first published in Barthes' journal of theatre studies *Théâtre Populaire*. This short text was the object of considerable media speculation following a polemical attack on it by the Sorbonne-based academic Raymond Picard in his pamphlet *Nouvelle critique ou nouvelle imposture?* Barthes responded in his *Critique et Vérité*. Barthes' essays on Racine repeatedly contrast themselves with the traditional critical approach laid down for the French academy by Gustave Lanson in the first half of the twentieth century. While no great shakes as Racine scholarship the essays combine psychoanalysis, Marxism and structural linguistics to provide an early version of what we would now call literary theory.

LA TOUR EIFFEL, 1964 (photographs by André Martin). *The Eiffel Tower and Other Mythologies*, trans. Richard Howard (New York: Hill and Wang, 1979).

An extended 'mythology' on its eponymous subject, which first appeared in French as a short artistic publication accompanied with photographs. It was first published in English along with texts not included in the 1972 translation of the *Mythologies*.

ESSAIS CRITIQUES, 1964. *Critical Essays*, trans. Richard Howard (Chicago: Northwestern University Press, 1972).

A collection of texts from Barthes' early work on theatre and literature in journals and the quasi-academic press before 1964. Included essays cover topics such as Baudelaire's drama, Brecht, Greek theatre and its staging, the nouveau roman, Kafka, critical method and latterly the question of structuralism. Here we can see Barthes struggling to emerge from his engagements with existentialism, Marxism, psychoanalysis and the question of history, prior to his establishment as a major literary theorist.

ELÉMENTS DE SÉMIOLOGIE, 1964. *Elements of Semiology*, trans. Annette Lavers and Colin Smith (New York: Hill and Wang, 1967).

First, and practically last, serious presentation by Barthes of a sustained engagement with structuralism (see also *Système de la Mode*). The schematic divisions of 'Myth Today' are expanded at length, following Saussure's account of language and speech, and signifier and signified. Barthes also borrows from Jakobson and Hjelmslev in discussions of idiolect, denotation and connotation, syntagm and system. The book is presented in short fragments and is intended as a primer for structuralist enquiry rather than an expansion of its primary literature. Barthes concludes with an outline for an extended semiological project.

CRITIQUE ET VÉRITÉ, 1966. *Criticism and Truth*, trans. Katrine Pilcher Keuneman (London: Athlone, 1987).

Barthes' response to Raymond Picard's *Nouvelle critique ou nouvelle imposture?* Paul de Man described the first half of Barthes' text, a discussion of the academic apparatus in France, as his greatest mythology. Barthes discusses the disciplinary divisions of the humanities in France and the historically contingent and constructed nature of the seemingly natural status of the critical vocabulary and method Picard wishes to defend. He goes on to propose a project of semiological analysis in the field of literary studies that provides the resources for the concepts of literary theory and cultural studies in the Anglophone academy.

SYSTÈME DE LA MODE, 1967. *The Fashion System*, trans. Matthew Ward and Richard Howard (New York: Hill and Wang, 1983).

Structural analysis of the discourse on fashion arising from a failed research project at the CNRS. Barthes had intended this work as a doctoral thesis but instead published it as a monograph, having taught its contents in his seminar. It is profoundly influential in the study of fashion in art schools as one of the few serious reflections on the subject. Barthes not only outlines a terminology for the semiology of fashion but offers us an example of what his often vaunted semiological research project might look like. The text is in fact one of Barthes' few attempts at a sustained monograph (as opposed to a fragmentary series of reflections or a collection of essays) and should therefore be considered of singular importance in Barthes' extended corpus.

S/Z, 1970. *S/Z*, trans. Richard Miller (New York: Hill and Wang, 1974).

An extended study of reading based upon Barthes' close analysis of a short story by Balzac ('Sarrasine'). The monograph arose from Barthes' seminar on the same topic. In this study Barthes has moved some distance from his formulaic account of signification in 'Myth Today' or the structuralist essays that make up *Elements of Semiology*. His reading works at the minimal unit of sense, which he calls proposing that textuality combines five discursive codes: hermeneutic code (the voice of truth), proairetic code (empirical voice), semic code (the voice of the person), symbolic code (the voice of symbols), referential code (the voice of science). Barthes seeks to argue for a looser and more fluid interweaving of the codes as the source of meaning rather than a hierarchical and rigid narratological system. In this sense, his thinking has begun in this book to depart from structuralism towards somewhere else.

L'EMPIRE DES SIGNES, 1970. *Empire of Signs*, trans. Richard Howard (New York: Hill and Wang, 1982).

Barthes' extended treatment of Japanese culture refracted through a semiological analysis. It is constructed from a number of trips Barthes made to Japan to teach and swings between the acute and the touristic in its insights. He is equally concerned with writing and vestmentary traditions as he is with the pop cultural significance of the chopstick. The text is a curious mix of Barthes' own deconstruction of the French idea of the Orient, and a certain complicity with its assumptions and models. It stands as a remarkably interesting historical document, before the rise of the vocabulary and method of 'post-colonial' theory and before the globalisation of academic travel and exchange.

SADE, FOURIER, LOYOLA, 1971. *Sade, Fourier, Loyola*, trans. Richard Miller (New York: Hill and Wang, 1976).

Barthes celebrates three 'logothetes', the founders of language, in this consideration of writing, conceptualisation and categorisation. One can see the influence of Foucault's genealogical project played out in this book. Barthes is concerned with Sadean writing as the sensual pleasure of classification and the madness of cutting; he sees a similar divine impulse in the text of Loyola. 'From Sade to Fourier, sadism is lost', writes Barthes, but the division of categories remains. The book then works around a series of fragments and quotations as so much of Barthes' reading does. It is, then, as much a consideration of his own mania for indexing and fragmentation as it is a history of discursive innovation.

NOUVEAUX ESSAIS CRITIQUES, 1972. *New Critical Essays*, trans by Richard Howard (New York: Hill and Wang, 1980).

A collection of essays written between 1967 and 1971 collating work that demonstrates Barthes' shift from card-carrying structuralist to his work after *S/Z*.

LE PLAISIR DU TEXTE, 1973. *The Pleasure of the Text*, trans. Richard Miller (New York: Hill and Wang, 1976).

A short text that continues the work of *S/Z* by building upon the '*lisible*' and '*scriptible*' distinction. Barthes identifies here the further categorisation between the text of '*plaisir*' (pleasure) and '*jouissance*' (bliss, or literally orgasm); the latter text aligned to the scriptable as being preferable in Barthes' line of thinking. However, as with any such binary model Barthes' own work merely demonstrates the ways in which a supposedly '*lisible*' text of simple '*plaisir*' can be more fascinating and writerly than its alternative.

ROLAND BARTHES PAR ROLAND BARTHES, 1975. *Roland Barthes by Roland Barthes*, trans. Richard Howard (New York: Hill and Wang, 1977).

Self-reflexive and autobiographical series of fragments related to the likes and dislikes of Roland Barthes. Following the manner of his own book on Michelet, Barthes does not attempt to roll his concerns towards the presentation of a coherent whole but rather insists on the heterogeneity as an affirmation of the complexity of authorial presence. Some judge this text to be the extreme of Barthes' decline as a theorist of structure and symptomatic of his disengagement with politics. It is undoubtedly beautifully written and full of extraordinary insights into literature and meaning that explain the complexity and generosity of Barthes' later writing. It contains a set of Barthes family photographs.

IMAGE-MUSIC-TEXT, essays selected and translated by Stephen Heath (New York: Hill and Wang, 1977).

Heath's collection and translation of some of Barthes' most significant essays remains a primary opening for readers of his oeuvre. The volume did more than any other single Barthes text to embed Barthes into the Anglophone academic mainstream, in particular securing the importance of Barthes for film theory and art theory in the late 1970s. Essays included are: 'The Photographic Message', 'Rhetoric of the Image', 'The Third Meaning' (on Eisenstein), 'Introduction to the Structural Analysis of Narratives', 'The Struggle with the Angel', 'The Death of the Author' and 'From Work to Text'.

FRAGMENTS D'UN DISCOURS AMOUREUX, 1977. *A Lover's Discourse: Fragments*, trans. Richard Howard (New York: Hill and Wang, 1978). Films: *Mouvements du désir*, 1994, prod. Catpics Coproductions, dir. Léa Pool, featuring Valérie Kaprisky, Jean-François Pichette, Jolianne L'Allier-Matteau, William Jacques; *A Lover's Discourse: Fragments*, 2004 (short film), dir. Donna Vermeer, featuring Sarah Desage, Tracey Godfrey, Eleanor Hutchins.

Based on a seminar by Barthes, this was the first of his texts to break into the mainstream and to sell in substantial numbers, securing his celebrity and fortune. Through a series of fragments and quotations Barthes reflects upon unrequited love via a range of philosophical and literary texts. He deals with all aspects of the experience of the plaintive lover, from the madness of not knowing if one is loved in return to the pain of not receiving a letter, to the despair of suicide. The book has been frequently reinterpreted by film makers, dramatists and choreographers.

SOLLERS, ÉCRIVAIN, 1979. *Writer Sollers*, trans. Philip Thody (Minneapolis: University of Minnesota Press, 1987).

A collection of previously published texts and reviews of Sollers' work (published, reportedly, on Sollers' suggestion). Usefully demonstrates the importance of the *nouveau roman* for Barthes and is suggestive of the proximity between Barthes and Sollers as fellow travellers. The essays discuss narrative, language and the relation between politics and literature.

LA CHAMBRE CLAIRE, 1980. *Camera Lucida: Reflections of the Photography*, trans. Richard Howard (New York: Hill and Wang, 1982).

The last book published during Barthes' lifetime. It is not so much a general theory of photography as a consideration of representation in selected photographs that appeal to Barthes. His distinction between the 'studium' (the obvious symbolic meaning of a photohgraph) and the 'punctum' (that which 'pierces the viewer') has been widely taken up by theorists of photography but it is in truth a slight binary model. The wider significance of the book is as a study in mourning, theory and writing, notably around the justly famous account of the 'Winter Garden' photograph of his mother, who died in 1977.

LE GRAIN DE LA VOIX, 1981. *The Grain of the Voice: Interviews 1962–1980*, trans. Linda Coverdale (London: Jonathan Cape, 1985).

A collection of interviews given by Barthes since 1962. The interviews often coincide with the publication of a text by Barthes and so shed considerable light on the run of Barthes' work. Frequently, they solicit Barthes to talk on issues of the day or on general topics such as love or violence. The Barthes on display in interview is as cunning and subtle as his writing persona but is also worldly wise and alienated from the 'Barthes' who writes. As with any collection of interviews the book works well as a point of introduction to Barthes' thinking, but should be followed up by exploration of the primary texts.

L'OBVIE ET L'OBTUS, 1982. *The Responsibility of Forms*, trans. Richard Howard (New York: Hill and Wang, 1985).

A posthumous collection of Barthes' essays on art and music demonstrating the significance of Barthes for the study of visual culture. However, much of the important work of this volume is published elsewhere, notably in Stephen Heath's *Image-Music-Text*. Rarer material included here tends to be short and presents Barthes as a commentator on art, with essays on Arcimboldo and Cy Twombly. All of Barthes' writing on music and the voice is included here in one place. The texts mostly date from the 1970s and show the variety of Barthes' interests after his drift away from the structural analysis of literature.

LE BRUISSEMENT DE LA LANGUE, 1984. *The Rustle of Language*, trans. Richard Howard (New York: Hill and Wang, 1986).

A collection of forty-five essays written between 1967 and 1980, providing a useful resource of many primary texts by Barthes hitherto only available in English-language collections. These include: 'To Write: An Intransitive Verb?' (the text he presented at the Baltimore conference in 1967), 'The Death of the Author', 'Rhetorical Analysis' and 'The Reality Effect' (an important essay on nineteenth-century Realism). The collection also includes essays on the Baroque, Brecht, Michelet, Kristeva, pedagogy, history, language and science.

L'AVENTURE SÉMIOLOGIQUE, 1985. *The Semiotic Challenge*, trans. Richard Howard (New York: Hill and Wang, 1988).

Posthumous publication of collected texts by Barthes at the height of his structuralist phase, including a seminar at the *École pratique de hautes etudes* in 1964–5 on rhetoric. The collected essays include texts on Saussure and democracy, sociology, advertising, cuisine, urbanism and medicine. Notably, for a Francophone audience the book collected in one place the 'Introduction to the Structural Analysis of Narratives', 'Wrestling with the Angel' and the essay on Poe's 'Valdemar'.

INCIDENTS, 1987. *Incidents*, trans. Richard Howard (Berkeley: University of California Press, 1992).

A collection of short journalistic and personal texts by Barthes published in 1987 by François Wahl, his literary executor. The first, 'La Lumiere du Sud-Ouest' (published in *L'Humanité* 1977), deals with the south-west of France of Barthes' childhood; the second, 'Incidents' (1969), treats Barthes' sex-tourism in Morocco; the third, 'Au Palace Ce Soir' (first published in *Vogues-Hommes* in 1978), describes a fashionable Parisian nightspot; the final text, 'Soirées de Paris', is a journal from autumn 1979 recording Barthes' cruising in Paris. The book is significant for the way it has resulted in the refraction of Barthes' work through the lens of queer theory. It is available to download for free from the University of California Press.

LE SPORT ET LES HOMMES, 2004 (Les Presses de Université de Montréal). *What Is Sport?*, trans. Richard Howard (New Haven, CT: Yale University Press, 2007). Documentary film: *Le Sport et les hommes*, 1961, prod. National Film Board of Canada, dir. by Hubert Aquin, narrated by Robert Gadouas.

The text of a short Canadian documentary film produced in collaboration with Québécois writer Hubert Aquin during the spring of 1961. Following the manner of Barthes' mythology on the Tour de France it treats this event and four other national sports as social and poetic phenomenon: bullfighting in Spain, motor racing in Italy, football in Hungary and ice hockey in Canada. The text is not included in the Marty edition of the *Ouevres Completes*.

THE LANGUAGE OF FASHION, ed. and trans. Andy Stafford and Michael Carter (Oxford: Berg, 2007).

A series of essays, interviews and articles (including some from *Vogue* and *Marie Claire*) written by Barthes before and immediately after publication of *Système de la mode* in 1968. The texts were all published between 1956 and 1969 but only edited together as an English-language publication in 2007. The collection is at once a demonstration of the reach that the name of Barthes continues to have in the study of visual culture and in art education, and the risk attached to resurrecting an unquestioned semiology as the basis of disciplinary study (fashion as an art school discipline). Stafford expertly makes the case for the texts as a representation of classic Barthes of the 1950s and 1960s.

LE NEUTRE: NOTES DE COURS AU COLLÈGE DE FRANCE 1977–78, ed. Thomas Clerc and Eric Marty (Paris: Seuil/Imec, 2002). *The Neutral*, trans. Dennis Hollier and Rosalind Krauss (New York: Columbia University Press, 2005).

Seminar series taught at the Collège de France on the topic of the 'neutre', an important trope than runs through much of Barthes' work. The neutral is that which undoes binary paradigms that structure thought and discourse in the west. Barthes treats twenty-three figures that represent the work of the Neutral, such as silence, sleep, tact, or the anti-Neutral, such as anger or conflict. Clearly influenced by Derrida, Barthes draws on a wide range of philosophers and cultural producers from Rousseau to John Cage, Tolstoy to Walter Benjamin. The two years of Barthes' seminar at the Collège ('Le Neutre' and 'Comment vivre ensemble') are available as MP3s in French at www.ubu.com.

JOURNAL DE DEUIL, ed. Nathalie Légere (Paris: Seuil/Imec, 2009). *Mourning Diary, October 26 1977–September 15 1979*, trans. Richard Howard (New York: Hill and Wang, 2010).

The diary of Barthes' life after the death of his mother in 1977 (see the later *Camera Lucida* as a theorisation of this time in his life). A lucid and personal account of mourning from a man falling apart with grief, which he calls 'a sort of deposit, of rust, of mud … a bitterness of the heart'. Includes ample evidence of Barthes' theory-poetry 'I say to myself … how barbaric it is not to believe in souls – in the immortality of souls. What a stupid form of truth materialism is.'

CARNETS DU VOYAGE EN CHINE, ed. Anne Herschberg-Pierrot (Paris: Seuil/Imec, 2009).

The diary of Barthes' trip to China with the Tel Quel group (including Philippe Sollers and Julia Kristeva) in 1974. Not published during his lifetime, the journal tells of Barthes' disappointment with China (in comparison with the Japan of *The Empire of Signs*) and his sexual frustration in a drab and repressive Maoist regime. It would seem he visited China only to support his Tel Quel friends and out of worry for his Parisian public image. He published one short and bland journalistic article on the trip but reserved his thoughts for his journal.

Further Reading: Texts on Roland Barthes

Allen, Graham. *Roland Barthes*. London: Routledge, 2003.

Attridge, Derek. 'Roland Barthes' Obtuse, Sharp Meaning and the Responsibilities of Commentary'. In *Reading and Responsibility: Deconstruction's Traces*. Edinburgh: Edinburgh University Press, 2010.

Badmington, Neil, ed. *Roland Barthes: Critical Evaluation in Cultural Theory*, 4 vols. London: Routledge, 2009.

Batchen, Geoffrey. *Photography Degree Zero: Reflections on Roland Barthes's Camera Lucida*. Cambridge, MA: MIT Press, 2009.

Bowie, Malcolm. 'Barthes on Proust'. *Yale Journal of Criticism: Interpretation in the Humanities*, 14:2, 2001, 513–18.

Brown, Andrew. *Roland Barthes: The Figures of Writing*. Oxford: Oxford University Press, 1992.

Burke, Sean. *The Death and Return of the Author: Criticism and Subjectivity in Barthes, Foucault and Derrida*. Edinburgh: Edinburgh University Press, 1998.

Calvet, Jean Louis. *Roland Barthes: A Biography*. Trans. Sarah Wyke. Bloomington: Indiana University Press, 1995.

Caygill, Howard, 'Barthes and the Lesson of Saenredam'. *Diacritics*, 32:1, 2002, 38–48.

Centre Georges Pompidou, ed. *R/B: Roland Barthes*. Paris: Centre Georges Pompidou, 2002.

Culler, Jonathan. *Roland Barthes*. New York: Oxford University Press, 1983.

De Man, Paul. 'Roland Barthes and the Limits of Structuralism'. In *Romanticism and Contemporary Criticism*. Ed. E. S. Burt, Kevin Newmark and Andrzej Warminski. Baltimore: Johns Hopkins University Press, 1993.

Derrida, Jacques. 'The Deaths of Roland Barthes'. In *Psyche: Inventions of the Other, Vol. 1*. Ed. Peggy Kamuf and Elizabeth G. Rottenberg. Stanford, CA: Stanford University Press, 2007.

Engh, Barbara. 'Loving It: Music and Criticism in Roland Barthes'. In Ruth A. Solie (ed.), *Musicology and Difference: Gender and Sexuality in Music Scholarship*. Berkeley: University of California Press, 1993, pp. 66–79.

ffrench, Patrick. 'Barthes in Tangiers: Renegotiating Perversity'. *Nottingham French Studies*, 36:1, 1997, 53–62.

Ha, Marie-Paule. *Figuring the East: Segalen, Malraux, Duras and Barthes*. Albany: State University of New York Press, 2000.

Hill, Leslie. *Radical Indecision: Barthes, Blanchot, Derrida, and the Future of Criticism*. Notre Dame, IN: University of Notre Dame Press, 2010.

Hollier, Dennis. 'Notes (on the Index Card)'. *October*, 112, 2005, 35–44.

Iversen, Margaret. *Beyond Pleasure: Freud, Lacan, Barthes*. University Park: Pennsylvania University Press, 2007.

Jay, Paul. *Being in the Text: Self-representation from Wordsworth to Roland Barthes*. Ithaca, NY: Cornell University Press, 1984.

Johnson, Barbara. 'The Critical Difference: Balzac's "Sarrasine" and Barthes's S/Z'. In Robert Young (ed.), *Untying the Text: A Post-structuralist Reader*. London: Routledge and Kegan Paul, 1981.

Knight, Diana. *Barthes and Utopia: Space, Travel, Writing*. Oxford: Clarendon Press, 1997.
—— ed. *Critical Essays on Roland Barthes*. New York: G. K. Hall, 2000.

Lavers, Annette. *Roland Barthes, Structuralism and After*. Cambridge, MA: Harvard University Press, 1982.

Mavor, Carol. *Reading Boyishly: Roland Barthes, J. M. Barrie, Jacques Henri Lartigue, Marcel Proust, and D. W. Winnicott*. Durham, NC: Duke University Press, 2007.

Miller, D. A. *Bringing out Roland Barthes*. Berkeley: University of California Press, 1992.

Modern Critical Theory Group, eds. 'Roland Barthes', *Paragraph*, 11:2/3, 1988.

Moriarty, Michael. *Roland Barthes*. Stanford, CA: Stanford University Press, 1991.

Payne, Michael. *Reading Knowledge: An Introduction to Barthes, Foucault and Althusser*. Malden, MA: Blackwell, 1997.

Pieters, Jurgen and Kris Pint, eds. *Roland Barthes Retroactively: Reading the Collège de France Lectures*. Edinburgh: Edinburgh University Press, 2008.

Rabaté, Jean-Michel, ed. *Writing the Image after Roland Barthes*. Philadelphia: University of Pennsylvania Press, 1997.

Rylance, Rick. *Roland Barthes*. New York: Harvester Wheatsheaf, 1994.

Scheie, Timothy. *Performance Degree Zero: Roland Barthes and Theatre*. Toronto: University of Toronto Press, 2006.

Shawcross, Nancy. *Roland Barthes on Photography: The Critical Tradition in Perspective*. Gainesville: University of Florida, 1997.

Sollers, Philippe. 'R.B: La plus forte des transgressions, celle du langage'. *Tel Quel*, 47, Autumn 1971.
—— *Women*. Trans. Barbara Bray. New York: Columbia University Press, 2004.

Stafford, Andy. *Roland Barthes, Phenomenon and Myth: An Intellectual Biography*. Edinburgh: Edinburgh University Press, 1998.

Thody, Philip. *Roland Barthes: A Conservative Estimate*. Atlantic Highlands, NJ: Humanities Press, 1977.

Trifonas, Peter Pericles. *Barthes and the Empire of Signs*. London: Ikon Books, 2001.

Wasserman, George Russell. *Roland Barthes*. Boston: Twayne Publishers, 1981.

Wiseman, Mary Bittner. *The Ecstasies of Roland Barthes*. London: Routledge, 1989.

Ungar, Steven. *Roland Barthes, The Professor of Desire*. Lincoln: University of Nebraska Press, 1983.
—— and Betty R. McGraw. *Signs in Culture: Roland Barthes Today*. Iowa City: University of Iowa Press, 1989.

Index

Note: n. after a page number denotes a note number on that page.